"High Nonsensical Words"

Standish O'Grady supporting himself between the tables
Speaking to a drunken audience high nonsensical words;

—W. B. Yeats, "Beautiful Lofty Things"

"High Nonsensical Words":

A Study of the Works of Standish James O'Grady

by

Edward A. Hagan

The Whitston Publishing Company
Troy, New York
1986

Copyright 1986
Edward A. Hagan

Library of Congress Catalog Card Number 85-52067

ISBN 0-87875-306-0

Printed in the United States of America

For Mom and Dad

Table of Contents

Acknowledgments

I am indebted to Mr. Standish DeCourcey O'Grady and the following libraries for permission to use and quote from unpublished O'Grady documents: The New York Public Library, the Milton S. Eisenhower Library at Johns Hopkins University, and the Library at the State University of New York at Stony Brook. I am also indebted to the National Library of Ireland, the Kenneth Spencer Research Library at the University of Kansas, the Stanford University Libraries, and the Colby College Library for providing me with xerox or microfilm copies of unpublished O'Grady documents.

Mr. Standish DeCourcey O'Grady was especially helpful in providing me with a large cache of his grandfather's unpublished work.

The Royal Irish Academy was most gracious in providing me with a microfilm copy of John O'Daly's translation of the *Tán-bo-Cooalney*, MS.24 M.39. I thank the Academy for allowing me to quote from the MS.

I gratefully acknowledge the kind attention and encouragement of Prof. David R. Clark of the University of Massachusetts. Without his skillful and patient direction, this study would never have been completed.

There were many other people who assisted me in this project, and I thank them all. In particular, I wish to mention the help of the late Joseph T. Bennett, Paul Dolan, the late Erwin Geissman, Denis J. Hynes, Herbert Janick, Richard J. Lundy, Peter Poland, Thomas Rogers, Norman Wallis, and John Wrynn, S. J. And lastly, I owe special thanks to my wife, Denise Lepicier, who offered much appreciated editorial assistance.

I am indebted to M. B. Yeats and Macmillan & Co. Ltd., London, for permission to quote from the poetry and prose of W. B. Yeats. The USA rights are as follows: the extracts from *Collected Poems* by W. B. Yeats are reprinted with the permission of The Macmillan Company, New York. Copright 1903, 1906, 1907, 1912, 1916, 1918, 1919, 1924, 1928, 1931, 1933, 1934, 1935, 1940, 1944, 1945, 1946, 1950, 1956, by the Mac-

Introduction

For Thomas Carlyle, "the one thing needed" from England's future heroes was a history of England. In "Shooting Niagara: and After?" he described the kind of history he had in mind: "To write the History of England as a kind of Bible (or in parts and snatches, to *sing* it if you could), this were work for the highest Aristos or series of Aristoi in Sacred Literature (really a sacred kind, this); and to be candid, I discover hitherto no incipiencies of this; and greatly desire there were some!"[1]   While Carlyle was displeased with the "dryasdust" history of his contemporaries, he was hardly more upset with them than an Irishman who heeded his call.   But it was the history of Ireland, not England, that Standish James O'Grady turned "into a kind of Iliad, almost perhaps into a kind of Bible."[2]

O'Grady's *History of Ireland* was published in two volumes in 1878 and 1880, and those volumes became the Bible of the Irish writers of the next several decades.   In fact, O'Grady's stature was so great in the following decades that he was called the "Father of the Irish Literary Revival."   Of him, W. B. Yeats wrote: "I think it was his 'History of Ireland, Heroic Period,' that started us all. . ."[3]   Yeats's "us all" refers to the writers of the Irish Revival, and almost every one of them echoed Yeats's statement.   Lady Gregory, for example, said in her autobiography that "Standish O'Grady's Homeric paraphrases had long been an inspiration and a delight."[4]   But O'Grady's *History* was not history in the usual sense of the word.   He had rescued ancient Irish tales, which he regarded as semi-historical, from "dryasdust" scholarship.   It was from O'Grady that the Irish writers learned of heroes such as Cuculain and Finn Mac-Cool, for they were virtually unknown otherwise.   AE, T. W. Rolleston, John Todhunter, Katherine Tynan, Aubrey de Vere, and Austin Clarke among others acknowledged their debt to O'Grady.

These writers were stirred by the high, noble tone which

O'Grady's *History* sounded.   The Homeric quality of his rendition made them feel heirs to a great tradition.   In the following one-sentence paragraph, O'Grady describes Cuculain's
feelings after he has killed his boyhood friend, Fardia:

> But Cuculain plucked out the spear, and stood above
> him, panting, as a hound pants returning from the chase,
> and the war demons passed out of him and he looked
> upon Fardia, and a great sorrow overwhelmed him, and
> he lamented and moaned over Fardia, joining his voice
> to the howl of the people of Fardia, the greathearted
> children of Mac Erc, and he took off the cathbarr from
> the head of Fardia, and unwound his yellow hair, tress
> after bright tress, most beautiful, shedding many tears,
> and he opened the battle-dress and took out the queen's
> brooch—that for which his friend had come to slay him—
> and he cursed the lifeless metal, and cast it from him
> into the air, southwards over the host, and men saw it
> no more.[5]

O'Grady closes his chapter with this paragraph, and the dying
fall of "men saw it no more" produces the cosmic, epic effect
he wanted.   He does not use the definite article before "men"
and shows thereby that the audience for the duel between
Cuculain and Fardia is not merely *the* men who were there.

Yet despite the fact that so many Irish writers were inspired by such passages, O'Grady may be known only to those
who have read Yeats's *Autobiography* very closely or remember
that Yeats placed him among the Olympians in "Beautiful Lofty
Things."   This study therefore attempts to make a somewhat
comprehensive knowledge of O'Grady possible without requiring the reader to engage in an intensive study of his works.
Since O'Grady's principal importance lies in his use of early
Irish literature in his early works, I have concentrated on those
works but have surveyed his other writings, his politics, and
his influence as well.

O'Grady's use of the early Irish literature is especially
important because, as Ernest Boyd pointed out in 1916,
O'Grady made possible an Irish national literature in English
by opening the literary wealth of Gaelic Ireland to writers in
English.   Boyd devoted a chapter of his book, *Ireland's Literary
Renaissance,* to O'Grady, and it is still valuable because it shows

how O'Grady's work made the movement more than a mere continuation of the Anglo-Irish literature of the eighteenth and early nineteenth centuries.

I have found only four critics who have examined O'Grady since Boyd. His study is limited to his assertion of O'Grady's importance and a recapitulation of the high points of O'Grady's work. The studies of the four critics contain some valuable insights but are similarly limited in scope.

Vivian Mercier's 1958 article is little more than an annotated catalog of O'Grady's work.[6] It was written to introduce a list of the items in the O'Grady collection at Colby College, and this purpose explains its limited scope. Mercier sees O'Grady's main significance in his contribution to the "hard blow" the Irish revival struck at "Ireland's inferiority complex."[7] This point is well taken since the surge in Irish nationalism in the late nineteenth and early twentieth centuries can be traced in part to the literary revival and O'Grady in particular although he did not like the form the nationalism took.

In a 1960 article,[8] Sean J. White provides the first intensive discussion of O'Grady's literary relations with prominent literary figures such as Walt Whitman, W. B. Yeats, Ernest Dowden, AE, Lady Gregory, and George Moore among others. White's article provides much biographical detail about O'Grady, which White was able to gather from various sources including O'Grady's son.[9]

William Irwin Thompson was the next to consider O'Grady and the first to analyze his stylistic method. A few pages of Thompson's excellent book, *The Imagination of an Insurrection,* show how in the *History of Ireland* O'Grady interweaves the past with the more distant past in his narrative and thereby accomplishes his design of showing how the past lives in the present and prophesies the future (a Carlylian notion).[10]

Lastly, Phillip Marcus's 92-page book, *Standish O'Grady,* appeared in 1970 as part of Bucknell University Press's Irish Writers Series. It is intended as an introduction to and short overview of O'Grady's life and work. It is valuable as far as it goes. Marcus's main contribution is his discussion of how O'Grady manipulated the saga material to suit his own didactic purposes. At times O'Grady would invent a character or incident to illustrate a point.

But Marcus makes no attempt to explain O'Grady's work in terms of any artistic precept, and it is precisely an understanding of his theory of art that is necessary to an intelligent reading of his work. The theory helps place O'Grady in his late nineteenth century milieu and explains the selectivity in his use of his sources. There is a need to "place" O'Grady because placing him gives us insight into the roots of not only the Irish movement but also other national literary movements.

The theory illuminates the manner in which O'Grady treats his two major historical interests—pre-Christian Ireland and Tudor Ireland. In addition to his two volume *History of Ireland*, O'Grady wrote several novelistic accounts of the bardic period—*Finn and his Companions, The Coming of Cuculain, In the Gates of the North,* and *The Triumph and Passing of Cuculain.* The style of these novels is similar to that used in his Tudor novels—*Red Hugh's Captivity, Ulrick the Ready,* and *The Flight of the Eagle.* O'Grady chose these periods for didactic reasons: he wanted to provide models for his Irish readers to emulate. Art was a didactic matter for O'Grady, and he expended considerable effort in producing stories which would teach the young especially. All his novelistic books have a "boyish" flavor to them, and, in addition, he also wrote three boys' stories—*Lost on Du-Corrig, The Chain of Gold,* and *Mr. Goodenough.* Although the above critics have not taken full account of these books, they have the same purposes as O'Grady's other works, and they reveal a great deal about the ideology he was trying to inculcate. As such they are a useful gloss on those other works. Moreover we know from Yeats's review of two of them that they were part of the body of books out of which the Irish Renaissance grew.[11]

While it is doubtful that O'Grady succeeded in molding many boys in the manner he desired, we do know that his works did influence many other writers. But it is important to note O'Grady's influence transcends the normal usage of that word because his was the result of conscious effort. In his preface to Vol. II of the *History of Ireland,* he wrote: "I desire to make this heroic period once again a portion of the imagination of the country, and its chief characters as familiar in the minds of our people as they once were."[12] In short, O'Grady set out to "father" an Irish national literature. But O'Grady's notion of what that literature ought to be and what it ought to do for the country was not limited to the idea that it would be nice if Irish writers wrote on Irish subjects.

O'Grady wanted a literature that would set up national,

"racial" archetypes suitable for emulation by all Irish people. Indeed, O'Grady believed that these archetypes already existed in the bardic literature of Ireland. However, the Christianization of the country had stalled the development of this literature into a national epic. Thus, for O'Grady, art had an evolutionary character—a theory that he expounded most explicitly in his *History of Ireland: Critical and Philosophical:*

> The legend-making faculty, and what is akin to it, never cease and never can cease. Romance, epic, drama, and artistic representation are at all times the point to which history continually aspires—there only its final development and efflorescence. Archaeology culminates in history, history culminates in art.[13]

This passage explains in great part the motivation behind O'Grady's entire career: he spent his life trying to make art out of history. He regarded the fragmentary early bardic literature as semi-historical and thus but a stage in the development of a great national epic. With characteristic self-assurance, O'Grady saw it as his function to resume what Christianity had interrupted.

O'Grady's method of making art out of history required the artist to bring both imagination and knowledge to his task. This method was similar to Carlyle's, and O'Grady wrote his histories and, later, his historical novels under the influence of Carlyle's free use of the imagination in *The French Revolution* and *Frederick the Great.* In those works O'Grady found that Carlyle had achieved that "complete escape from positive history and unyielding despotic fact" necessary to produce "results . . . so typical. . ."[14] While O'Grady's allegiance to such a notion of the writing of history might disturb some, he was an unabashed follower of Carlyle. Many now consider Carlyle's "Shooting Niagara: and After?" the work of a man in his dotage, but O'Grady called it Carlyle's "maturest and most sober utterances on the subject of history."[15] Indeed it was "Niagara" that O'Grady quoted in his essay, "Imagination in History," "to show that in the opinion of this great modern man of letters [Carlyle] history is not a science but an art, and the greatest of the arts."[16]

As Carlyle was didactic, O'Grady was exceedingly so. He believed that art should teach great moral lessons, and he was especially earnest in his desire that the chief characteristics of the Irish should be their truthfulness. Consequently, he goes to great lengths to depict Cuculain's high standards of honor. O'Grady's desire probably arose from the popular Victorian notion that the Irish were deceitful.[17] He evidently agreed with that notion and wanted to remake them into a truthful "race" or, rather, to recall them to the truthfulness of their ancestors.[18]

Now this recall was no simple matter to O'Grady. He, like many nineteenth century ethnologists, believed that such qualities were a matter of genetic inheritance. Christianity (and especially jesuitical Catholicism) had prohibited their full development. Indeed even the art of the "race" was a matter of inheritance. His analysis of the value of the ancient literature shows this clearly: "But perhaps the most valuable work achieved for Ireland by those ancient shapers of legend and heroic tale, is like all that is best done in the world, incapable of being definitely grasped and clearly exhibited. Their best work is probably hidden in the blood and brain of the race to this day."[19]

Such thinking was by no means original with O'Grady, but most Victorian ethnological writing disparaged the racial inheritance of the Irish.[20] Ernest Renan's *The Poetry of the Celtic Races* and Matthew Arnold's *On the Study of Celtic Literature* were two of the most notable attempts to counter the tide of prejudice. Arnold's essay is especially important because O'Grady's motivations for studying Irish Literature were similar to Arnold's. Arnold estimated that all Englishmen were at least in some part Celtic, and therefore they ought to know what inheritance they had from their Celtic blood. Arnold believed that the Celt in them would be the antidote to their Philistinism. O'Grady follows Arnold by constantly justifying his historical researches by showing how they will supply a missing link in the history of the Aryan race. O'Grady seems to be nervous that someone might not consider the Irish to be Aryans.

This strong national tendency in O'Grady's work is paralleled by similar movements in other countries, most notably Germany, where the belief in an *Ur* culture eventually led to the Nazi madness.[21] In Ireland it led to the idealization of the peasant (cf. Yeats's "The Fisherman"), and O'Grady himself tempered his aristocratic views considerably when he became disgusted with the aristocracy. O'Grady, like Carlyle, always had reservations about democracy, but eventually he developed great faith in the peasantry and became a "communist" when he came to feel that his class, the Anglo-Irish Protestant Ascendancy, was thoroughly worthless.

Yet O'Grady was never quite as extreme as Carlyle, and we have O'Grady's own testimony that it was his association with Walt Whitman which kept him from becoming so. In an 1881 letter to Whitman, he wrote: "I dare say like most men but for you I would have swung round to the theory of strong govts., an aristocratic ruling class, &c."[22] Whitman's influence on O'Grady served mainly to temper Carlyle's pessimism, while at the same time Whitman's desire to create an American national literature was consonant with O'Grady's own aims. O'Grady could easily have written these lines from "Democratic Vistas": "The literature, songs, esthetics, &c., of a country are of importance principally because they furnish the materials and suggestions of personality for the women and men of that country, and enforce them in a thousand effective ways."[23]

To shape Irish character O'Grady used not only the early bardic literature but also the history of Tudor Ireland. His Tudor novels were set in the period when the old Irish aristocracy was being supplanted by the Anglo-Irish aristocracy. O'Grady's major point is that while it was time for the nation-state to supplant the old Irish petty chiefdoms, some members of the old Irish aristocracy acted nobly to the very end. O'Grady hoped to inspire the modern Anglo-Irish aristocracy to act similarly.

O'Grady not only made this point through his novels, but he also wrote several political tracts on this subject—*The Crisis in Ireland, Toryism and the Tory Democracy,* and *All Ireland.* Throughout his career he was active politically, and his politics could well be the subject of a separate study. For years, he was a leader writer for the most conservative newspaper in Ireland, *The Daily Express,* until he could take the decadence of the ascendancy class no longer. He constantly pointed out not only the rights but also the obligations of the gentry. He never lost his belief in the aristocracy entirely, and even after he became a communist, he saw a function for the old aristocrats as the managers of a communal system. It was always his desire to bring all Irish people together, to reconcile even the most extreme opposites. At times his art suffers from this desire because his manipulation is too artificial and inconsistent. Yet in his politics he constantly attempted this synthesis, and the name of the review he edited for seven years—*The All Ireland Review*—indicates his purpose of reconciliation. It was published from 1900 to 1907, and almost all the major Irish writers of the time contributed to it.

Among those contributors was W. B. Yeats, whose aristocratic notions and whose idealization of the peasant are consonant with O'Grady's views. Indeed, Yeats's notion of the tragic hero—"Proud, open-eyed and laughing to the tomb"[24]— is precisely O'Grady's model for aristocratic emulation.

O'Grady himself believed that he had been born to live that model. At the least he tried to convince others to live it as he believed it had been lived by the ancient Irish heroes. This study examines the heroic ideal he formulated and the aesthetic he used to embody it.

Notes

[1]Thomas Carlyle, "Shooting Niagara: and After?" in *Critical and Miscellaneous Essays,* vol. IV, vol. XVI of *Carlyle's Complete Works* (Boston: Dana Estes and Charles E. Lauriat, 1884), p. 445.

[2]Carlyle, p. 445.

[3]W. B. Yeats, quoted in George Russell [AE], "The Dramatic Treatment of Heroic Literature," *Samhain,* (Oct. 1902), p. 12.

[4]Lady Isabella Augusta Gregory, *Seventy Years: Being the Autobiography of Lady Gregory* (Gerrards Cross, England: Colin Smythe, 1974), p. 391.

[5]Standish James O'Grady, *History of Ireland: The Heroic Period*, I (1878; rpt. New York: Lemma, 1970), 238.

[6]Vivian Mercier, "Standish James O'Grady," *Colby Library Quarterly,* 4 (1958), 285-290.

[7]Mercier, p. 290.

[8]Sean J. White, "Standish O'Grady," *Kilkenny Magazine*, 2 (Autumn 1960), 10-26.

[9]White also wrote his M. A. Thesis on O'Grady at an Irish University. I have not been able to procure a copy of it.

[10]Cf. pp. 68-70.

[11]W. B. Yeats, *Uncollected Prose by W. B. Yeats,* ed. John P. Frayne and Colton Johnson (New York: Columbia University Press, 1976), II, 515.

[12]Standish James O'Grady, *History of Ireland: Cuculain and His Contemporaries,* II (1880; rpt. New York: Lemma, 1970), 17.

[13]Standish James O'Grady, *History of Ireland: Critical and Philosophical,* I (London: Sampson Low & Co.; Dublin: H. Ponsonby & Co., 1881), 56-57.

[14]*History of Ireland: Critical and Philosophical,* p. 57.

[15]Standish James O'Grady, "Imagination in History," *The New Review,* 17 (1897), 659.

[16]"Imagination in History," p. 659.

[17]L. P. Curtis, Jr.'s Study of Victorian anti-Irish prejudice, *Anglo-Saxons and Celts* (Bridgeport U. P., 1968), shows how extensive that belief was.

[18]O'Grady's passion for truthfulness was so extreme that he was capable of classing lying with robbery and murder. This attitude perplexed a reviewer of O'Grady's *The Story of Ireland* so much that he felt compelled to ask: "Surely lying is scarcely a worse crime than stealing or killing? Apparently Mr. O'Grady thinks it is, for he pours forth the vials of his wrath on the native Irish for their deviations from strict truthfulness, and regrets that the Danes did not completely conquer the country." In "History and Biography," *Westminister Review,* 141 (1894), 221.

[19]*History of Ireland: Critical and Philosophical,* p. 61.

[20]Cf. Curtis, *passim.*

[21]For a comprehensive study of the development of the Aryan myth in Europe in the late nineteenth and the twentieth centuries, cf. Leon Poliakov, *The Aryan Myth,* tr. Edmund Howard (New York: Basic Books, 1974).

[22]Standish James O'Grady, Letter to Walt Whitman, 5 Oct. 1881 in Horace Traubel, *With Walt Whitman in Camden* (New York: Rowman & Littlefield, 1961), p. 400.

[23]Walt Whitman, "Democratic Vistas," in *Leaves of Grass and Selected Prose* (New York: Modern Library, 1950), pp. 485-486.

[24]W. B. Yeats, "Vacillation" in the *Variorum Edition of the Poems of W. B. Yeats,* ed. Peter F. Allt and Russell K. Alspach (New York: Macmillan, 1957), p. 501.

Chapter I

Early Life and Work

Some writers consciously set out to change the course of literature. Standish O'Grady did, and at times his task was a lonely one. His poem "I Give My Heart to Thee" reveals in the speaker a self-pity that O'Grady himself may sometimes have felt:

> I give my heart to thee, O Mother-land—
> I, if none else, recall the sacred womb.
> I, if none else, behold the loving eyes
> Bent ever on thy myriad progeny
> Who care not nor regard thee as they go,
> O tender, sorrowing, weeping, hoping land![1]

Such a cry is the lament of a man who feels himself called to a special mission. His early training and the influence of his parents' religious sensibility disposed O'Grady to see his life's work in terms of calls to be answered. He heard many calls during his life, and many could not be reconciled with one another. For this reason, O'Grady's works may often appear self-contradictory and confusing. Yet one may understand his temperament and see a certain consistency to his life by observing the facts of his early years and the ideas developed in his early work.

Standish James O'Grady was born on September 18, 1846 to Thomas and Susanna O'Grady. Thomas O'Grady was the Church of Ireland Rector of Castletown Berehaven in County Cork, and his brand of Protestantism was strongly Evangelical in character. Though Standish later rejected the tenets of his parents' religion, he, like his mentor Carlyle, never lost his respect for the spirit of Evangelicalism.[2] His son has told us that the parents in O'Grady's boys' stories are based on Thomas and Susanna O'Grady.[3] In *Mr. Goodenough*, the narrator, Charles Randon, tells us that his parents "were both very serious-minded and pious, and perhaps a little strait-laced in certain directions, awfully strict Sabbatarians, and so forth; but, however things may have altered since then, I rather think that in my time all really god [sic] people were religious, and professed Evangelical principles.   All the great clergymen of the day—Pope, Gregg, Brooke, Alcock, and soforth [sic], were Evangelical."[4]

Implicit in this passage is a belief that "all really good people" now more properly owe their allegiances to something more than Evangelical Protestantism.   Yet during the narrator's youth they were properly given to that religious movement. O'Grady's thinking here follows Carlyle's, especially in *Sartor Resartus.*   For, to use Carlyle's words, the "clothes" of Evangelicalism are worn out, and the seeker of truth is constantly looking for the new "clothes" which are the visible manifestation of the "celestial invisible."[5]   O'Grady exhibited this attitude of unrest throughout his life.   Yet he probably regarded the changes he went through as more apparent than real, just as he regarded visible changes as mere "new clothes."

During his early years, O'Grady changed his life's work several times.   He began as a divinity student at Trinity College in 1864, but, as his son reports, O'Grady "had to believe and disbelieve too much."[6]   He turned to the law and was called to the Bar in 1872. Then, some time after 1873, he found his true range of interests: he became a journalist for the Dublin *Daily Express* and devoted himself to the study of early Irish literature.

His discovery of Irish literature has all the earmarks of a religious conversion, and it follows the pattern of Evangelical religious experience.   Indeed O'Grady's account of the experience reminds me of Moses hearing God's voice in the desert:

> . . . I believe that this account of the accident of the wet day and an old library at hand, which started me as a writing man, will be not unwelcome to those who take an interest in the history of Anglo-Irish literature.   It looks like an accident, a mere chance; and yet I don't think it was quite such. If the fall of a sparrow is provided for, possibly so was that wet day in the West of Ireland.[7]

That "wet day" "providentially" compelled O'Grady to remain indoors where he happened to pick up and read a book on Irish history. The book was Sylvester O'Halloran's *History of Ireland* (1778),[8] and for the first time O'Grady discovered that Ireland had a history. O'Grady found a calling, and he had found it in a curiously Evangelical way. Apparently this kind of experience was common in the nineteenth century. Indeed, the novelist Wilkie Collins saw fit to satirize the Evangelical practice of leaving devotional pamphlets where people might pick them up and be touched by the word of God. In *The Moonstone*, Miss Clack leaves devotional pamphlets all over Lady Verinder's house, "under the sofa cushions, half in, and half out, close by her [Lady Verinder's] handkerchief, and her smelling bottle. Every time her hand searched for either of these, it would touch the book; and sooner or later (who knows?) the book might touch her."[9] While Collins thought such notions were nonsense, O'Grady did not. For him the "wet day" was "provided for" as a mode of perceiving how to live his life, and O'Halloran's book was there that it might touch him.

   In one way at least O'Grady was right. Sylvester O'Halloran's *History of Ireland* was "provided for" by O'Grady's ancestors. The list of subscribers in O'Halloran's *History* includes six O'Gradys, one of whom was Standish's great-grand-father.[10] Such a point would not have been lost on O'Grady. He came from an old family, and he was keenly aware that his ancestry conferred both rights and responsibilities on him. Indeed his insistence on the responsibilities of his fellow land-lords during the Irish Land War of the 1880's shocked them.[11] Yet O'Grady felt that he was following in the traces of a high noble family. A cousin of his father's and a namesake had been a hero at the Battle of Waterloo, and another of his father's cousins had been one of Nelson's captains. The Irish had shared in the "glories" of the British Empire, and when later in his life O'Grady began to speak of the "Anglo-Irish Empire,"[12] he could cite as evidence the exploits of his own ancestors. As O'Grady's family heritage had acted upon him by providing O'Halloran for him to read, so O'Grady's life became an attempt to make his and Ireland's past work in the present. He had learned from Carlyle, most notably in *Past and Present*, that the future could only be made by the work he did in the present, a present shaped for him by his ancestors.

   The recognition that the work of his ancestors was an *Irish* contribution to the British Empire, however, was certainly not "provided for" in his education. O'Grady attended Protestant Irish schools where history was taught from an English perspective. For this reason O'Halloran's *History* came as a shock to him. Yet in other respects he received a good education. His son credits the Tipperary Grammar School for giving his father "training in minute and accurate scholarship."[13] From there, O'Grady went to Trinity College, where he won the classical scholarship, the University Silver Medal in Ethics and Psychology, and the Philosophical Society's silver medal in oratory and gold medal in essay writing. His schoolmate at Trinity, Alfred Percival Graves, claims that O'Grady "surprised all of us would-be scholars in his class by the beauty of his Greek verse."[14] O'Grady's later epical treatments of the Irish bardic literature bear witness to the classical studies of his youth.

During his time at Trinity, however, he and the other members of the literary circle put their classical learning to use by writing poems in Greek and Latin and translating English poems into those languages. One of O'Grady's first published articles[15] was written to introduce *Kottabos*—a magazine that had been started by his Trinity circle to publish its Latin and Greek poems and translations. The article's significance lies not so much in his statements about the poetry itself, as in his encouragement and recognition of Irish literary efforts. O'Grady spent the rest of his life combating the inferiority complex of Irish writers. *Kottabos,* his article contends, proves that Trinity College writers can produce first-rate poetry: "This witty and spirited little periodical . . . will go far towards dissipating the reproach of silence that has clung, so long, and so unjustly, around the University of Dublin."[16] A collection of verse by *Kottabos* contributors had "earned the warm praise of English literary organs."[17] Later in his career, O'Grady became more interested in pleasing the Irish, but his comment does reveal the state of Irish literary affairs at the time. An Irish writer achieved success by pleasing English audiences.

O'Grady himself contributed to *Kottabos.* A poem, "On Reading the Fragments of Early Greek Lyric Poetry,"[18] gives evidence of the kind of literary interest that later sparked his study of early Irish literature. The poem records O'Grady's fascination with the remnants of early Greek poetry, "whose broken harmony / Makes discord shriek where music seem'd to flow. . ." In contrast to that now lost harmony, the speaker

in the poem reports that "We have all Tupper—not one thunder-
tone / Hath ceased to bellow through the British sky. . ." Martin
Farquhar Tupper's verse was the quintessence of trite morality
during the Victorian era, yet it achieved overwhelming popularity.[19]   In the face of that popularity, the speaker wonders
what has become of the early Greek poems. He answers his
own question in lines strongly reminiscent of Matthew Arnold's
description of Hebraism and Hellenism in *Culture and Anarchy:*

> The law that bound the Israelites of old
> Slays you, the firstlings of Apollo's fold.

Arnold regarded the Hebrew and Greek cultures as the
two primary influences on British culture. However, he saw the
Hebraic spirit which emphasized strict conscience and righteous
conduct as the dominant influence during his time. Its
dominance over the clear-eyed symmetry and spontaneity of
Hellenism encouraged the philistinism of the English middle
class which idolized the works of Tupper. Accordingly,
O'Grady's speaker's words record not only the action of time,
but also the triumph of the Hebraic spirit, in bringing to pass
the death of the early Greek poems. In the ensuing years
O'Grady came to see the near-death of early Irish literature
in similar terms.
        However, that view of Irish literature awaited the "wet
day" of O'Grady's conversion expience. The available evidence
suggests that prior to that time O'Grady was a young man in
search of an object of belief. A letter to John Stuart Mill in
1869[20] shows O'Grady looking for grounds on which it is
possible to establish a legitimate belief in the supernatural.
The manner in which O'Grady phrases his question to Mill
suggests that it is not an abstract matter for him. He is not
looking for grounds for *a* believer; rather he asks, ". . . why
could not *my* belief in that supernatural being be established
and legitimately established?"[21]
        The evidence of O'Grady's life and his writing during the
period between his graduation from Trinity with a B. A. in
1868 and the publication of Volume I of the *History of Ireland*
in 1878 suggests that his letter to Mill was part of a search for
a *raison d'etre.* During that time he made the move from law
to journalism and literature although the move was probably
gradual. His son suggests that he continued to practice law

even after he began writing for the *Daily Express.*[22]   Under the pseudonym Arthur Clive he also published many articles and one pamphlet which he later described to John Quinn as the product of his "metaphysical student days."[23]   The pamphlet, *Scintilla Shelleiana,* was published in 1875.   That O'Grady should look back on a time so much after his graduation from Trinity as part of his "metaphysical student days" supports my contention that the entire period was spent in a restless search for his life's work and meaning.   Restlessness was to remain essential to O'Grady's character, yet at this time he formed many ideas and attitudes which stayed with him to the end.   The articles and the pamphlet that he published in the 1870's reveal the development of his thought.

The fact of the publication of *Scintilla Shelleiana* is in itself telling.   The pamphlet was a republication with O'Grady's own preface of the agnostic tract, "The Necessity of Atheism," which had resulted in Shelley's expulsion from Oxford.   Even though O'Grady published it under a pseudonym, doing so was still an audacious act because agnostic tracts were not received kindly in Ireland and discovery of the editor's real name might have been severely prejudicial to his ability to make a living. But O'Grady had a great deal of the imp in him, and he seems to have been drawn to the unpopular simply because it was unpopular.   Many years later, in a letter to John Quinn, O'Grady acknowledged as much.   He had written a short study of the king who had first brought the English to Ireland.   The study, *The Departure of Dermot,* praised the great virtue of Dermot, about whom a kind word had not been uttered by a patriotic Irishman for centuries.   O'Grady says of this work: "I think it was perhaps love of mischief made me do it, partly; because our patriots always treat that unlucky dynast as an Irish Iscariot."[24]

O'Grady was an instigator who constantly sought to introduce new ideas.   Whether his *History of Ireland* was or was not the spark that ignited the Irish Literary Revival, O'Grady was very happy to think it so since he spent most of his life trying to light fires.   Much has been made of O'Grady's modesty,[25] but I find him shy rather than modest.   In a 1905 letter, he tells John Quinn, "If you ever have a conversation with the President [Roosevelt], you might say *truly*, that, as to the intellectual, literary, Gaelic-Irish Movement, it was I who set them all in motion."[26]   Indeed in a 1914 letter he is even able to become sentimental about himself. He tells Quinn that he "noticed that you regarded all this princely hospitality [during O'Grady's New York trip] as a mere trifle; save for your desire to do something for the pleasure and entertainment, while with you, of an Irish man, who once gave a very little time and labor to the interests of the poor old country."[27] O'Grady deserves admiration for what he set out to do and what he accomplished. It should be noted, however, that he was willing to take the credit he deserved.

O'Grady's works influenced many people, and almost everything he wrote had a didactic purpose. The preface to *Scintilla Shelleiana* was no exception to the latter point, at least. O'Grady dedicated the pamphlet to the youth of Ireland in the hope that it would stir in them a passion for truth. He states the problem simply: "Pure speculation does not flourish in these countries. There is always something which we prefer to truth. Trinity College, of whose large and generous spirit we are all so proud, plainly postpones the interests of truth to those of religion."[28] While O'Grady's appeal has an academic framework here, the same passion later motivates him to make the Fenians' chief characteristic that "they always told the truth."[29]

In those later works, O'Grady's purpose is to provide heroic models, and the heroic call is also present in his preface to the *Scintilla Shelleiana*. He feels compelled to publish this atheistical document because Trinity's curriculum "includes the best written defences of Theism and of Christianity, but does not contain a single hostile work. If this be the way to make Christians, it is not the way to make men, and the latter object, not the former, should at all times guide the action of an institution which boasts itself to be national and is unsectarian."[30] In short, the university should mold the future heroes of the country.

In those future heroes, O'Grady placed his entire faith. He considered Ireland a country with a still-born history. Yet the heroic past that he found in the bardic literature prophesied a great future, and that future belonged to the young to whom O'Grady dedicated his pamphlet.

In publishing the *Scintilla Shelleiana*, O'Grady was taking on two institutions—the Established Church (although in essence he was confronting all religions) and Trinity College. On the one hand, O'Grady's Evangelical background made him suspicious of established religion; on the other hand, he admired the spirit of primitive religions because he believed that they did not alienate people from primal realities as institutionalized religions did.

O'Grady shared a dislike of institutions with Shelley, and it is no accident that it was Shelley's agnostic tract that he chose to republish. O'Grady was sympathetic to the romantic sensibility, and he had written an article on Shelley's "Prometheus Unbound" in 1874 which reveals how close in spirit he was to Shelley. O'Grady concludes that article by praising Shelley for having "raised the ideal of human excellence so far as almost to make us hate the word 'progress' and grow weary of 'civilization' whose results up to the present have been so meager and disheartening."[31]

With such an attitude towards progress and civilization, it is not surprising that O'Grady became interested in the literature of primitive Ireland. He shared an aversion to material progress with the Romantics who had rebelled against the eighteenth-century thinkers who had been convinced of the value of progress and civilization. Where they had looked at the primitive as backward and unevolved, the Romantics saw the primitive as natural and unspoiled. In the nineteenth century, the historian Macaulay was still glorifying progress much as his eighteenth-century predecessor Gibbon had done. A man of O'Grady's propensities could only dislike such views. With an Irish consciousness added to his Evangelical spirit, O'Grady gravitated naturally to the Romantics. For Macaulay and Gibbon, Ireland was primitive and therefore wild, untameable, and savage. For O'Grady, Ireland was primitive and therefore unspoiled. Like many Romantics, O'Grady hated the city and saw it as the center of the cash-nexus that Carlyle had declaimed against so vehemently. Later in his life, O'Grady tried to encourage Dublin clerks to leave the city and form communes in the country because he believed that communes were the primitive form of human organization.[32]

The fact that Ireland was primitive meant also that it was young. The country's potential greatness in the future inspired O'Grady with tremendous optimism. He saw the same optimism in Shelley in whose "first-rate works there lives a confident and sanguine spirit which is infectious" despite the "pale modern spirit."

> The "Prometheus Unbound" is of this character—it is
> a splendid lyrical drama in which through the medium
> of superhuman characters of the utmost sublimity and
> loveliness, the poet depicts the sufferings and endurance
> of the unconquerable spirit of freedom through its night
> of tribulation and suppression, the ultimate overthrow
> and annihilation of that Evil One that brooded over the
> world threatening the extinction of the human race,
> and concludes with the joy of all created things at their
> liberation and the glory and beauty that start up on
> all sides on the destruction of that "sceptred curse"
> which had so long darkened the world.[33]

Despite the ghastly occurrences which accompany the
"destruction of that 'sceptred curse,' " O'Grady, with Shelley,
dwells on the glory that is to come but recognizes that the
horror must come first. O'Grady seems to have read enough
Carlyle by this time to see a modern counterpart for the dark
hours before the triumph of Prometheus. As the dark hours
came, so "rose the French Revolution when its fatal hour drew
nigh."[34] Carlyle believed that French Revolutions were "fated"
and necessitated by the "shams" that preceded them.

Despite his agreement with Carlyle on the causes of French
Revolutions, O'Grady disliked Carlyle's pessimism and was
willing to attack him for it. Another 1874 article, "Boswell
and His Enemies," took Carlyle to task for his lack of sympathy
with James Boswell. The main thrust of O'Grady's criticism is directed at Macaulay, but at times he includes Carlyle. Given the
fact that O'Grady became so wildly enthusiastic about Carlyle in
his later work, his criticism here is surprisingly severe: "Boswell's book lives and has power because it is true. In proportion
as men are themselves genuine they will admire and like the
man. It was beyond the limit of possibility that either Macaulay
or Carlyle should have any close and sympathetic relations
with one who above all others calls a spade a spade, and never
swells and foams in the vein of 'Ercles.' "[35] The explanation
for this criticism, however, lies in O'Grady's passion for truthfulness. He cannot brook any deviation from the highest
standards of truthfulness even from Carlyle, nor does he particularly like Carlyle's bombast (which O'Grady probably regarded as a species of untruthfulness). Carlyle's strident criticism
of the social ills of the time lacked the optimism which marked

O'Grady's attitudes.

The Boswell article itself reveals more than O'Grady's attitude towards Carlyle. Characteristically, O'Grady writes it to champion a man who was unpopular at the time, although Boswell hardly compares in unpopularity with King Dermot. (The article on "Prometheus" was written to examine "the profoundest and most perfect, yet at the same time the *least popular,* of his [Shelley's] more elaborate compositions.")[36] While Boswell may have been an unpopular type in the nineteenth century, he was O'Grady's ideal man. O'Grady attributes to Boswell many of the qualities that he would later see in Irish heroes:

> Boswell's talents are denied, his virtues degraded into vices, his vices exaggerated into crimes; his noble and passionate affection for the place of his birth and the seat of his ancestors, his feudal pride in a long and distinguished lineage, his sincere and manly admiration for talent and all forms of spiritual courtesy, eminence, his flowing and universal courtesy, his generosity, *bonhomie,* and conviviality, his frank and winning ways, his, at times, spirited and gallant behaviour, his manly outspokenness and his no less manly reticence, the grand passion of his life, his high and heroic devotion to his type and ideal of moral and intellectual grandeur, Samuel Johnson, are all denied, or ignored, or ridiculed.[37]

O'Grady's Boswell is the chivalric man of feudal times, and in O'Grady's later work this role is filled by the "grand old heroes of the Red Branch of Ulster, from whose strength and courage and other manly attributes sprang the rude beginnings of European chivalry, which was strong in Ireland before its beautiful laws began to be understood in the rest of Europe."[38]

Those heroes abided by a moral code, and this morality is what most impresses O'Grady about Boswell. He says that "it is not Boswell's literary so much as his moral worth that I feel pleasure in substantiating."[39] O'Grady might have taken this a step further by denying that there can be literary worth without moral worth. Indeed, almost all of O'Grady's works are written with express moral purposes.

Since the "moral message" of a work is most important to O'Grady, its literary form is secondary. And in the "Boswell" article O'Grady begins to justify the use of prose where poetry would normally be expected. He finds much in Boswell's *Life of Johnson* that

> . . . is grand as the Iliad and the Odyssey. If not writ in the high epic style it treats of high epic matter, and treats thereof in the mode best suited to the times. To sympathise tenderly and deeply with character and with mental suffering, attach oneself to it with passionate devotion, and so to write in loose prose what is great as the greatest poem, has fallen to few, and it has fallen to James Boswell.[40]

Less than a year later, in 1875, O'Grady wrote another essay, "The Trammels of Poetic Expression," which openly attacked meter and rhyme as artificial poetic constructs imposed by custom. In so doing, he was paving the way for the writing of his epic *History of Ireland* in prose. Here he praises Walt Whitman for the first time and singles out the absence of rhyme and meter in Whitman's works as "a very remarkable and significant fact."[41] He even goes as far as to declare that it

> . . . is plain that Plato was as great a poet as he was a philosopher. Yet even for his highest and most soaring flights of thought and imagination he employed unmetrical language. Still, it may be said that as the scheme of all his great works was didactic and philosophical he would naturally select the mode of expression which was best suited for teaching and illustration, and that, though his mind at times rose to the ethereal region of sacred enthusiasm and lyric frenzy, he could not disturb the integrity of his work by a change in the form of his language. Yet if metre is the natural expression of poetic thought, How [*sic*] happens it that as his mind rose to the lyric mood, as his thought soared heavenward, his language did not naturally and gradually assume the character of the thought, as the bird that soars or desires to soar beats its wings the faster? . . . Believing that metre is an artificial mode of speech, I can understand how Plato became a poet without writing in metrical language.[42]

Besides Plato, O'Grady found great poetry in the writings

of the "Hebrew bards." They, too, had addressed their people free from the "bonds" of meter. In particular, O'Grady was impressed by the suitability of the absence of meter to their moral purposes. Its absence allowed the Hebrew people to comprehend the message of their bards clearly. In his own time, O'Grady believed that Whitman was performing the same function, for the absence of meter facilitated Whitman's moral purpose of spiritualizing democracy. O'Grady looked also to the Romantic poets as the "teachers and schoolmasters of the young men of the present day."[43] They had made literature "the organ through which high moral natures address themselves to the improvement and elevation of man."[44] The Romantics had begun by giving literature moral purpose, and from this beginning O'Grady hypothesized that the "desire to influence the mind of man will inevitably urge poets to break through the flimsy barriers which metre sets up between them and the hearts of men."[45]

Here O'Grady was viewing the writing of literature as an historical process and was boldly prophesying the future course of poetry. A response to this kind of thinking was not long in coming. In the next issue of *The Gentleman's Magazine*, T. S. Omond (who later became a linguist of some note) called O'Grady to task for his article the previous month:

> . . . the critic can at best only collate the past; he cannot
> predict the future. It is his to say what poets have done,
> in what forms they have expressed their visions; but he
> steps beyond his province when he attempts to dictate
> what, therefore, the future poet shall do.[46]

In so attacking O'Grady, Omond was hitting at the core of O'Grady's theory of literature. Not until he writes his *History of Ireland: Critical and Philosophical* does O'Grady fully articulate his historical theory of literature. But his notion that art has an historical development is implicit in his belief that the future course of literature can be predicted, or for that matter, influenced by conscious design as he and Whitman tried to do. For Omond, such designs are impossible because "Great movements grow themselves."[47] Whitman cannot "write the poetry of democracy, such as on *a priori* grounds it must and will be."[48]

However, both O'Grady and Whitman had decided *a priori*

that meter must go. Omond's defense of it is the commonly held notion that "the highest truths of insight and imagination tend naturally and most perfectly to express themselves" in metered poetry.[49]   Indeed, Omond finds that in Whitman's "most passionate poems, whenever the thoughts are earnest and glowing and 'poetical,' the language instantly assumes a metrical cadence."[50]   But, in fact, the differences between O'Grady and Omond lie more in their notions of the nature of poetical truth, not its form.   For O'Grady, truth teaches. Omond found that quality objectionable in Whitman: "He is too self-conscious, too much wedded to certain theories, in fact a little too much of a doctrinaire, to attain that high self-forgetfulness which is essential to poetic fire."[51]

O'Grady would probably have regarded "high self-forgetfulness" as decadence. He was very "self-conscious," and, in fact, he begins his article by saying, "I believe that I am now breaking up virgin soil that has felt no plough before mine . . . if I can turn for awhile the minds of men of letters to an examination of the issue raised, I believe that the results will be in the highest degree salutory and mark an era in the history of our literature."[52]   O'Grady usually knew what he was doing, and he was usually trying to instigate others to do likewise.

While O'Grady did not manage to banish meter from poetry, he did manage to inaugurate an era in Irish literature, and his first essay on an Irish subject had appeared only one month before his essay on meter. The essay, "Stone Worship: Ireland," reveals once more O'Grady's great respect for the primitive.   His thesis is that Ireland had a highly developed religious sensibility before the advent of Christianity and that "the divine instincts of reverence and sacred awe are ours by inheritance from them."[53]

The respect O'Grady shows for the ancient religion is remarkably akin to his respect for the spirit of the Evangelical movement even though he did not believe in its tenets. Indeed, his ideas are much like those expressed in Carlyle's *On Heroes and Hero Worship*. There Carlyle praises the spirit that worships despite the fact that the visible object of its worship changes throughout the centuries. If anything, the primitive worship most directly comprehended what Carlyle called the "celestial invisible" since the object of the hero worship was a god.[54] The Norse god Odin was Carlyle's exemplar for the most primitive state of hero worship.

In his essay, O'Grady was trying to engender respect for that primitive religious sensibility. In doing so, he was fighting the notions of progress which the empiricists and *philosophes* of the Enlightenment had promulgated and which were still being nurtured by historians like Macaulay in the nineteenth century. Most Enlightenment writers generally valued reason and the abstract and saw civilization as real progress. Thus, the religion of the primitive which was passionate rather than rational, and concrete rather than abstract, was seen by the empiricists and *philosophes* as the state of religion which befitted such a low level of civilization.[55]   French *philosophes* such as Bernard Fontonelle and Pierre Bayle and the British empiricist David Hume were skeptics who were very close to regarding all religious belief as superstition. German Romantics, such as Johann Georg Hamann and Johann Gottfried von Herder, revolted against this skepticism and saw belief as a mode of perceiving truth. Carlyle was well acquainted with German Romantic thought, and O'Grady probably developed some acquaintance with it by way of Carlyle.

Herder's ideas are particularly pertinent to a study of O'Grady because Herder allied his notion of the development of religion to the development of races, and O'Grady's "Stone Worship" article follows this notion closely. Herder differed

> . . . from virtually all the western theorists in one vital respect: the divine revelation took place not in an individual, all men being equal, or in an archetype of a primitive, all aborigines being identical in the state of nature, but in the *Volk*. The *Völker* were at once the same and different. While the birth of the idea of God and the genesis of myth were in form similar historic events among all nations throughout the world, each people had enacted a unique version of the drama. . . . Herder's theory of the *Volk* focused upon divergences. Religion and mythology were the central character-forming agents, the crucial experiences of every *Urvolk*, and each history was a separate individual manifestation of the creative organic capacity of mankind.[56]

O'Grady saw in the artifacts of ancient Irish stone worship the remnant of the primitive religion and mythology of the

Aryan race—the *Urvolk* of Europe. Accordingly, study of these artifacts should shed light on the characteristics of that race which supposedly had spawned most European peoples. Indeed, O'Grady makes Christianity an Aryan growth and Irish paganism the font of the high Middle Ages:

> Scarcely was Ireland converted from paganism, when her piety became remarkable across the Continent, and through England and Scotland, founding schools, and monasteries, and churches, or rather sowing the tiny seeds, which afterwards grew up into noble abbeys and great cathedrals. But it was not Patrick and his successors who kindled that divine flame. It was kindled in the remote East, and the grey unnoted past. It was kindled in Iran, in Central Asia, when first the rude Aryan looked with awe upon aught which was awful, and taught his fellow to feel with him the same awe, and fixed a recurring time on which they should surrender their spirit to this emotion, and fixed upon an outward form by which that emotion might be reverently manifested, and a set of words by which it might be reverently expressed.[57]

Indeed, if O'Grady is right, Irish antiquarian studies ought to command the attention of most of Europe. But O'Grady was primarily interested in stimulating Irish interest, and the main thrust of his argument is directed towards his fellow Irish. On one level, O'Grady's logic is merely clever: he is trying to make the Irish see that their well-developed respect for Christian religious places should also dictate a respect for their pagan predecessors.[58] He even proposes a program for preserving the artifacts of the ancient religion. Its details are not important, but it is very typical of O'Grady to propose practical solutions to problems. During his life he devised many practical political schemes for the implementation of his theories.

The subject of his next 1875 article, Lord Chesterfield, appealed to him on precisely these grounds, for O'Grady found in him a man who had incorporated the noble virtues into a practical scheme of life. Chesterfield had perfected the practical art of good manners, in which was embodied "his strong sense of what conduced most to happiness in the intercourse of man with man. . . ."[59]

O'Grady admired Chesterfield for the traits that he had found praiseworthy in his previous essays. Chesterfield's prime consideration in the education of his son was that he "knew that young Stanhope would never succeed unless as a man of honor and truth, and accordingly he [plied] him with every conceivable reason by which he might induce him to love truth."[60]   O'Grady liked Chesterfield's optimism and thought it no fault that Chesterfield's life was happy. Because a "horror of thick darkness brooded for ever over the sick soul of Johnson,"[61] Chesterfield's great contemporary, O'Grady found no reason to condemn Chesterfield for his happiness. Once again, O'Grady chose to champion the unpopular. Johnson was popular in the nineteenth century, while Chesterfield was not.

In explaining Johnson's popularity, O'Grady wrote one startling sentence in which he sounded a note of absolute authority worthy of the Doctor himself. Without preparing his readers (he begins a paragraph with it), he declares: "A great deal of the praise which is lavished upon Johnson is to be ascribed to our Teutonic love of the vast and the horrible."[62] This boldness became characteristic of O'Grady's style. He goes on to explain what he means, but the sentence has a way of making the reader pause and read it again before going on. While it may not have been unusual to attribute a national characteristic so glibly and so absolutely to race, the certainty with which O'Grady speaks is still surprising, and indeed the rest of his paragraph does not warrant such certainty:

> A splendid drama of the Sophoclean type, in which might be represented Hamlet, not tottering on the verge of insanity, but as he was in the days when the sweet bells of his brain rang out the music of health, and vigorous, joyful activity, would never have stirred the English and German soul so deeply as the wild and ghastly career of the madman. It is as evident as anything can be that we, in these northern climates, whether from race or from whatever cause, are in love with sorrow, and hold it as one of our most cardinal beliefs that greatness is necessarily more or less closely allied to melancholy.[63]

This passage is also noteworthy because O'Grady casts himself in the role of a Northerner with strong affinities to England. He does so in the *Dublin University Magazine*, no less, despite the fact that he has already undergone his conversion to Irish interests. He remained confused about his identity for the rest of his life, for his ancestral loyalties to England often swayed him.

O'Grady's confusion was not limited to his sense of national identity. He often made errors and contradicted himself. In his next essay, "Druidism" (November, 1875), he returned to Irish subject matter and managed to make statements which are hard to reconcile. On the one hand, he says that there is "no evidence that any of these northern peoples, who have since received the inapplicable name of Aryan, ever emerged from barbarism. . ."[64] On the other hand, he holds out the hope that knowledge of druidical learning "would rescue the north of Europe from that ignominy and imputation of unmitigated barbarism which the ignorance and prejudice of Roman writers have attached to it."[65]

This assignation of barbarism to the north and civilization to the south is one of O'Grady's favorite theories. Northern barbarism implied an heroic code, while the south was the cradle of the imagination. O'Grady believed that it was "beyond question that, up to the time of Christ, all the civilizations of the world arose in the south of Europe and the south of Asia, that is, in the heart of the Euskarian or Semitic tract of the world's surface. . ."[66] These peoples were constantly invaded by northern people who imposed their languages on them but who "were totally destitute of even the germs of a civiliza-tion. . ."[67] In Vol. I of his *History of Ireland,* O'Grady des-cribed the Irish as part Basque and part Celtic, or, in effect, part southern and part northern.[68] Therefore, the Irish should be the perfect amalgam of the qualities of both.

The Basque part of the Irish was particularly important to O'Grady, and it was on his mind when he wrote his article on druidism. He believed that the Basque inhabitants of Spain were the remnants of the original civilizing tribes of Europe. Druidism had been an institution among these tribes, and its practice "involved learning and intellectual superiority."[69] Since Rome conquered all the people who practiced druidism except the Irish, Ireland alone through its descent from the Basques had some record of that druidical learning, and for this reason O'Grady appealed for its study. Ireland was originally Christianized from the East and maintained a druidical culture until *Roman* Christianity came, or so O'Grady thought. He was appalled by the Roman character of the Christianity which St. Patrick brought and which destroyed the druidical culture. Then, "[f]anaticism and superstition invaded the country in the form of continental ecclesiastics, revolutionized the whole tone of thought and feeling in the country, and in that revolution Druidism, and all of good or evil which it contained, passed away as a living and effective influence."[70]

Here, O'Grady reveals a mind totally given over to the idealization and glorification of pre-Christian Ireland. It is the attitude which fires his *History of Ireland,* and the article justifies such a history:

> . . . history, and especially that of the so-called pre-historic times, require more often than other departments of research new and still new popularizations of the accumulated information, on account of the greater number of sources from which fresh facts may be drawn to elucidate it, and the great importance of this science when compared with those which treat of inorganic things, or of the lower animals.[71]

It was not enough that scholars should uncover the facts and artifacts of druidism; they had to be made accessible to the people through "new popularizations." This theory follows naturally from O'Grady's Carlylian belief that the past lives in the present and the present must be aware of it so that the past can exercise its capability to "spiritualize" the present.

A month after the "Druidism" article, O'Grady wrote an article in praise of the poet who sought to "spiritualize" democracy. In Whitman's "Democratic Vistas," the reader would find "an eager brooding anxious pondering over and statement of the great problem of how to spiritualize and refine the gross, crude, vulgar American mind. . ."[72] While Carlyle looked on democracy with horror, Whitman saw it as the wave of the future and sought ways to attach to it the spiritual qualities that Carlyle himself admired. While Carlyle realized that the exterior manifestations of those spiritual qualities kept changing, he seems always to have clung to the manifestation that was passing away instead of the one that was on its way. Whitman and O'Grady both look to the future, and O'Grady admired Whitman's optimism. O'Grady felt genuine enthusiasm for Whitman, while his other cherished guides, Ruskin and Carlyle,

merely had his respect. The "Whitman" article makes O'Grady's
reasons clear: "Ruskin is evidently more affected by the oyster
shells in the stream than by the pretty stream itself, and the
sombre and funereal imagination of Carlyle extends itself over
the whole universe. Read the 'French Revolution.' Who in
perusing that powerful performance would imagine that France
was a sunny country?"[73]

While O'Grady approved of Whitman's artistic purpose,
he criticized him for pursuing it too consciously. O'Grady's
only comment about Whitman that is even slightly negative
could ironically be made about some of O'Grady's own work.
In Whitman, O'Grady finds:

> . . . this detraction from his genius, that he works after
> ideals and models in a conscious manner. His notions on
> the subject are singularly profound and just, but one is
> prejudiced slightly against poetry which may be the
> result of effort, and the striving after a preconceived
> ideal. Whitman sees that in everyday life one must be
> natural in order to please, that there is an indescribable
> charm and freshness about persons who are natural.
> And so with industry prepense he labours to be so and
> to appear so.[74]

Except for this criticism, O'Grady is heeping praise on a
kindred spirit. Whitman read the article and was "deeply
pleased" by it, for O'Grady dwelt "on *what I like to have dwelt
on*."[75] Whitman sent his photograph to O'Grady, and thus
began their correspondence which continued intermittently
until Whitman's death in 1892.

After the Whitman essay, O'Grady published three more
essays on Irish subjects prior to his publication of Vol. I of
the *History of Ireland* in 1878. The three essays—"St. Patrick"
(March 1876), "Irish Archaeology" (December 1876), and
"The Milesian Invasion of Ireland" (June 1877)—reveal O'Grady
wrestling with historical method. All three demythologize
longstanding beliefs about characters and events in Irish history
and literature. O'Grady saw St. Patrick as but one saint among
many who brought about the Christianization of Ireland. He
achieved preeminence over the others by the need of the bards
to have a central hero for all the legends of the Christianizing
process.[76] In "Irish Archaeology," O'Grady argued that Brian

Borom did not win the battle of Clontarf and banish the Danes from Ireland. O'Grady held that, in fact, Brian was fighting an indigenous population.[77] In "The Milesian Invasion of Ireland," O'Grady argued that the story of the Milesian invasion was really an allegory "and transformed history of the subjugation of Ethnic Ireland by Spanish Christian missionaries."[78]

In demythologizing, O'Grady applied what he called the "critical and philosophical spirit" to the historical accounts. He believed it would enable him to find the true facts which lay behind the legendary accretions of centuries. O'Grady saw the "critical and philosophical spirit" as an historical development, and called it

> . . . a plant of slow and late growth. In the development of nations, in the progress of civilization, it never precedes the artistic, the creative spirit, but if it comes at all, succeeds it generally with a long interval. To the critical spirit the first question is—Is this true? To the artistic— Is it beautiful? Does it satisfy the imagination? For this reason, those personages whom we see in the forefront of every history must be unreal. Even when they have had a real historical existence, their figures, as they have come down to us, are strangely magnified and altered.[79]

In adopting this spirit, O'Grady was following the nineteenth century passion for "scientific history," i. e., history which treated sources with skepticism and tried to distill out the irreducible truths. F. G. Collingwood's description of this nineteenth century historiographic method is useful:

> The historians of the early and middle nineteenth century had worked out a new method of handling sources, the method of philological criticism. This essentially consisted of two operations: first, the analysis of sources (which still meant literary or narrative sources) into their component parts, distinguishing earlier and later elements in them and thus enabling the historian to discriminate between the more and the less trustworthy portions; and secondly, the internal criticism of even the more trustworthy parts, showing how the author's point of view affected his statement of the facts, and so enabling the historian to make allowance for the distortions

thus produced. The classical example of this method is [Barthold] Niebuhr's treatment of Livy, where he argues that a great part of what was usually taken for early Roman history is patriotic fiction of a much later period; and that even the earliest stratum is not sober historical fact but something analogous to ballad-literature, a national epic (as he calls it) of the ancient Roman people. Behind that epic, Niebuhr detected the historical reality of early Rome as a society of peasant-farmers. I need not trace the history of this method back through Herder to Vico; the important point to notice is that by the middle of the nineteenth century it had become the secure possession of all competent historians, at least in Germany.[80]

I have quoted Collingwood at such length because this theory together with some ideas of his own was the "secure possession" of Standish O'Grady. In "Irish Archaeology," he argued that it ought to be part of the method for writing the history of Ireland. For to "write a great and valuable history of Ireland, one should combine the science of Niebuhr and the imagination of Livy."[81] Given the fact that Niebuhr's *History of Rome* was credited with "unmasking" Livy's political purposes, it is hard to see how an historian could manage to combine both methods in a single history. This O'Grady tried to do in his *History of Ireland,* and the marriage of the two methods is not happy. O'Grady's sympathies seem always to lie with the way of the imagination, yet he constantly feels the obligation to the "critical and philosophical method." This obligation probably accounts for his *History of Ireland: Critical and Philosophical,* which was written after his mostly imaginative two-volume *History of Ireland.*

Even as O'Grady made his statement about the ideal method of writing Irish history, he tipped the scales toward the imaginative. He follows his statement about Niebuhr and Livy immediately with a recognition of the value of an imaginative history:

I am very far from saying that a history of Ireland, written as Livy wrote his history of Rome would not be in the highest degree valuable. Those splendid and glowing myths deserve a literary as well as a scientific treatment;

Livy made the history of his country as interesting as
the best tale.   And there are sufficient materials preserved in the Irish manuscripts for the pictorial history
of ancient Ireland. . . .   Of course, it would not have
supplied the place of a more scientific and rational narrative, but it would have fulfilled many important ends,
and, also, might be a delight when the scientific history
is forgotten.[82]

Niebuhr's "scientific" *History of Rome* is now nearly
forgotten, and it is no delight to read.   Yet, it strongly influenced
O'Grady, and it had a tremendous vogue in the nineteenth
century.   It was a powerful influence on the Liberal Anglicans
including the leading poet of the age—Tennyson.[83]   Niebuhr
and O'Grady held many of the same ideas.   For example, like
O'Grady, Niebuhr regarded meter as an artifice which limited
poetic expression.   Niebuhr believed that "now . . . every one
knows how poetry maintains its existence in every people,
until metrical forms, forein models, the various and multiplying
interests of every-day life, and general inertness or luxury,
stifle it, so that poetical minds are the very class whose genius
most rarely finds a vent. . ."[84]

Niebuhr further believed that the literary accretions of
centuries covered over the original poetry which was at the root
of Roman history.   This poetry is the ballad literature that
Collingwood described, and it takes a cold, scientific eye to
regard the literary reshapings it underwent through the centuries
as disfigurements.   Yet, that was Niebuhr's view and he saw it
as his task

. . . to restore the ancient tradition, to fill it up by re-
uniting such scattered features as still remain, but have
been left out in that classical narrative which has become
the current one, and to free it from the refinements with
which learning has disfigured it.   That distinct and lively
view, which his [the modern historian's] representation
also should aim to give, should be nothing more than the
clear and lively perception of the outlines of the old lost
poem.[85]

The "old lost poem" was the epic at the root of Roman
history which Niebuhr believed marked the Roman people out

for special ends.   This idea was very much like Herder's idea
of the supreme importance of the *Urvolk*.   Niebuhr believed
that these sacred songs or lays (*carmina*) embodied the mark
by which Providential fate had singled out the Roman people
for greatness.   Only certain "races" were so marked, and only
those marked were capable of civilization.   Niebuhr held that

> . . . not a single instance can be produced of a really
> savage people which has become civilized of its own
> accord, and that, where civilization has been forced
> upon such a people from without, the physical decay
> of the race has ensued. . . . For every race of men has
> received its destination assigned to it by God, with the
> character which is suited to it and stamps it.[86]

Niebuhr further believed that the quintessential document that
recorded God's stamp on a particular people was their national
epic.   For Rome, that epic was embodied in the lost sacred
songs and lays.

    With Niebuhr's theory in mind, O'Grady viewed the Irish
bardic literature as the providential stamp that marked out the
Irish for great things.   Unlike Niebuhr, who was viewing Roman
history as "a foreiner and a critic,"[87] O'Grady could make his
scholarship serve great national purposes.   He could be both the
"singer" that Carlyle called for in "Shooting Niagara"[88] and
the scientific scholar that Niebuhr wanted.

    Now the science that Niebuhr wanted was no simple ab-
stracting of facts.   He saw uses for the imagination in writing
history (not in the way that Livy used it), and O'Grady sub-
scribed to his view also.   Professor Loebell, a contemporary of
Niebuhr, described his method:

> . . . to form to himself a consistent picture of the whole,
> he [Niebuhr] was often compelled to foresake established
> opinions, and to throw out new hypotheses, which he
> was enabled by the rich variety of his learning, the acute-
> ness of his criticism, and his genius for combination, to
> suggest and maintain. Criticism here showed itself as not
> merely negative, but as the stimulant and assistant to
> creative energy, while a vivid imagination helped the
> author to perfect his production. For imagination, if
> understood, not in the sense of an absolutely unfiltered

invention, but as the gift of restoring distinct outlines and coloring to dim and faded forms, is as essential to the historical inquirer as to the poet, who does not decorate the materials furnished by history at his own free will, but colors the given outlines, according to conditions involved in their very nature.[89]

O'Grady expressed almost exactly the same view of the use of the imagination in his 1897 essay, "Imagination in History."[90] That theory of the imagination also informed a postscript to *The Flight of the Eagle* (1897) in which he criticized J. A. Froude for not properly disciplining his imagination. At the same time, O'Grady distinguished his own kind of imagination from Froude's:

Of conscious imagination there is in this tale no doubt a little, but of unconscious imagination I hope none. By 'unconsciousness' I mean that sort of imagination which led Mr. Froude, for example, in a highly picturesque manner to slay the old chieftain, Feagh MacHugh, some twenty years before the date of this story. Mr. Froude slew him brilliantly one snowy day, under a wrong surname, and chased his O'Byrnes into the mountains, tracking them by the blood of their wounded.[91]

It was with such a conscious imagination that O'Grady set about writing his *History of Ireland*. He believed firmly in searching out his facts and then allowing his imagination to recreate the actual people and events.[92] This method he learned from Niebuhr. He believed it would reveal the truth of the past. Like Carlyle, he believed that truth teaches and that therefore the truth of the past has a moral function in the present. Like Livy, he thought to write his history to instill his own moral ideas in his people. To be true to all these models was to be a difficult balancing act, but it was in the nature of this Anglo-Irish Protestant Nationalist Unionist to try to reconcile the irreconcilable.

Notes

[1] Standish James O'Grady, "I Give my Heart to Thee," in Hugh Art O'Grady, *Standish James O'Grady: The Man and the Writer* (Dublin and Cork: Talbot, 1929), p. 50.

[2] O'Grady's Evangelical proclivities pervaded many of his stances: his sympathies lay with the Dissenters in Church matters, he admired Milton and the Puritans, and he shared the Dissenters' dislike of institutions.

[3] Hugh Art O'Grady, *Standish James O'Grady: The Man and the Writer* (Dublin and Cork: Talbot, 1929), p. 25.

[4] Standish James O'Grady, *Mr. Goodenough*, in *All Ireland Review*, 3 March 1900, p. 3.

[5] Thomas Carlyle, *Sartor Resartus*, in *Sartor Resartus and Selected Prose* (New York: Holt, Rinehart and Winston, 1970), pp. 86, 183, and *passim*.

[6] Hugh Art O'Grady, p. 33.

[7] Standish James O'Grady, "A Wet Day," *The Irish Homestead*, 5 (1899—Christmas number), 9. The "fall of a sparrow" idea is not original with O'Grady. Cf., *Hamlet*, V, ii, 190-191: "Not a whit, we defy augury. There's special providence in the fall of a sparrow." Cf. also, Matthew 10:29: "Are not two sparrows sold for a farthing? And one of them shall not fall to the ground without your Father."

[8] Cf. the next chapter for an extensive discussion of O'Halloran's *History*.

[9] Wilkie Collins, *The Moonstone* (London, Dent; New York: Dutton, 1971), p. 206.

[10] Sylvester O'Halloran, *A General History of Ireland* (London: Printed for the author by A. Hamilton, 1778), p. xi.

[11] Cf. O'Grady's *The Crisis in Ireland* (Dublin: E. Ponsonby; London: Simpkin and Marshall, 1882).

[12] Cf., e. g., Standish James O'Grady [Luke Netterville], *The Queen of the World* (London: Laurence and Bullen, 1900), p. 118.

[13] Hugh Art O'Grady, p. 31.

[14] Alfred Percival Graves, "Foreword," in Hugh Art O'Grady, p. 10.

[15] Standish James O'Grady [Arthur Clive], "*Kottabos*," *Dublin University Magazine* 84 (1874), 565-579.

[16] "*Kottabos*," 565.

[17] "*Kottabos*," 566.

[18] See Appendix A.

[19] Martin Farquhar Tupper (1810-1889) was an "English versifier whose facile, moralizing *Proverbial Philosophy* (four series, 1838-1867) went through some 50 editions and attained international vogue. A man who could write anything (e. g., *Some Verse and Prose about National Rifle Clubs*, 1858), his name became synonymous with pretentious twaddle." William Rose Benet, *The Reader's Encyclopedia*, 2nd ed. (New York: Thomas Y. Crowell, 1965), p. 1029.

[20] See Appendix B. For Mill's answer, see John Stuart Mill, "To Standish O'Grady," 16 January 1869, Letter 1378, *The Later Letters of John Stuart Mill, 1849-1873*, ed. Francis E. Mineha and Dwight N. Lindley (Toronto University Press, 1972), XVII, 1545-1546.

[21] Standish James O'Grady, Letter to John Stuart Mill, 9 January [1869], Hutzler Collection, Milton S. Eisenhower Library, Johns Hopkins University, Baltimore, Maryland (See Appendix B).

[22] Hugh Art O'Grady, p. 34. I do not accept everything Hugh Art O'Grady says about his father as certain fact.

[23] Standish James O'Grady, Letter to John Quinn, March [1918], John Quinn Memorial Collection, Manuscripts and Archives Division, The New York Public Library, Astor, Lenox and Tilden Foundations. The entire paragraph of his letter to Quinn reads: "I am not obliged to Mr. [Ernest] Boyd, his great industry and thoroughness, for hunting up the 'Scintilla Shelleyana' [sic]. It was only the pamphlet which caused Shelley's expulsion from Oxford and was printed by me in my metaphysical student days. Nothing to be ashamed of but a rather silly thing to do in a country like Ireland where the clerical mind has been and is so potent."

[24] Standish James O'Grady, Letter to John Quinn, 10 October 1917, John Quinn Memorial Collection, Manuscripts and Archives Division, The New York Public Library, Astor, Lenox and Tilden Foundations.

[25] This is rather a popular conception of O'Grady, and I have seen it stated many times in my reading about him. B. L. Reid's *The Man from New York* (New York: Oxford University Press, 1968) and Ella Young's *Flowering Dusk* (New York and Toronto: Longmans, Green, 1945) contain many anecdotes about O'Grady which support this view. Yet most of the anecdotes reveal O'Grady's shyness, not his modesty. For example, Reid reports the great difficulty John Quinn had in persuading O'Grady to sit for a portrait by J. B. Yeats.

[26] Standish James O'Grady, Letter to John Quinn, 13 April 1905, John Quinn Memorial Collection, Manuscripts and Archives Division, The New York Public Library, Astor, Lenox and Tilden Foundations.

[27] Standish James O'Grady, Letter to John Quinn, 15 March 1914,

John Quinn Memorial Collection, Manuscripts and Archieves Division, The New York Public Library, Astor, Lenox and Tilden Foundations.

[28]Standish James O'Grady [Arthur Clive], ed. *Scintilla Shelleiana* (Dublin: William McGee; London: Simpkin and Marshall, 1875), p. 6.

[29]Standish James O'Grady, *Finn and His Companions* (Dublin: Talbot; London: T. Fisher Unwin, 1921), p. 110.

[30]*Scintilla Shelleiana*, pp. 6-7.

[31]Standish James O'Grady [Arthur Clive], "Shelley's 'Prometheus Unbound,' " *The Gentleman's Magazine*, NS 12 (1874), 421-437.

[32]Cf. O'Grady's series of letters to Dublin clerks published under the title "Life and Liberty" in *The Peasant* and *The Irish Nation*. See bibliography for publication data.

[33]" 'Prometheus,' " 423.

[34]" 'Prometheus,' " 432.

[35]Standish James O'Grady [Arthur Clive], "Boswell and His Enemies," *The Gentleman's Magazine*, NS 12 (1874), 73.

[36]" 'Prometheus,' " 421 (italics added to quotation).

[37]"Boswell," 73.

[38]Standish James O'Grady, *The Story of Ireland* (London: Methuen, 1894), p. 25. Implicit in O'Grady's statement here is his belief that Ireland was the font of the High Middle Ages. Cf., pp. 23-24. In pointing out the importance of "moral worth," O'Grady reveals his "Hebraic" tendencies despite his early poems in condemnation of Tupper (cf., pp. 13-14).

[39]"Boswell," 75.

[40]"Boswell," 74-76.

[41]Standish James O'Grady, "The Trammels of Poetic Expression," *The Gentleman's Magazine*, NS 14 (1875), 184.

[42]"Trammels," 185-186.

[43]"Trammels," 196.

[44]"Trammels," 196.

[45]"Trammels," 196.

[46]T. S. Omond, "Is Verse a Trammel?" *The Gentleman's Magazine*, NS 14 (1875), 344.

[47]Omond, 349.

[48]Omond, 349.

[49]Omond, 354.

[50]Omond, 349.

[51]Omond, 348.

[52]"Trammels," 184.

[53]Standish James O'Grady [Arthur Clive], "Stone Worship: Ireland," *Dublin University Magazine*, 85 (1875), 70.

[54]Thomas Carlyle, *On Heroes, Hero-Worship and the Heroic in History*,

ed. Carl Niemeyer (Lincoln: Nebraska University Press, 1966), pp. 9-10 and *passim.*

[55]For a history of eighteenth-century religious thought, cf. Frank E. Manuel, *The Eighteenth Century Confronts the Gods* (New York: Atheneum, 1967).

[56]Manuel, p. 291.

[57]"Stone Worship," 70. Note that the religion-making process is the activity of a people as Herder said it was.

[58]Carlyle said that the "old clothes" deserved respect. Cf. *Sartor Resartus*, pp. 221-225.

[59]Standish James O'Grady [Arthur Clive], "Lord Chesterfield," *Dublin University Magazine*, 86 (1875), 65.

[60]"Lord Chesterfield," 54. Note that love of truth has practical advantages.

[61]"Lord Chesterfield," 53.

[62]"Lord Chesterfield," 53.

[63]"Lord Chesterfield," 53.

[64]Standish James O'Grady [Arthur Clive], "Druidism," *Dublin University Magazine*, 86 (1875), 515.

[65]"Druidism," 522.

[66]"Druidism," 515.

[67]"Druidism," 515.

[68]*History of Ireland: the Heroic Period*, pp. 15-18.

[69]"Druidism," 515.

[70]"Druidism," 522.

[71]"Druidism," 513.

[72]Standish James O'Grady [Arthur Clive], "Walt Whitman, the Poet of Joy," *The Gentleman's Magazine*, NS 15 (1875), 713.

[73]"Whitman," 704.

[74]"Whitman," 711.

[75]Walt Whitman, "To Edward Dowden," 4 March 1876, Letter 720, *Walt Whitman: The Correspondence*, ed. Edwin Haviland Miller (New York University Press, 1961), III, 27.

[76]Standish James O'Grady [Arthur Clive], "St. Patrick," *Dublin University Magazine*, 87 (1876), 270-271.

[77]Standish James O'Grady [Arthur Clive], "Irish Archaeology," *Dublin University Magazine*, 88 (1876), 642.

[78]Standish James O'Grady "The Milesian Invasion of Ireland," *Dublin University Magazine*, 89 (1877), 674.

[79]"St. Patrick," 258-259.

[80]R. G. Collingwood, *The Idea of History* (New York: Oxford University Press, 1956), pp. 129-130.

[81]"Irish Archaeology," 650.

[82]"Irish Archaeology," 650.

[83]Cf. Henry Kozicki, "Philosophy of History in Tennyson's Poetry to the 1842 *Poems*," *ELH*, 42 (1975), 88-106.

[84]Barthold G. Niebuhr, *The History of Rome,* Vol. I, tr. Julius Charles Hare and Connop Thirlwall (London: Taylor, Walton and Maberly, 1851), p. 256.

[85]Niebuhr, p. 510.

[86]Niebuhr, p. 83.

[87]Niebuhr, p. 510.

[88]Thomas Carlyle, "Shooting Niagara: and After?" in *Critical and Miscellaneous Essays,* Vol. IV, Vol. XVI of *Carlyle's Complete Works* (Boston: Dana Estes and Charles E. Lauriat, 1884), p. 445.

[89]Prof. [?] Loebell, "On the Character of Niebuhr as an Historian," in *The Life and Letters of Barthold George Niebuhr* (New York: Harper, 1852), pp. 541-542.

[90]Standish James O'Grady, "Imagination in History," *The New Review,* 17 (1897), 657-665.

[91]Standish James O'Grady, *The Flight of the Eagle* (Dublin: Phoenix, [n.d.]), pp. 308-309.

[92]Cardinal Newman's *Apologia pro Vita sua* provides an intriguing parallel to O'Grady's method. Newman did his scholarship first. He traced all the theological arguments which had led the Anglican Church to separate from Rome. Yet the scholarship was not enough to make Newman move to Rome. It required an act of the whole person—mind, will, and heart—to accomplish this move. Newman later defined this as the "illative sense." Cf. his *Grammar of Assent.*

Chapter II

O'Grady's Sources and the Tradition
of Irish Historiography

Between 1878 and 1882 O'Grady published the works that were to become his most important contributions to the Irish Literary Revival. The five books that he published during those years repeat parts of one another, and thus it is important to know the differences among them as well as to understand the differing designs that produced the changes in each book.

In 1878 the first volume of what was commonly called his "bardic history" appeared. The book, *History of Ireland: the Heroic Period*, contains two distinctly different kinds of chapters: some, mostly the opening, chapters are "scientific," descriptive accounts, while most of the chapters are narrative, or "bardic," renderings of the deeds of the ancient heroes, especially Cuculain. O'Grady was trying to present the facts or the "archaeology," as he termed it, of Ireland's progress from prehistory to the bardic times as well as the tales produced by the bards in those later times. He presented the tales with a liveliness that the "archaeology" could not possibly possess, and as a result, the two kinds of chapters do not mesh well. The narratives make the "archaeological" chapters seem very dry by contrast.

O'Grady seems to have had some awareness of this problem, for in the following year (1879), he published an 88-page essay entitled *Early Bardic Literature, Ireland* in which he described his mistakes in Vol. I and outlined the changed emphasis he planned for Vol. II. In Vol. I he "did not permit it to be seen with sufficient clearness that the characters and chief events of the tale are absolutely historic. . ." He believed his rendering of the tale partook more of the "nature of legend and romance than of actual historic fact seen through an imaginative medium."[1] While the narrative chapters may well partake of the "nature of legend and romance," it is their sharp contrast with the "archaeological" chapters that so pronounces their fanciful qualities.

Vol. II, *History of Ireland: Cuculain and his Contemporaries,* appeared in 1880, and O'Grady reprinted *Early Bardic Literature, Ireland* as the introduction to that volume. Vol. II proper followed that introduction with a long first chapter in which O'Grady sketched Irish history up to the time of Cuculain.[2] This sketch has the air of strict historicity about it in accordance with the design outlined in the introduction. However, the second chapter takes up the story of Cuculain where O'Grady leaves it at the end of Vol. I, and the decorum of the remainder of the volume does not differ markedly from the narrative chapters of Vol. I. Thus, O'Grady seems to have realized that it was the mixing of the two kinds of chapters that had created the wrong impression.

In O'Grady's next book, Vol. I of *History of Ireland: Critical and Philosophical,*[3] he reprinted many of the "archaeological" chapters from Vol. I of the "bardic history" and added to them many chapters written in the same vein. These chapters contained O'Grady's most explicit and best explanations of his theories of history and literature, yet on several occasions his imagination led him to launch into "bardic" renderings of some events.

Finally in 1882 O'Grady combined the narrative sections of Volumes I and II of the "bardic history" and published a single volume with the title, *Cuculain: an Epic.*[4] The first six pages of the book are new, but they are followed by pp. 109-267 of Vol. I and pp. 121-348 of Vol. II. In his preface to this volume, O'Grady admits the incompatibility of the "archaeological" matter with the narratives:

> . . . it having been suggested to me that the passages in question being divested of irrelevant matter, . . . [the narrative portions], being grouped around and integrally related with a single vital theme, would form a complete whole, and arrest and detain that attention which was dissipated by the multiplicity of details not interesting in this context, and by the various disquisitions and unrelated stories comprised in those volumes.[5]

The stylistic problem in these works resulted partly from O'Grady's attempt to write history in the manner of both Niebuhr and Livy.[6] On the one hand, he wanted to present the original, unembellished facts of the history; on the other hand, he wanted to inspire the Irish nation with the heroism of its ancestors. However, the stylistic problem also had a specific origin in the materials of Irish history as O'Grady found them, and partly for that reason it is necessary to examine his sources before proceeding to a full discussion of his works.

Irish history had been preserved in two principal ways: in annals, or sketchy, factual accounts of the principal events of each high king's reign, and in the bardic literature which bore some relation to the accounts in the annals. O'Grady was living in the age of Heinrich Schliemann, and the latter's excavations were revealing the historicity of the *Iliad*.[7] O'Grady quite naturally thought it fit to reconcile the more obviously historical documents with the predominantly imaginative literature.

O'Grady's sources influenced him in more ways than simply their mode of composition or arrangement, however. Indeed, it is necessary for a full appreciation of his works to understand that he was following a long tradition of Irish historiography.[8]   There is an edge to O'Grady's writing which he shared with his predecessors, i. e., they saw history as a vehicle for the vindication of Ireland from all kinds of charges, e. g., barbarism, treachery, and the like. They did not write history merely to have an account of Ireland's chronology. For these Irish historians, history argues for the greatness of the Irish people and serves as an instrument for the development of a positive national consciousness.   In short, their Ireland, as did O'Grady's, required the heroic vision.

Not surprisingly then, many of O'Grady's favorite ideas are not at all original with him and may be found in his sources. However, the sources also contain information that O'Grady chose to ignore. The discarded information is important, too, because it reveals the standard of judgment O'Grady exercised. For example, some of the stories in the sources about Cuculain did not contribute to the heroic image that O'Grady considered the correct image of Cuculain, so he dismissed them as not "canonical."[9]

O'Grady began his study of Irish history with his momentous discovery[10] of Sylvester O'Halloran's two volume work, *A General History of Ireland* (1778). O'Grady never referred to O'Halloran's work as a source, but he must have found O'Halloran's treatment of the ancient Irish legends appealing.   O'Halloran, with no apology or explanation, regarded them as containing a great deal of fact. His sense of vindicating the Irish even led him to connect them with the Greeks, the great progenitors of Western civilization. He treated the legends of a Greek ancestry for the Irish as factual and boldly stated that "our ancestors were the first reformers and improvers of Greece."[11]

O'Halloran wrote his history somewhat in the manner of an Irish annalist, i. e., he catalogued the kings of Ireland and the principal events of their reigns. He also embellished the account with the legends of ancient Ireland and his own speculations on the meaning of events. O'Grady, however, had available to him an English translation of the original annals, *Annals of the Kingdom of Ireland, by the Four Masters, from the Earliest Period to the Year 1616.* These annals, *The Annals of the Four Masters,* as they are commonly known, were translated and heavily annotated by John O'Donovan. They are dry, extremely factual renderings of the "bare bones" of Irish history. O'Grady liked to think of them as typical of the learning of the Irish monks, i. e., representative of the minds which had inherited only one-half of the bardic legacy, a concern for strict, almost scientific, accuracy. The monks, O'Grady believed, had no interest in the products of the imagination.[12] They simply took over the task of preserving the annals which the bards had preserved orally for centuries.

The entry in *The Annals of the Four Masters* for the time of Cuculain is typical and contains no mention of the most famous ancient Irish hero:

> The Age of the World, 5084. Eocaidh Aireamh, after having been fifteen years in the sovereignty of Ireland, was burned by Sighmall, at Freamhainn.[13]

O'Donovan embellished this entry with a footnote in which he described the events surrounding Cuculain's lifetime. O'Grady's *History of Ireland: Critical and Philosophical* resembles *The Annals of the Four Masters* in the sections in which it "catalogues" the reigns of the Irish kings. Many of O'Grady's entries in that volume are as sketchy as the quoted entry.

The task of transcribing *The Annals of the Four Masters* was finished in 1636, just seven years after Geoffrey Keating had finished his *History of Ireland.* Keating's *History* resembles *The Annals* in format, i. e., it proceeds by listing the kings of

Ireland from the earliest times and by describing the events of each king's reign. Keating's descriptions, however, are quite full, and he tries to find meaning and pattern in the events. *The Annals* are sheer chronology.

O'Grady used Keating extensively, and there are many footnote references to his *History* in Vol. II of O'Grady's *History of Ireland.*[14]   A new translation from the Irish of Keating's *History* by John O'Mahony had appeared in 1857, and O'Grady considered O'Mahony's edition to be the best.[15]   O'Mahony footnoted the book heavily, and many of the footnotes take Keating to task for including barbaric and salacious incidents. O'Grady's good Victorian soul found a kindred spirit here in O'Mahony as O'Grady could not bear to think that his heroes might not have been chaste.

O'Grady considered Keating, like O'Halloran, to have treated much of the bardic literature as "pure historic fact."[16] In *Early Bardic Literature, Ireland* O'Grady records his strong endorsement of this treatment.   Yet, in his introduction to Vol. I, he did criticize Keating for going too far.   He found that Keating had purged the bardic tales of "those qualities which have alone value to me, viz., the epic and dramatic."[17]

The epic and dramatic are qualities that make for good stories, so to find these in the records of early Ireland, O'Grady had to become acquainted with the bardic tales themselves.   In 1861, Eugene O'Curry had published his *Lectures on the Manuscript Materials of Ancient Irish History*, more commonly known by the short title *MS. Materials*.   These lectures were comprehensive, albeit very dry, descriptions of the principal manuscripts then available to scholars.   O'Grady found them valuable, for they described many of the tales and the appendices contained many translations.   Yet there was no order to the tales that would make for good reading.   Indeed, the lectures are really a catalogue and have the features that make a catalogue dull as a whole but interesting in parts.   O'Curry recommended that a successor use the bardic tales to fill in *The Annals of the Four Masters*.   O'Grady did so to some extent in his *History*, but O'Curry's notion was more scholarly, i. e., he simply wanted to insert the tales into the chronology of *The Annals* without reshaping them.   He probably did not conceive of the kind of imaginative rendering that O'Grady undertook for his "bardic history."

O'Curry, too, along with W. K. Sullivan, was responsible

for producing an archaeological and anthropological study to which O'Grady was very much indebted. The three volume study, *On the Manners and Customs of the Ancient Irish,* was published in 1873. Sullivan wrote the first volume to introduce the series of O'Curry lectures that were printed in the second and third volume. The three volumes describe in detail the class structure, the legal system, the use of metals, the armaments, and the music of the ancient Irish among other subjects. O'Grady incorporated much of this information into his *History,* often assuming that the reader would either know or would learn the technical meaning of the terms he borrowed from Sullivan and O'Curry.

The following sentence is an extreme example of the demands O'Grady placed on his readers by this kind of incorporation:

> Now, when there was no justification, the Ardollav computed first the enechlan on account of the insult, and this was determined according to his rank, and after that the corp-diera for the wounding.[18]

The context, however, usually conveys the general meaning of such terms, and, in a way, the terms give a certain appealing quaintness to the text.

In addition to O'Curry's *MS. Materials,* O'Grady found translations of the bardic tales in periodicals such as *Revue Celtique, Publications of the Ossianic Society,* and *New Atlantis.* He was especially indebted to the translation by John O'Daly of the *Tan-bo-Cooalney (The Cattle Raid at Cooley)* which he found in Royal Irish Academy.[19] The *Tan* is the most important tale in the Red Branch cycle of Irish sagas. It describes the raid on the North by the men of the four provinces of Ireland led by Queen Maeve. The tale focuses on the actions of Cuculain in single-handedly holding off the huge invading force.

O'Daly's translation uses archaic English throughout, which produces some appealing effects in parts. But he seems to have been more interested in rendering a literal translation than in creating a literary work of art. O'Grady's language is not as consistently archaic as O'Daly's, but he does use the archaic form for the second person.

O'Daly's translation provided the basis for O'Grady's rendering of Cuculains's exploits,[20] and there are many footnotes to the manuscript in Vol. II of the *History*. However, O'Grady was quite selective in his use of the translation, and his standard of selectivity was informed by many ideas that he shared with the authors and editors of his sources.

O'Grady shared with several of them a belief in the European significance of ancient Irish history and literature. Although the architectural ruins of ancient days can be found throughout Europe, O'Grady believed, however, that it was possible only in Ireland to know what those ruins had meant to the people who raised them. This knowledge was made possible by the surviving ancient Irish literature: "In world-history the value of the Irish bardic literature is this, that it clings close to rath and cairn, the source of all ancient Aryan literature. In the Iliad and the Nibelungen Lied the life-cord had been cut."[21] O'Grady believed that all European (or Aryan—he sometimes used the words interchangeably) peoples had evolved their institutions in the same manner. Only the Irish could tell other Europeans the history of European development.

O'Halloran had made exactly the same point: "Our history is the only means left to arrive at any tolerable knowledge of the ancient state of Europe. . ."[22] And Keating before him had made a point of the unsullied nature of Irish historical records: ". . . none of these plunderers had ever conquered Ireland, even according to Cambrensis, who tells us that Ireland had been always free from the incursions of any enemies by whom its history or antiquities could be destroyed—a thing that was not the case with any other European nation."[23] In the first volume of *Manners and Customs*, W. K. Sullivan gave the idea particular relevance to England, and the sense of vindication in his statement is strong:

> The results which I have obtained are very different from the current views about the political and social condition of the ancient Irish and their ethnological relationships. They also throw such an unexpected light upon the early institutions of the Anglo-Saxons, and upon the origin of the English representative system, of Gilds, and of the feudal system, as must give to ancient Irish history an importance it never possessed before, and secure for it a high place in early European and Aryan history.[24]

Almost a corollary of this notion about the importance of Irish history is the belief of O'Grady and his predecessors that Irish history reveals a high degree of civilization and learning in the country prior to Christianization.   Since the history of Europe was the history of the progress of civilization, it followed naturally that the only country with a record of that progress from its very early stages should exhibit more than a barbaric state of affairs in its early years.

O'Grady was particularly keen on this point especially since he regarded the advent of Christianity as a mixed blessing. He believed that Ireland had been highly civilized before the arrival of St. Patrick, and he was annoyed by the glib dismissals of Irish civilization by English historians.   Without evidence Gibbon had dismissed the early Irish as savage[25] and incapable of conquering Britain.   Macaulay likewise had disparaged the Irish and had indicated that they were uncivilized even as late as 1686:

> The Roman Catholic of Lancashire or Staffordshire had only to turn Protestant; and he was at once, in all respects, on a level with his neighbors: but, if the Roman Catholics of Munster and Connaught had turned Protestants, they would still have continued to be a subject people.   Whatever evils the Roman Catholic suffered in England were the effects of harsh legislation, and might have been remedied by a more liberal legislation.   But between the two populations [English and Irish] which inhabited Ireland there was an inequality which legislation had not caused and could not remove.   The dominion which one of these populations exercised over the other was the dominion of wealth over poverty, of knowledge over ignorance, of civilized over uncivilized man.[26]

O'Grady continually refuted such thinking by arguing that the Irish Church would not have reached such a high state of learning so soon after the Christianization of the country had not there been a highly developed culture prior to that time. O'Grady found precisely the same reasoning in O'Halloran:

> If then Ireland, in these early days of Christianity, became so renowned for arts and sciences, that when a lettered man of Britain, or of the continent, was for any

time absent, it became a common proverb—Amandatus
est ad disciplinam in Hibernia!—Is it not a strong pre-
sumptive proof that she must have possessed them before
this period, even though our histories had been silent
on this head, which we see was not the case?[27]

And in Sullivan's and O'Curry's *Manners and Customs,*
O'Grady found ample evidence of a highly developed culture.
Sullivan and O'Curry had provided a detailed explanation,
for instance, of the complex legal system that had existed in
pre-Christian Ireland. O'Grady used that information in his
History to demonstrate the sophisticated nature of early Irish
society. The inclusion of such information in his text is more
than mere decoration.[28] It is part of his argument on Ireland's
behalf.

In pre-Christian Ireland also, O'Grady and his sources
found evidence of an heroic, chivalric code, which they believed
had given birth to the chivalric code of the Middle Ages.
O'Grady always characterizes Cuculain as a "knight," and he
continually points out that warfare was carried out under high
standards of fair play. A knight's word was his bond, and no
knight would take unfair advantage of his opponent in battle.
Warfare was not to be avoided; rather the knight should seek
it to prove his mettle. O'Grady's Cuculain loves to fight.

O'Halloran expressed the same idea:

> To outlive a general defeat; to exist after the loss of the
> diadem, was to entail an eternal disgrace on the family.
> It was acknowledged by the princes; it was constantly
> practised by them; and in this they were imitated by the
> knights and the great nobility. *Is buane blath, na Saoighal*
> —"Glory is preferable to the world," was a constant
> maxim amongst our heroes.[29]

Indeed, O'Halloran went so far as to trace the existence
of the code to his ancestors back in Greece and even wondered
how much farther back it could be traced.

> So extremely ancient has the institution of chivalry
> been amongst us, that we scarce know where to trace
> its origin. We find our ancestors had it in Greece; and
> the Curetes, or knights amongst the first reformers of

Greece are mentioned with particular honor, and such
is to this day, the name of a knight in Irish.[30]

There is a point at which this heroic code becomes outright
Spartan militarism.[31]   O'Grady usually stopped short of advocating violence for its own sake, but his Cuculain is a blood-
thirsty sort.   On the day of his knighting, he immediately jumps
into his chariot, goes south and slays three of Ulster's enemies,
and brings back their heads.[32]   Indeed, O'Grady seems to be en-
dorsing Spartan schooling in the following passage in which
Cuculain and his charioteer, Laeg, visit their schoolboy haunts:

> . . . Cuculain and Laeg looked around them with great
> affection upon that noble park, where they knew well
> every nook and tree, and much they conversed with the
> knights who surounded [sic] them, recalling old adven-
> tures and pleasant incidents of that happy life, for as yet
> books had not imposed their tyranny over youthful
> minds; but the boys were there taught the management
> of steeds and chariots, and to close or let out the deadly
> shining blade and run forward upon the chariot-pole,
> also to fight from the chariot . . . and all that pertained
> to such warfare.[33]

O'Halloran, too, saw positive benefit in a military culture.
A nation with a faculty for war also had a faculty for the arts
and sciences:

> In countries where the fine arts are protected, war will
> not injure, much less destroy them. The reign of Francis
> I was one continued scene of war, yet he first introduced
> letters into France. The reign of Louis XIV was long and
> bloody, and still learning was never more flourishing
> there. Britain and Germany equally involved in war, yet
> still protected letters; whilst Ireland in peace for near a
> century, for want of countenancing, science had in a
> manner fairly left them![34]

Of O'Grady's sources, O'Halloran was perhaps the most
extreme in his espousal of the heroic code, but O'Grady found
it also in Keating and O'Curry.   Both used the knightly
terminology in talking about the ancient heroes, so O'Grady was

hardly exercising any license when he followed suit.

In speaking of the necessary personal qualifications of the king of Tara, Keating reported that the king must "have first received the degree of Knight of Chivalry."[35] The heroic code applied also to the bards, and Keating spoke of the unswerving truthfulness of the bards. "In Pagan times no person could hold the rank of Ollamh-re-senchas, or doctor of history, who had been once discovered to have falsified a single fact."[36] O'Grady would have liked this for two reasons: he believed that the modern Irish needed a code of strict truthfulness, and he believed that it was Christianity that had corrupted the strict Pagan code.[37]

Like O'Halloran, O'Curry spoke of chivalry as an institution among the ancient Irish. By "the strict laws of ancient Gaedhilic Chivalry," Cuculain is able to demand that the invading forces advance no further "into his territory until the victory of their champion and his own defeat should justify their progress."[38] Similarly, a standard of fairness is evoked in the contest between the Firbolgs and the Tuatha De Danann, centuries prior to the time of Cuculain. The king of the Firbolgs sends a messenger to the camp of the Tuatha De Danann to discuss the rules of warfare (somewhat like baseball managers and umpires discussing the ground-rules before a ballgame). Despite the chagrin of the Firbolgic king whose forces had the advantage in numbers, "it was agreed, on the demand of the *Tuatha De Danann*, that it should be fought always with equal numbers. . ."[39]

O'Grady could also find such respect for fair play in O'Daly's translation, although there was just as much unfairness. Indeed, the comic features of the following story overshadow the sense of fairness. Dubthach has wearied of the single combats with Cuculain, and he has become especially annoyed at the admiration of the women for Cuculain. Having made up his mind to break the pact with Cuculain, he

> . . . gave a deceitful and destructive advice to the host,
> viz. that they should act deceptiously and seem to fight
> amongst themselves on every side of him [Cuculain]
> until he might be slain by them. When Fergus mc Roith
> heard of it he was much enraged at the treacherous and
> destructive advice against Cuchullin that Dubthach had
> given; and he pursued him thru the host till he gave him
> a strong speedy surpassing powerfully mighty push of

> his two feet from him that drove Dubthach on before
> him in anger and he publicly showed all the evil and the
> disgrace and the treachery and the embroidered linen that
> reached up to the top of his brown armour. . .[40]

In this instance the ignoble action is performed by a warrior, Dubthach, but in O'Grady's *History* ignobility is usually the preserve of the merchant or a person whose motives are mercenary. If O'Halloran is to be believed, O'Grady's contempt for the merchant has a long tradition:

> The Irish, though they knew the value of trade, and
> highly encouraged and protected it, yet deemed it dis-
> honorable. Enthusiastically fond of arms and letters,
> they looked upon other avocations with contempt. . . .
> Even at this day Ceanuighe, which is the Irish for mer-
> chant, conveys with it a contemptible idea; and from the
> old law word Cain, tribute, is the word Ceanuighe de-
> rived.[41]

O'Curry also followed this tradition by attributing high honor to a prince who determined that Ireland's history "should not be altogether lost," "although himself and his country might sink for ever under the impending tempest." O'Curry says this was "no mercenary or ignoble sentiment."[42]

The bardic literature of Ireland is filled with allusions to magical and mystical practices. Like trade, such practices were deemed ignoble by O'Halloran. O'Grady, too, was unwilling to countenance them, so he explained their existence as the result of awe felt by the succeeding generations for the deeds of their ancestors. The stories grew in their imaginations as the centuries passed until it seemed that certain deeds could only be explained as the results of magic. O'Halloran dismissed the magical stories as "instances of pitiable credulity in our annalists" "since nothing can be more absurd, then recuring [*sic*] to preternatural causes in accounting for facts which we know may happen, and often happen. . ."[43] In speaking of the attempts of druids to find water by magic, he is more incensed: "We are disgusted with the superstition of these times."[44]

O'Grady and O'Halloran are close on many points,[45] in-cluding the typically Protestant belief that the Irish Church developed independently of Rome and was "Romanized" later on.[46]   O'Grady, a Protestant, saw Roman Catholicism as a corruption—the practice of "priestcraft" and saw this theory of Irish Christianization as an argument for the legitimacy of the Church of Ireland.   O'Halloran, a Catholic,[47] while agreeing about the history of Irish Christianization seems to have been oblivious to the legitimacy he was lending to the Church of Ireland.   Significantly, O'Curry, another Catholic, did not accept this view of Irish Christianization.[48]

Both O'Grady and O'Curry, however, agree in believing that the Irish bardic literature would have developed into a great national epic had it not been cut off prematurely. They differ on the nature of the check to the development, however, and their religions probably explain the difference.   O'Grady believed that the heroic temper had been completely trans- formed into the saintly temper with the arrival of Christianity, and thus an heroic epic became an impossibility because the heroic temper was no longer the national ideal.[49]   Since Christianity became very Roman in practice in Ireland, O'Grady felt no qualms about questioning the whole value of the Christianizing process.   O'Curry, on the other hand, makes no reference to religion and attributes the checked development of the literature to the invasions of the Danes and the Anglo- Normans.   In Ireland, an historian's religion is likely to be reflected in his writing, and it helps in reading O'Grady to bear in mind that he was a Protestant.

However, it is a more important fact that both O'Grady and O'Curry agreed that the bardic literature had been cut off prematurely.   And O'Grady probably owed many of his ideas on literary theory to O'Curry, for the latter's theories resemble O'Grady's closely.

O'Grady and O'Curry believed that both the fact and the myth in the bardic literature were valuable.   This belief led O'Grady on the next-to-last page of his "scientific" history, *History of Ireland: Critical and Philosophical,* to ask the reader who was still skeptical about the historicity of the early Irish literature to view it as "a portion at least of the history of the Irish mind."[50]   In *MS. Materials* O'Curry wrote in a similar vein:

> Some of these pieces [in the *Book of Ballymote*] are, doubtless, mixed up with mythological fable; but as the main facts, as well as all the actors, are real, and as to these mythological fables may be traced up many of the

> characteristic popular customs and superstitions still
> remaining among us, these pieces must be looked upon
> as materials of no ordinary value by the historical and
> antiquarian investigator.[51]

O'Curry, however, was more interested in both the myth
and the fact from a scholarly, historical point of view. At
times he regarded the poetic as mere embellishment or even
disfigurement of the original history. He shows the influence
of Niebuhr[52] in his belief in an unembellished original form:

> Of this class [Imramh—Expeditions by Sea] of our
> ancient tales, the number that have come down to us
> is but small, but they are very ancient; and though in-
> definite in their results, and burdened with much matter
> of a poetic or other romantic character, still there can be
> no rational doubt that they are founded on facts, the
> recital of which, in the original form, would have been
> probably found singularly valuable, though, in the lapse
> of ages, and after passing through the hands of story-
> tellers, whose minds were full of imagination, these
> tales lost, in a great measure, their original simplicity
> and truthful character, and became more and more
> fanciful and extravagant.[53]

Yet O'Curry was not without respect for the tales as
literature. Unlike O'Grady he believed that he ought to keep
his purely historical concerns divorced form his literary
appreciation. As if aware that he has gone too far in condemning
the products of the imagination, he reminds his readers that

> . . . in estimating the literary value of the compositions
> of this class . . . you are not to be guided by the remarks
> I have made respecting their merely *historical* importance.
> Perhaps their chief claim, after all, to your attention
> would be found to lie in their literary merits, and in the
> richly imaginative language in which they are written.[54]

O'Grady did not particularly like the "richly imaginative
language" of the bardic literature, and his rendering of the tales
reduced their linguistic lushness. However, he believed that this
reduction would not diminish their appeal to the imagination.

His task, "to make this heroic period once again a portion of the imagination of the country,"[55] is work for a literary artist, not a scholar such as O'Curry. Unfortunately, O'Grady did not always keep the difference between artist and scholar firmly in mind. Vol. I of the *History* in particular suffers from his failure to do so.

Yet O'Grady's fault may well have resulted from an attempt to write history as O'Curry suggested in this passage in *MS. Materials:*

> But the recital of the facts of history, however detailed, cannot satisfy those who seek in a history properly so called a lively as well as truthful report of the life and character, the thoughts and manners, of their ancestors, as well as a record of their government, and of the heroic achievements of the kings and chieftains among them. History is only really valuable to a people for the lessons it gives them of what their race has succeeded or failed to do,—for the lesson it gives them in the capacities as well as the faults of the men whose blood is in their own veins today, and whose peculiar virtues and vices their descendants have probably inherited, and will perpetuate to the end of time. History is really valuable when it revives and strengthens the bond which connects us with our forefathers,—the bond, of sympathy, of respect towards themselves,—or pride in and emulation of their brave deeds and their love of country. We want to know not merely of the existence of the kings of ancient Erinn, but we want also to become acquainted with themselves, to be able to realise in our minds how they and their people lived. To do this, the historian must introduce us to their laws, to their social customs, to their mode of education, and, above all, to so much of their private life as shall exhibit to us the relation in which the stronger and the weaker sex stood to one another; in short, to the nature of the civilization of ancient Erinn in detail.[56]

In his *History of Ireland* O'Grady followed O'Curry's prescription for a proper history to a great extent. However, O'Grady found much in O'Curry and his other sources that he chose to ignore. This was especially true of gory and salacious detail, which could be used to argue that the ancient Irish were barbaric and debauched.

Cuculain is O'Grady's type of Irish heroism, but there are many stories in O'Curry's *Manners and Customs* that show Cuculain to be far from pure. For example, on one occasion Cuculain kills a king and carries the king's wife off to Ulster with him. On another occasion Cuculain is unfaithful to his wife, Emer, and marries another woman.[57] In fact, Cuculain violates the heroic code constantly and demonstrates cowardice and knavery on several occasions. The most noteworthy example of this kind of behavior occurs in the aforementioned story of the killing of a king in order to abscond with his wife. On that occasion Cuculain plotted with Blathnaid, the wife of Curoi MacDaire, to kill Curoi. Blathnaid contrived to make sure that Curoi would be caught off guard by Cuculain. At a signal from Blathnaid, Cuculain approached Curoi's house or *Cathair:*

> . . . which he found, as was promised to him, open and unguarded. He found the royal mansion within in the same condition; and, on entering that, the lady *Blathnaid* sitting on a couch by the side of her husband, who lay asleep with his head in her lap, his sword and spears hanging on a rack over the couch. *Cuchulaind's* first care was to secure the sword and spears; and then giving the sleeping warrior a smart prick of his sword in the side, to awaken him—so that it should not be said he slew him while in his sleep—he cut off his head.
>
> The court was next stripped of all its valuables; and *Cuchulaind* with the treacherous *Blathnaid,* taking with them a quantity of rich spoils gathered from all parts of the world, returned in safety to Ulster.[58]

The stories in O'Curry, however, pale in comparison to those in Keating's *History.* Keating had no objection to repeating the most licentious stories of the pagan times since they demonstrated the moral improvment Christianity had wrought. So, for example, Concobar, the king of Ulster in Cuculain's time, is lured to his death by Connaught women.[59] O'Grady would never allow that noble warriors should demonstrate such lust or that they should be killed as the result of a stratagem. Concobar comes in for even worse treatment: Keating reports that Concobar committed incest with his mother.[60] Yet even incest pales before the two stories of cannibalism that

Keating reports. In one, during a time of famine, "men were known to eat their kind."[61] Even then famine might be some excuse, but the other story is incredible: Ethni Uathach "was fed upon the flesh of infants by the Desi, in order that she might the sooner become marriageable. . ."[62]

Less spectacular but also important were the incidents that O'Grady came across in O'Daly's translation of the *Tan-bo-Coolaney.* The most tragic single combat in which Cuculain engages in O'Grady's *History* is with his boyhood friend, Fardia. O'Daly's translation makes it very clear that Cuculain succeeds in defeating Fardia only because he is possessed of a weapon that Fardia does not have. This puts them on unequal terms and violates the chivalric code. Fardia dies, telling Cuculain, " 'It is not fairly thou hast slain me.' "[63]

On another occasion, Cuculain displays real treachery and breaks the code immediately after saying that he is always governed by it. This time he meets Ollamh, the son of Ailleel and Maeve (the king and queen of Connaught) alone and unarmed in the forest. Cuculain tells him, " 'Fear not! . . . for I never wounded warrior knight or man that is unarmed. . .' " Cuculain then tells him to go back to his leaders and warn them " 'that if I encounter them in single combat they will surely fall by me.' Off went the young man for to seek his leaders; but, however quickly sped the youth Cuchullin went still quicker and he cut off the head of Ollamh and took it and displayed it before the Men of Eire."[64]

O'Daly's translation also contains many sexual references that O'Grady ignored. Maeve is frankly sexual, and in discussing the qualifications her husband ought to have, she says: " 'And if the man were jealous we could not be one; for I never was myself without having a man concealed from another man with me. . .' "[65] It is strongly suggested also that Cuculain delays before meeting the invading force because he has an appointment with a woman. Fergus calls Cuculain "the man of assignations,"[66] and Cuculain does "not get up early that morning [after the assignation], for, there had been a feast on shipboard. . ."[67]

The last reference is oblique, but the context strongly suggests sexual activity. O'Grady ignored this as well as most of the humor that runs throughout O'Daly's translation. The humor often has sexual overtones, and there are many amusing incidents and comments in the original contrary to O'Grady's

statement in the *History of Ireland: Critical and Philosophical*
that in "the Tan-bo-Cooalney there is not a comic character,
and not more than three amusing incidents."[68]   O'Grady did
not believe that the bardic literature was very sophisticated.
Many modern scholars have rejected this view and have seen
the literature as satiric, ironic, humorous, and therefore
sophisticated.   Thomas Kinsella's modern rendition of the
Tan-bo-Cooalney is written with this idea in mind.[69]

O'Daly's translation provides ample evidence for viewing
the tale as the moderns have done.   For instance, although
O'Grady treats the following scene straight-forwardly, O'Daly's
version is grimly humorous.   Eidercomhal, a young warrior,
visits Cuculain under the protection of Fergus. After a parley
between Cuculain and Fergus, Eidercomhal offers to fight
Cuculain.   Cuculain refuses because Eidercomhal has come
under the protection of Fergus.   Eidercomhal persists and
finally they arrange to fight the next day. Eidercomhal is still
not satisfied, so he asks his "squire" if he should fight Cuculain
that night or the next day.   The "squire" replies, " 'I think it
would be best for thee . . . to do so [tonight] , for thou wilt
not reap a victory tomorrow and it is just as well for thee to
be vanquished tonight.' "[70]   Needless to say, Cuculain helps
him to "get it over with."

There are many such incidents in O'Daly's translation,
but the fact that O'Grady chose to ignore them does not mean
that he was totally blind to them. He probably felt that they
were not "canonical." The above incident can be used to show
the humor in the original, but it also shows Cuculain abiding by
the heroic code.   O'Grady chose to emphasize the latter and
could not do so by including the former. The humor would
have distracted attention from the observance of the code as
in fact it does in O'Daly's text. O'Grady's times called for the
heroic vision, and it may well be argued that modern scholars
are eqully subject to the temper of their times since the ironic
vision has been much in vogue in the last several decades.

Modern scholars, too, may feel less need to vindicate
Ireland and may also feel that sexual frankness is no indication
of barbarism. O'Grady wrote his *History* in the militant spirit
of his forebears—in the spirit of Keating, O'Halloran, and
O'Curry. In O'Grady's time, Ireland still needed an advocate.

Notes

[1] Standish James O'Grady, *Early Bardic Literature, Ireland* (1879; rpt. New York: Lemma, 1970), pp. 31-32.

[2] O'Grady followed his sources in placing the floruit of Cuculain around the time of Christ.

[3] O'Grady never published another volume in this series. A review of Vol. I in *Hibernia*, (2 Jan. 1882), p. 14, stated that the second volume was "in the Press." I have found nothing to confirm that assertion.

O'Grady's notion of archaeology was much broader than the current definition of the word. To him it signified the purely scientific side of historical investigation.

> . . . the province of archaeology has so extended its frontiers, as to have swallowed up the dominion of pure history altogether. Nearly every work one takes up affecting to treat of the past in a rigid and conscientious spirit, is merely archaeological. It is an accumulation of names, dates, events, disquisitions, the balancing of probabilities, the testing of statements and traditions, categorical assertions concerning laws and customs. All works of this character are of the nature of archaeology; they are the material of history not history itself.

History of Ireland: the Heroic Period, p. iv.

[4] A copy of this volume is inscribed from O'Grady to William Morris. It is located in the library of the University of Kansas.

[5] Standish James O'Grady, *Cuculain: an Epic* (London: Sampson, Low, Searle, Marston & Rivington; Dublin: E. Ponsonby, 1882), p. i.

[6] Cf. pp. 30-33.

[7] Schliemann's major discoveries were made during the 1870's and 1880's. For a sketch of his work, see John Edwin Sandys, *A History of Classical Scholarship* (New York: Hafner, 1958), III, 224.

[8] Cf. Russell K. Alspach, *Irish Poetry from the English Invasion to 1798* (Philadelphia: University of Pennsylvania Press, 1959), p. 102. Alspach makes this point also: ". . . the line of descent from Keating to O'Halloran to Standish James O'Grady is direct."

[9] *History of Ireland: the Heroic Period*, p. xiii.

[10] Cf., pp. 11-12.

[11] O'Halloran, I, 72.

[12] In *Early Bardic Literature, Ireland*, p. 36, O'Grady quotes a monk's remark to this effect. The monk had been the scribe who had transcribed the eleventh century manuscript, the *Leabhar na Huidhre*. The monk wrote the following comment on the manuscript's contents: " 'Quaedam autem poetica figmenta, quaedam ad delectationem stultorum.' "

[13] John O'Donovan, ed. and tr. *Annals of the Kingdom of Ireland, by the Four Masters, from the Earliest Period to the Year 1616* (1854; rpt. New York: AMS Press, 1966), I, 89.

[14] O'Grady did not use footnotes in Vol. I, but it is very likely that he used the same sources in that volume as he did in Vol. II.

[15] *History of Ireland: Cuculain and His Contemporaries*, p. 89.

[16] *History of Ireland: the Heroic Period*, p. viii.

[17] *History of Ireland: the Heroic Period*, p. ix. O'Grady's statement here contrasts with his avowed intention later expressed in *Early Bardic Literature, Ireland* to emphasize the historicity of the bardic literature. Cf., p. 39.

[18] *History of Ireland: the Heroic Period*, p. 81.

[19] John O'Daly, tr. *Tan-bo-Cooalney*, Royal Irish Academy MS. 24. M. 39. I have found some evidence in this manuscript that O'Daly may only have been the transcriber of the translation. A note on p. 92 of the MS. reads: "P. S. a blank in Mr. Kelly's translation here." However, I will refer to the MS. as O'Daly's work since it has been attributed to him.

[20] I am not able to judge the accuracy of O'Daly's translation, but Phillip Marcus reports that O'Grady "had to rely primarily upon a manuscript which a later and ,more accomplished Gaelic scholar has termed 'wretched.' " *Standish O'Grady*, pp. 17-18.

[21] *History of Ireland: Critical and Philosophical*, p. 51 n.

[22] O'Halloran, I, xxiv.

[23] Geoffrey Keating, *The History of Ireland*, tr. John O'Mahony (New York: P. M. Haverty, 1857), p. lxvi.

[24] W. K. Sullivan, *On the Manners and Customs of the Ancient Irish* (London and Edinburgh: Williams and Norgate; Dublin: W. B. Kelly; New York: Scribner, Welford, 1873), I, 11.

[25] Edward Gibbon, *The History of the Decline and Fall of the Roman Empire*, ed. William Smith (New York and London: Harper and Brothers, 1880), III, 441.

[26] Thomas Babington Macaulay, *The History of England*, ed. Charles Harding Firth (1913; rpt. New York: AMS Press, 1968), II, 786.

[27] O'Halloran, I, xxiv.

[28] Cf., the example given on p. 44. Phillip Marcus was disturbed by

such information, and I do agree that at times O'Grady includes too much of that kind of information.   Yet an understanding of O'Grady's purpose makes the inclusion of such material seem less arbitrary, and, at times, the odd sound of the Irish terms gives the text an appealing antique ring, as I have noted. Cf., Marcus, pp. 26-28.

[29] O'Halloran, I, 124.

[30] O'Halloran, I, 191.

[31] O'Grady's later writings often praised Sparta at the expense of Athens.   Cf., e. g., "An Event of World History," *The Irish Review*, 1 (1911), 161-164.   Yet he seems to have been unwitting of the encouragement he was giving to Irish rebels by praising *the* city noted for militarism.

[32] *History of Ireland: the Heroic Period*, pp. 128-129.

[33] *History of Ireland: Cuculain and His Contemporaries*, pp. 315-316. O'Grady's conception of Cuculain probably had a great influence on the Irish revolutionaries of 1916 particularly Padraic Pearse.   On Mar. 20-22, 1909 the boys of Pearse's school, St. Edna's, performed O'Grady's play, "The Coming of Fionn," along with Douglas Hyde's "*An Naomb ar Iarraidb*" ("The Lost Saint").   Pearse quoted W. P. Ryan's description of the scene:

> "In the "Coming of Fionn" one could easily lose sight of the fact that it was a dramatic representation; the boys for a time were a part of the heroic antiquity; dressed in the way they were, and intense and interested as they were, one could picture them in Tara or Eamhain with out much straining of the imagination. The heroic spirit had entered into their hearts and their minds, and one realized very early indeed that the evening's life and spirit were not something isolated, a phase and charm to be dropped when they reappeared in ordinary garb.   The evening's sense was a natural continuation of that and many other evenings and days when the spirit of Fionn and his heroic comrades had been instilled into their minds by those for whom the noble old-time love had a vivid and ever-active and effective meaning. Fionn and Cuchulain and their high-heroic kin had become part of the mental life of the teachers and the taught."

Padriac H. Pearse, *The Story of a Success* (Dublin and London: Maunsel, 1917), pp. 16-17.

[34] O'Halloran, I, 127.

[35] Keating, p. 391.

[36] Keating, p. 413.

[37] Cf., pp. 4-6.

[38]Eugene O'Curry, *On the Manners and Customs of the Ancient Irish* (London and Edinburgh: Williams and Norgate; Dublin: W. B. Kelly; New York: Scribner, Welford, 1873), II, 296. Hereafter *Manners and Customs.*

[39]O'Curry, *Manners and Customs,* II, 238.

[40]O'Daly, pp. 194-195. O'Daly's translation is full of barbarisms such as "deceptiously," so it would be senseless to insert *sic* after every such word. I follow O'Grady's spelling of Irish words except where they are spelled differently in quoted material.

[41]O'Halloran, II, 211.

[42]Eugene O'Curry, *Lectures on the Manuscript Materials of Ancient Irish History* (1861; rpt. New York: Burt Franklin, 1964), p. 140. Hereafter *MS. Materials.*

[43]O'Halloran, I, 94.

[44]O'Halloran, I, 264.

[45]Russell K. Alspach found it difficult to understand what O'Grady saw in O'Halloran:

> Just what it was about O'Halloran's history that inspired O'Grady is hard to say. The chronological portions are as dull reading as such stuff generally is; the treatment of legend is by no means so full nor so interesting as Keating's. No distinction of any kind is apparent in O'Halloran; O'Grady must have been attracted to his history simply because it was the first account of Ireland he read that told him anything about his native country before the English invasion. Further, since O'Grady's own history is notable especially for its retelling of the heroic tales, the hints of the old stories that he got in O'Halloran undoubtedly inspired him to further research.

Irish Poetry from the English Invasion to 1798, p. 99. I believe I have established that O'Grady and O'Halloran were much closer than Alspach allows.

[46]Cf. O'Halloran, I, xxxi. Cf. pp. 26-27 for O'Grady's view.

[47]The available evidence suggests that O'Halloran was a Catholic, but a contemporary fictionalized account of O'Halloran's early life suggests that some suspected O'Halloran, a medical doctor of some note, of switching to Protestantism for professional reasons. Cf., Ronan Sheehan, *Boy with an Injured Eye* (Dingle: Brandon, 1983), pp. 41-45.

[48]*MS. Materials,* pp. 372-373.

[49]*Early Bardic Literature, Ireland,* p. 24.

[50]*History of Ireland: Critical and Philosophical,* p. 463.

[51]*MS. Materials,* p. 189.

[52]O'Curry must have been acquainted with Niebuhr's work, although he does not mention him by name. Sullivan, the editor of *Manners and Customs* and the author of the first volume, makes many direct references to Niebuhr.

[53]*MS. Materials*, p. 289.

[54]*MS. Materials*, p. 319.

[55]*Early Bardic Literature, Ireland*, p. 17.

[56]*MS. Materials*, p. 455.

[57]O'Curry, *Manners and Customs*, II, 370.

[58]O'Curry, *Manners and Customs*, III, pp. 80-82. Cf. also II, 371 n., for another example of Cuculain's trickery.

[59]Keating, p. 272.

[60]Keating, p. 278.

[61]Keating, p. 311.

[62]Keating, p. 338. I can't resist wondering whether Jonathan Swift was aware of this story.

[63]O'Daly, p. 252.

[64]O'Daly, pp. 95-96.

[65]O'Daly, p. 3.

[66]O'Daly, p. 39.

[67]O'Daly, p. 41.

[68]*History of Ireland: Critical and Philosophical*, p. 337.

[69]Thomas Kinsella, tr. *The Tain* (Oxford University Press, 1970).

[70]O'Daly, p. 128. Cf. *History of Ireland: the Heroic Period*, pp. 162-164, for O'Grady's version of this story.

Chapter III

History of Ireland: The Heroic Period

In his *History of Ireland: Critical and Philosophical,* O'Grady set forth his theory of art most explicitly:

> Romance, epic, drama, and artistic representation are at all times the points to which history continually aspires—there only its final development and efflorescence. Archaeology culminates in history, history culminates in art.[1]

The introduction to Vol. I of his "bardic history" reveals that O'Grady had this theory in mind when he wrote that book:

> The treatment which I have . . . adopted consists in the reduction to its artistic elements of the whole of that heroic history taken together, viewing it always in the light shed by the discoveries of modern aracheologians, frequently using the actual language of the bards, and as much as possible their style and general character of expression.[2]

He goes on to describe just what the "artistic elements" are:

> Through the loose chaotic mass of bardic story and monkish chronicle, I have endeavoured to trace the mental and physical personality of the heroes and heroines in their essential elements, and to discovery that order of events which best harmonises with the records and traditions of the poets, and the characters of the heroic personages (p. x).

In short, O'Grady sought to distill out the elements that would make for a good story, in which the history would "culminate" in art. At the same time he believed himself capable of giving to the artistic elements, refashioned into a whole, a truth that they lacked in parts. The process, however, would not require him to change the often contradictory originals simply for the sake of his story. "Instinctively" he would be able to "feel" the characteristics of the heroes that are "essential" and the tales that are "canonical" (p. xiii).

This instinctual sense is very similar to Niebuhr's notion of the historian's intuition.[3] By the use of this faculty the historian is able to realize the actual, original history that has come down to him or her in a distorted state. O'Grady's description of the history as it had come down to him shows the strong influence of Niebuhr:

> The old heroic history is overlain and concealed, but much of it is still there. In the bardic account of the Milesian invasion, we find a multitude of ancient tales reduced to their essence, or rather their anatomies, and then poured pell-mell together. By looking closely into these relics, we see that the real history was something very different from that which the last redactor desired to represent. The materials which he employs tell a different tale (p. xv).

In his *History of Rome* Niebuhr had uncovered the original history which the "last redactor," Livy, had distorted for his own patriotic purposes. In his *History*, despite the influence of Niebuhr, O'Grady was the "last redactor" whose purposes were as patriotic and political as any of Livy's. Thus in 1878 O'Grady saw a need to popularize ancient Irish history and literature by giving a "fitting form" to the mass of antiquarian material his nineteenth century predecessors had turned up (p. v). His notion of that "fitting form" cast him in the role of a Livy or a Homer, i. e., the artist who "tones down to epic proportion and reasonableness" (p.48) the chaotic, fragmentary stories which are the bardic legacy.

O'Grady was not unaware that he would be bringing the prejudices of his own time to the *History*. He frankly admitted that was "certainly the case" (p. v-vi). Apparently this problem did not particularly bother him because he still felt capable of judging what was "canonical" and what was not despite his time-bound imagination. O'Grady was never particularly bothered by inconsistency.

The dual role of Niebuhr and Livy that O'Grady undertook

goes a long way to explain the inconsistency in his style in Vol. I. The opening chapters resemble Niebuhr's dry *History,* while the narrative chapters tell the inspiring story of Cuculain with the patriotic fervor of a Livy. It is in these latter chapters that O'Grady appears to be using what he called "the actual language of the bards, and as much possible their style and general character of expression" (cf., p. 62). Since O'Grady did not know Irish, this assertion could only refer to the representations of the bardic style that he had come across in translations. Often he seems only to have imitated some of O'Daly's archaic usages since the "bardic history" and O'Daly's translation differ greatly in style.

O'Grady does state, however, that the chapter concerning "the death of Conairey Mor is almost a literal transcript from the tale" (p. x). That chapter does contain several devices that can be found in profusion in O'Daly's translation. For example, the following paragraph from the *History* is similar to many of O'Daly's passages where several sentences are used to make a point. Each sentence by itself is a synecdoche; together they become hyperbole.

> All Erin, say the bards, had peace in the days of Conairey. Nature herself, the rivers, soil, and winds of Erin, responded to the call of the son of Eterskel, and unlearned every evil propensity. In his reign the hazels and apple trees all but broke with the abundance of the fruit with which they were bent to the ground. The winters were not thunderous, or storm-producing, or cold. From March in one year, to April in the next, the hair of the kine was not roughened by any wind. The rivers teemed with salmon, and the sea annually cast up the secret treasures of her depths upon the strand of Inver Colpa (pp. 99-100).

This excess of description, however, is not typical of O'Grady's style. He found many similar passages in O'Daly's translation and either ignored or diminished them. His narrative is full of direct action, while O'Daly's translation moves very slowly.

Indeed, when O'Grady wishes to slow his narrative down, his style becomes more like O'Daly's. For example, in that same chapter on Conairey Mor's death, he uses a device which occurs over and over again in the original, and infrequently in his own rendition. It is a mark of O'Grady's skill that in this case he chooses an appropriate moment to use it. The device is a question-and-answer routine often used in the reporting of information. The question and answers take on a parallel form. Here Ferrogane, the leader of those who eventually kill Conairey Mor, the High King, questions Inkel, who has returned from spying on Conairey Mor and his forces. Each time Ferrogane asks Inkel whom he saw in Conairey Mor's camp. Each time Inkel replies by describing in detail a warrior or some personage of the king's retinue. As the questioning proceeds in parallel form, the description of the nobility of the king's men reduces Ferrogane to tears. Ferrogane was banished previously by Conairey Mor, so the slow process of questioning reveals the full extent of what he has lost. It also establishes firmly the legitimacy of Conairey Mor's right to the throne: he is the best man. Thus the original text fitted very nicely with O'Grady's immediate purpose of dwelling on Conairey's virtues.

However, O'Grady never felt compelled to observe the precedence of the bards in either style or substance. In his introduction he pointed out that the "bardic mind affected a certain fastidiousness in its mode of treating the heroic period. A conventional set of ideas were deemed poetic and all outside that was unpoetic" (p. xi). This "fastidiousness" meant that the bards never referred to the commonplace realities of the Ireland of their time. In his *History,* however, O'Grady "departed wholly from the limited range of ideas permitted to themselves by the bards, and introduced boldly the ancient civilization of the country" (p. xi-xii). Even more boldly he announced: "In these volumes the heroic period reflects the actualities of the early historic time" (p. xii). Introducing the "ancient civilization of the country" meant mostly that O'Grady added information in Sullivan's and O'Curry's *Manners and Customs* to the bardic tales. With that amalgam, he believed he would achieve the historicity of Niebuhr as well as the inspiration of Livy.

While the degree of historicity in O'Grady's works is open to question, there can be no doubt that they have a strong inspirational tone. It is very important to understand the precise nature of the principles and sympathies that O'Grady was seeking to engender in his readers. To understand O'Grady, it is necessary to see how deeply imbued he was with the spirit and teachings of Thomas Carlyle. Indeed, the works of Carlyle are the best glosses on O'Grady's "bardic history."

In *Early Bardic Literature, Ireland* O'Grady referred to Carlyle as "the first man of letters of the day, his the highest name as a critic upon, and historian of, the past life of Europe."[4] In that context, however, he criticized Carlyle for his ignorance of Irish antiquities. O'Grady's high regard for Carlyle did not include respect for the latter's ill-informed opinions on Ireland. O'Grady's esteem for Carlyle, however, grew more and more during the next 30 years. In fact, Vol. II of the "bardic history" shows increased Carlylian influence, if that is possible. In 1886, O'Grady wrote: *"En passant* I would request the more inquiring and reflective amongst my readers to study closely and again, and again Carlyle's political treatises—'Chartism,' 'Past and Present,' the 'Essay on the Jamaica Question,' and over and over and over again, 'Shooting Niagara and After.' "[5] In 1878 O'Grady may not have acknowledged his debt to Carlyle so directly, but Vol. I of his *History* clearly follows Carlyle's favorite *dicta.*

Cuculain is O'Grady's type of ancient Irish heroism, and Cuculain's attributes closely resemble those of the Carlylian hero. Like O'Grady, Carlyle believed firmly in the importance of a great national epic, indeed an epic molded from the actual history of the country. Creating the epic was not so much a matter of the poet arranging words on a page as it was a matter of the hero providing the deeds that by themselves would write the epic. In this vein Carlyle writes:

> Great honour to him whose Epic is a melodious hexameter Iliad; not a jingling Sham-Iliad, nothing true in it but the hexameters and forms merely. But still greater honour, if his Epic be a mighty Empire slowly built together, a mighty Series of Heroic Deeds,—a mighty Conquest over Chaos; *which* Epic the "Eternal Melodies" have, and must have, informed and dwelt in, as it [the epic] sung itself! There is no mistaking that latter Epic. Deeds are greater than Words.[6]

This last being the case, the doer of deeds becomes the great man in the country, the man everyone looks for and toward. Carlyle described the hero in a series of lectures first given in 1840 and later published under the title, *On Heroes, Hero-Worship, and the Heroic in History*. The following long paragraph is his most succinct statement of the relationship of the hero to his time:

> For if we will think of it, no Time need have gone to ruin, could it have *found* a man great enough, a wise man and good enough: wisdom to discern truly what the Time wanted, valour to lead it on the right road thither; these are the salvation of any Time. But I liken common languid Times, with their unbelief, distress, perplexity, with their languid doubting characters and embarassed circumstances, impotently crumbling-down into ever worse distress towards final ruin;—all this I liken to dry dead fuel, waiting for the lightning out of Heaven that shall kindle it. The great man, with his free force direct out of God's own hand, is the lightning. His word is the wise healing word which all can believe in. All blazes round him now, when he has once struck on it, into fire like his own. The dry mouldering sticks are thought to have called him forth. They did want him greatly; but as to calling him forth—!—Those are critics of small vision, I think, who cry: "See, is it not the sticks that made the fire?" No sadder symptom of a generation than such general blindness to the spiritual lightning, with faith only in the heap of barren dead fuel. It is the last consummation of unbelief. In all epochs of the world's history, we shall find the Great Man to have been the indispensable saviour of his epoch;—the lightning, without which the fuel never would have burnt. The History of the World, I said already, was the Biography of Great Men.[7]

In short, the hero has the ability to transform his Age, which, without him, might well go to ruin. In O'Grady's *History*, Cuculain is the lightning that comes to ignite his people and dispel their unbelief. He is the great man who knows what has to be done and does it. Like the Carlylian hero who is marked by his lack of self-consciousness, Cuculain does not dream; he acts. He follows the Carlylian Gospel:

> The latest Gospel in the world is, Know thy work and do

> it. 'Know thyself:' long enough has that poor 'self' of
> thine tormented thee; thou wilt never get to 'know' it,
> I believe! Think it not thy business, this of knowing
> thyself; thou art an unknowable individual; know what
> thou canst work at; and work at it like a Hercules![8]

O'Grady's Cuculain knows what he can work at: he never intellectualizes about it and never hesitates to act immediately. Because "his free force" comes "direct out of God's own hand," to use Carlyle's words, his actions always bring good. That good overcomes all unrest and dispenses with the conditions that bring about the horror, as Carlyle termed it, of French Revolutions. The presence of the hero at the right moment obviates all need for revolution, and O'Grady's description of Cuculain's heroic action thoroughly realizes Carlyle's theory of the hero.

Even the fact that Cuculain is a warrior and that O'Grady's *History* frankly glorifies militarism is in keeping with the tenor of Carlyle's ideas. Carlyle is not at all behindhand on this score; indeed he considers fighting to be in the very nature of man and all of life to be a battle:

> Man is created to fight; he is perhaps best of all definable
> as a born soldier; his life "a battle and a march," under
> the right General. It is forever indispensable for a man to
> fight: now with Necessity, with Barrenness, Scarcity, with
> Puddles, Bogs, tangled Forests, unkempt Cotton;—now
> also with the hallucinations of his poor fellow Men.[9]

A page later he adds:

> A Battlefield too is great. Considered well, it is a kind
> of Quintessence of Labour, Labour distilled into its ut-
> most concentration; the significance of years of it com-
> pressed into an hour.[10]

The parallels between O'Grady and Carlyle do not end with their common militarism. Both men shared similar notions about history. Central to Carlyle's thought is his belief that the past prophesies and forms the present and the future. He expressed this belief most directly in *Past and Present.* In that book he intended:

. . . from the Past, in a circuitous way, to illustrate the
Present and the Future. The Past is a dim indubitable
fact: the Future too is one, only dimmer, nay properly
it is the *same* fact in new dress and development. For the
Present holds in it both the whole Past and the whole
Future;—as the *Life-tree Idgrasil,* wide-waving, many-
toned, has its roots down deep in the Death-Kingdoms,
among the oldest dead dust of men, and with its boughs
reaches always beyond the stars; and in all times and
places is one and the same Life-tree![11]

Implicit in such a notion of history is a belief that history
teaches, or that, at least, it ought to do so.[12] O'Grady writes
his *History* not merely to have a record of the past but principally to teach his contemporaries in Ireland that their current
state[13] is the "*same* fact" as their ancient history. The ignorance
of that history in Ireland was appalling to O'Grady.

The appropriate embodiment of a nation's history for
both O'Grady and Carlyle was the epic. There a nation could
find a wellspring of inspiration from the past that it was fated
to repeat forever. Since the epic was the fit vehicle to convey
the messages of history, it followed that the best art ought to
be grounded in the facts of history, not the individual visions
of the artist. Carlyle espoused this view in his later writings
after he had distanced himself somewhat from the Romantics.
In a recent study of Carlyle's aesthetics, Peter Allan Dale dis-
cerned a "new realism" in Carlyle's "insistence that the highest
poetry is that which concentrates on the imitation of reality,
specifically historical reality, rather than bodying forth dubious
visions. . ."[14] O'Grady, no doubt, found this insistence very
congenial, as he himself disliked the "dubious visions" of Wordsworth, which attributed the genesis of the gods to the poet's
imagination. O'Grady dismissed Wordsworth's description of
the herdsman who might, "with small help from fancy," transform "Sunbeams upon distant hills," "Into fleet oreads, sporting
visibly." He found this description "pretty, but untrue."[15]
O'Grady, like Carlyle, insisted on tempering the imagination
with historical fact. For O'Grady, the historical fact was that
the gods resulted from the apotheosis of heroes.

The genuine poet, therefore, always writes with a strong
awareness of historical fact. His job is to interpret those facts
correctly, or as Carlyle says: " '. . . in the right interpretation of

Reality and History does genuine Poetry consist.' "[16] "Right interpretation" ultimately involves the poet in creating a vision of the pattern and meaning of events. Carlyle's "Historian of a national Poetry" (who seems to synthesize the works of epic poets) "will discern the grand spiritual Tendency of each period, what was the highest Aim and Enthusiasm of mankind in each, and how one epoch naturally evolved itself from the other. He has to record the highest Aim of a nation, in its successive directions and developments, for by this the Poetry of the nation modulates itself; this is the Poetry of the nation."[17]

In his "bardic history" O'Grady set out to "record the highest Aim" of Ireland "in its successive directions and developments." Implicit in Carlyle's ideas is a belief that history is cyclical: what we have seen before we shall see again. O'Grady, too, believed that history was cyclical, and, like Carlyle, he believed that the cycles bring progress. Unlike Carlyle, however, O'Grady optimistically emphasized the progress. He believed that what was good before would be good again. Indeed it would be better.

Vol. I of the *History of Ireland* opens with "factual," "scientific" descriptions of Ireland from prehistoric times. O'Grady describes briefly the epochs that have come and gone. At one point an ignoble race inhabited Ireland:

> The man of the ice-period was the antique representative of the modern Eskimo, if not actually his progenitor. He was short, flat-faced, and prognathous. He was filthy, brutish, and a cannibal. Fishing and hunting formed his occupation. The divine command to till the earth and to eat of the fruits thereof had not been obeyed, nor yet did he drive about flocks and herds, leading a nomadic and pastoral life, and subsisting on the milk of cows or mares. No gentle domestic animals roamed around his house. The wolf was still untamed. No watchdog's honest bark greeted him as he drew near home (p. 7).[18]

The Ice Age, however, sweeps away this brute, for there is better yet to come. O'Grady's inclusion of this description has enabled him to show how Ireland was destined for great things from the earliest days of the world: Ireland was not a place for such a low "breed." A better people were to come, a people part Basque and part Celt, and therefore composed of the two great "races" of Europe—the Scythian and the Turanian. The Scythians were the civilizers of Europe, the Turanians the warriors. Ireland, therefore, had the best of both stocks.

So O'Grady begins his *History* with the clear intent to demonstrate the growth of a great civilization. Much of what he says must have been sheer conjecture on his part, yet he states it with absolute assurance.[19] Some of his assertions are stunning in their certainty, e. g., "The original inhabitants of the country were Basque, but successive Celtic invasions obliterated the ancient language, and altered the physical appearance of the people" (p. 15). Such statements may not be factual in the sense of absolute truth, but for O'Grady they are the "facts" that inform Irish history. His *History,* therefore, demonstrates how the "fact" of the Basque and Celtic origin of the Irish people serves to make them both civilized and warlike. Similarly in a chapter entitled "The First Fact," O'Grady proclaims the political and military supremacy of Ulster over the rest of Ireland. Naturally, his *History* tells the story of the greatness of Ulster in the time of its greatest hero, Cuculain.

Before O'Grady arrives at the time of Cuculain, however, he slowly traces the growth of the great nation that will spawn that hero. He speaks of the ages which are now "a land of the dead" (p. 28), where no clear idea of their history may be ascertained. Then he moves to the tales surrounding the Fianna Eireen or the Fenians, whom he mistakenly placed long before the time of Cuculain. He corrected this mistake in *Early Bardic Literature, Ireland,* but his placement of the Fianna at this point satisfies more than his desire to trace the chronology. The Fianna enable O'Grady to point to the high nobility of the pre-Christian Irish and therefore to praise the ideals that Christianity had supplanted.

The Fianna were a band of warriors among whom were numbered Fionn mac Cool, Oscar, and Oiseen. Significantly, O'Grady makes it a point to demonstrate the love of the Fianna for their dogs and thus their superiority to their Eskimo-like Ice Age predecessors. But most importantly, he records the complaint of Oiseen against Patrick who has brought a life-denying Christianity to Ireland. Oiseen has returned to Ireland centuries after the time of the Fianna. He tells Patrick, " 'Life is a burden to you, not a pleasure. It is the journey of one travelling through desolate places hastening homeward' " (p.37).

Oiseen contrasts the Christian life with his life among the Fianna, and O'Grady gives Oiseen's words a clear resemblance to Swinburne's similar complaint in his "Hymn to Proserpine":

> "We did not weep and make mournful music. When we let our hounds loose at Locha Lein, and the chase resounded through Slieve Crot, there was no doleful sound, nor when we mustered for battle, and the pure, cold wind whistled in the flying banners of the Fianna of Erin; nor yet, in our gentle intercourse with women, alas, O Diarmait; nor in the banqueting hall with lights, feasting and drinking, while we hearkened to the chanting of noble tales and the sound of the harp and the voice."
>
> "How, then, hast thou conquered, O son of Calpurn" (p. 38).[20]

O'Grady has thus laid the groundwork for the appreciation of the heroic values that he clearly considered superior to the Christian values that succeeded them. At the least, he was not pleased with the current embodiment of the Christian values, and he longed to return Ireland to its ancient heroism.

O'Grady next turns to a description of the development of the Ard-Rieship, or High-Kingship, of Ireland, and he leaves little doubt that the evolution of such an institution is the mark of a civilized people with a destiny:

> But there is a pleasure more certain, more human, more subline, felt by one who contemplates out of the seething welter of warring tribes the slow growth of a noble people, the reclamation of a vast human wilderness, the stormful gloom of ignorance and hate growing less and less dense, shot through by the rays of imagination, knowledge, and love—the chaos of confusion and aimless strugglings concentre gradually into the wise and determined action of a nation fulfilling its part in the great national confraternity of the world (p. 39).

The growth of the Irish Ard-Rieship arose out of the custom of a triennial national fair or *feis* at Tara. The chieftain who secured for himself the power to preside at Tara became the High King. In this regard, O'Grady believed that the Irish were superior to the Greeks, for "the Irish did work out for themselves unity, which the Greeks did not. . ." (p. 43).

Up to this point almost all of the chapters have been of the descriptive, "archaeological" variety. Starting with Chap. XV, O'Grady's *History* becomes more "bardic" as he begins to deal with personalities. Significantly, his epic invocation occurs at this point:

> Spirits of the ancient bards, my ancestors, and ye sacred influences that haunt for ever the soil and air of my country, nameless now and unworshipped, but strong and eternal, be with me and befriend, that in circles worthy so glorious singing their praise upon whom nations looked back as upon their first and best, with a flight unfailing I may rise to regions where no wing of laborious ollav or chanting shanachie ever yet fanned that thinner air (pp. 48-49).

Following this invocation, O'Grady describes the foundation of the premier city of the North, or Ulla, and the kingship of that province. The story is very significant because it sets forth the grounds on which a king may establish his legitimate authority. The story begins with a goddess of War, Macha, coming to the North in search of a new home. Coming upon many of the kings of the North who are sleeping, she lures them one by one into the forest. As each offers to embrace her, she binds them easily. She does this to all the kings until she comes to Kimbay Mac Fiontann. As soon as she touches him, he rises up, seizes her, and brings her to the earth, "but in his arms she changed into a blooming and beautiful maiden, and she responded to his love, and became his bride" (p. 50). After that, Kimbay frees the other kings who, in turn, pledge their fealty to him. Kimbay then builds a city on that spot, Emain Macha, the sacred height of Macha. Thereafter that city was the seat of the High King of Ulla.

The story demonstrates two important points: that the king must be a good warrior, capable even of defeating a goddess of war, and that rule is a male prerogative. Kimbay establishes his kingship by defeating a woman, albeit a goddess. This last point was exceedingly important to O'Grady, for an essential problem with the four provinces when they raid the North in the time of Cuculain is that they are led by a woman, Queen Maeve. To

O'Grady's mind and probably also to the authors of the old tale, women were simply incapable of rule.

Immediately following the story of Kimbay, O'Grady shifts to a lengthy account of the High Kings of Ireland in the time shortly after the reign of Kimbay in Ulla. Here too, O'Grady's purpose is to show how the kings established legitimacy and on what basis. Their reigns provide the archetypal pattern for succeeding generations. O'Grady begins with Ugainey More, but quickly passes to Ugainey's son, Lorc, who succeeded him. Lorc is a good king: "For he preserved the precepts of his father, and kept in check the warlike tribes, and advanced the dignity of the ollavs [bardic historians], and discouraged border warfare and lawlessness between tuath [fiefdom] and tuath" (p. 52).

Lorc, however, has an older brother, Covac Coel-Bray, who is annoyed that he was passed over. Covac plots with other dissident petty-kings to kill Lorc. The nature of his plot shows his unfitness for kingship; indeed O'Grady regarded all stratagems as ignoble. A messenger sent by Covac to Lorc informs the latter that the former is dead. Lorc, good man that he is, rushes to Covac's side with only "a small retinue." Covac slays him as he leans over Covac's bed. After that Covac goes on a rampage and kills everyone who opposes him including all the sons and grandsons of Lorc except one. O'Grady makes it clear that this coup is a victory for illegitimacy, for Covac "depressed the ollavs and the druids, setting the kings and nobles above the law, whence, too, came his power" (p. 54). This last statement is very important because disrespect for the bards, in particular, in O'Grady's *History* becomes a sure sign of unfitness in a ruler. He is not always upset about disrespect to the druids, but in this case he includes them in Covac's disrespect to show Covac's completely unbridled nature.

However, all hope is not lost as one grandson of Lorc, Lara, is not slain. He escapes death by feigning insanity, and Covac's men "slew him not, partly from contempt, and partly for that they were sacred whose minds the divine people had disturbed" (p. 55). Lara grows up living with a swineherd of his father's and is secretly tutored by Ferceirtney the poet and Craivetheena the harper in the history and laws of his people and in the bardic tales of his ancestors.

Meanwhile under Covac Coel-Bray, the state of the country degenerates into absolute chaos. Among other things:

> The ollavs, too, fell away from their high place, and
> became dependent upon the kings, forgetting those lofty
> ranns in which were enshrined the wisdom and justice of
> the Gaeil, and the ramifications of far-spreading tribes
> preserving the ancestral rights of men, and they chanted
> now only songs praising lawlessness and strength; and the
> rights of women, too, and the laws of marriage were
> relaxed (p. 56).

This state of affairs, significantly the result of revolution, continues for some time, until one day Lara becomes involved in the quarrel of boys who are playing hurling. Dropping his pose of insanity, Lara fells the son of Covac and utters a "fierce imperious speech" (p. 59) which strikes fear into the hearts of the boys. Immediately thereafter Lara is forced to flee with Ferciertney and Craivetheena to friendly tribes.

At this point O'Grady interrupts the story of Lara, and, in three chapters, he tells the story of the Milesian invasion of Ireland which had supposedly occurred twelve centuries previously. Milesius was the king of Spain, and the ruling class of Ireland traced their ancestry back to his sons who had invaded Ireland and settled there. O'Grady relates the great trials the sons of Milesius had in establishing themselves in Ireland. Their arrival was a crucial moment in the fulfillment of the Irish destiny; they "were moved by an ancestral spirit prompting them to great deeds" (p. 61). They arrived as strangers, but they established their legitimacy by meeting the challenges of the Tuatha De Danan, the inhabitants of the island. Banba, the queen of the land, finally welcomed the Milesians and prophesied a great future for them in Ireland. "Moreover she said that now for the last time would she be seen of the Gaeil, but that she would dwell for ever invisible in the hollow folds of Slieve Mish, and that she would care for the children of Heber [a son of Milesius] to the end of time."

It is to Slieve Mish that Lara flees, the home of Banba and the place where Heber established his capital. It is the center of legitimate Irish rule. O'Grady's interjection of the Milesian invasion demonstrates how the Milesian past informs Lara's present much in the way the past is repeated in the present in Carlyle's *Past and Present*. At Slieve Mish, Lara finds the sustenance that the past provided for the present.[21] There the rule of law and the ancient customs are observed, unlike the practice at Dinn Rie where Covac rules. For in the latter place, "indeed, the kings and lords dealt out judgments as they pleased, and for firm law there was only the caprice of unjust men" (p. 79).

After marrying the daughter of the king and queen at Slieve Mish, Lara raises an army, and defeats and kills Covac despite an initial setback. Once more legitimacy is established, and from Lara and his wife "proceeded a race and monarchs and legislators whose fame was great amongst the Gaeil" (p. 86).

After this story O'Grady's text moves rapidly forward through the centuries and sets the stage for the central tale of this and the succeeding volume—the story of Cuculain. He begins by telling the story of the birth of Maeve, the daughter of the High King of Ireland and of a fairy queen. Maeve marries Aileel More, the king of the West, and O'Grady describes in detail (probably borrowed from O'Curry) the palace at Cruhane. Aileel had it built expressly for Maeve in order to receive pro- perly the daughter of the High King. The description is very straightforward and meticulous, yet the epigraph to the chapter entitled "Aileel More's Palace" reveals O'Grady's attitude to the Western enterprise and, ultimately, to Maeve. The epigraph comes from Book I, ll. 722-723, of Milton's *Paradise Lost*:

> "The ascending pile
> Stood fixed her stately height" (p. 94).

The context of these lines is the construction of Pandaemonium by the devils in Hell, the very seat of disorder and chaos. Maeve and her men come to represent the same forces in O'Grady's *History*.[22]

After telling the story of Conairey Mor[23] (which gives O'Grady another chance to demonstrate the virtues of a great king), he moves directly to the story of Cuculain. The arrival of Cuculain at Emain Macha as a boy closely parallels the scene in which Lara drops his pose of insanity. Once again the scene is a hurling field, and as an outsider like Lara, Cuculain faces the wrath of the boys who are playing:

> After this [a demonstration of Cuculain's superior
> hurling skill], the boys came together into a group, and
> held a council. Then commenced what seemed to be an

an attempt to force him out of the ground, followed by a furious fight. The strange boy seemed to be a very demon of war; with his little hurle grasped, like a war-mace, in both hands, he laid about him on every side, and the boys were tumbling fast. He sprang at tall youths like a hound at a stag's throat. He rushed through crowds of his enemies like a hawk through a flock of birds. The boys, seized with a panic, cried out that it was one of the Tuatha from the Fairy Hills of the Boyne, and fled right and left to gain the shelter of the trees (p. 109).

When heroism appears on the scene, it makes its presence felt, and like Lara, Cuculain is imperious in his speech, not even shrinking from rebuking the High King of Ulla, Concobar. He boldly announces himself by his given name: " 'I am Setanta, the son of Sualtam, and Dectera, your sister, is my mother; and it is not before my uncle's palace that I should be insulted and dishonoured' " (p. 110).

Lest there be any doubt about the nature of the personage who has arrived upon the scene, O'Grady interrupts the narrative to proclaim the importance of Cuculain:

This was the debut and the first martial exploit of the great Cuculain, type of Irish chivalry and courage, in the bardic firmament a bright particular star of strength, daring, and glory, that will not set or suffer aught but transient obscuration till the extinction of the Irish race; Cuculain, bravest of the brave, whose glory affected even the temperate-minded Tierna, so that his sober pen has inscribed in the annals of ancient Erin, this testimony: "Cuculain filius Sualtam fortissimus heros Scotorum" (p. 110).

O'Grady then narrates the story of the naming of Cuculain and shifts to the story of Deirdre, one of the essential reasons for the central conflict in the *History*. That conflict is a contest between the North and the other four provinces of Ireland. The four provinces are led by Maeve, and the ostensible purpose of their raid into the North is to obtain a prize bull which is kept at Cooley. Perhaps the most important warrior in her forces is Fergus Mac Roy who at one time had been the High King of the North, but who was now living in exile in the West.

The Deirdre story explains the exile of Fergus. Before Deirdre's birth, Cathvah, the druid, predicted that she would be the source of great trouble to Ulla. Therefore Concobar ordered that she be raised in a remote area. However, Deirdre meets Naysi, one of the sons of Usna, and they fall in love and flee to Scotland. Concobar banishes them forever, but after several years Concobar relents and allows Deirdre and the sons of Usna to return. Fergus pledges that he will insure their security. However, as soon as they return, Concobar goes back on his word and slays the sons of Usna. He keeps Fergus away by a stratagem while he does this.

Concobar has been clearly perfidious, and Fergus immediately goes into revolt. O'Grady gives some rationalization for Concobar's actions, "for he [Concobar] saw that his authority and sovereignty were set aside, and that now the wars predicted by Cathvah were about to burst, and that Fergus and the children of Usna were confederate against him" (p. 119). But these excuses are lame, and Fergus has good reason to revolt: the king has violated the heroic code. Concobar, however, succeeds in vanquishing Fergus and his adherents, and they are forced into exile with Maeve and Aileel in the West.

The character of Fergus is intriguing: he is very noble, but he pays no heed to the bards or the druids. In this instance the trouble is caused partly because Concobar, at the urging of Fergus, ignores the prophecy of Cathvah and allows the sons of Usna to return. Fergus had uttered "bitter gibes and scoffs against the High King and his star-gazers" (p. 177). O'Grady's own attitude towards the druids is ambiguous. At times he treats them as an institution to be respected; at other times he shares Fergus's contempt for them. O'Grady was suspicious of any species of priestcraft. On the other hand, he would brook no contempt for the bards, as the entire *History* makes clear. Fergus's notion of bravery, however, leads him to ignore the bards. Later in Vol. I when the suggestion is made that Maeve's forces break their pact with Cuculain to advance no farther until they have defeated him in single combat, Fergus lashes out at the would-be "treaty-breaker": " 'Fear, I plainly see, hath eaten away thy manly heart that thou dreadest the bard-loving captain of the Red Branch, and the crooning of the bearded poet, which the brave man no more regards than the idle rail that crakes at sunset in the meadows' " (p. 183).

In this instance Fergus comes off well because he is upholding the heroic code. O'Grady probably allowed Fergus's disrespect for the bards to remain unrebuked for that reason. Respect for the bards is necessary because they curb those who need curbing, especially for violations of the heroic code—"crimes" which Fergus does not commit. However, his leader Maeve is threatened by the bards and restricts them. Her un-heroic queenship is often the target of bardic satires and tales which demonstrate her unfitness for rule. Fergus is her one claim to rectitude, but his unrebuked criticism of the bards suggests that right action alone makes it unnecessary to worry about what the bards might say—a state of unconcern that Maeve's actions deny her.

Thus, in joining Maeve, Fergus tarnishes the purity of his rebellion against the perfidy of Concobar. While he has ample justification for his rebellion, alliance with Maeve is not the answer as the rest of the *History* makes clear.

The reaction of Cuculain to the Deirdre story is instructive in this regard. Cuculain does not go into rebellion. The ex-planation for his failure to do so makes sense in Carlylian terms. Cuculain stays with Concobar and by his heroic action trans-forms the situation and the time. Cuculain has the "wisdom to discern truly" what the Time wants; he becomes the "lightning out of Heaven" that kindles the "dry dead fuel" of this time when it is hard to know where the right lies.[24] After Cuculain's actions have purified the North, the details of Con-cobar's perfidy lose importance. The name of Cuculain is on everyone's lips. The first need of all people, according to Carlyle, has been satisifed; they have a hero to worship.[25]

O'Grady does not record Cuculain's reaction to the Deirdre story at the same point in the text as we hear about Fergus's rebellion. Instead, we hear the story almost at the end of Vol. I. Then a bard tells it to Laeg, Cuculain's charioteer, while Cuculain lies severely wounded. Significantly the details of Cuculain's heroic activity in single-handedly holding off Maeve's invading force are known to us at that point. We know the wonder Cuculain has worked, and we should be ready to see that as the greater good.

When the story of Concobar's perfidy reaches him, Cuculain's reaction is characteristic: he acts immediately.

> . . . a great wrath like a madness descended upon him
> when he heard of the slaughter of Illan and the others,

> for they had been dear comrades and school-fellows;
> and this wrath bore him onward like a dead leaf on a
> rushing torrent. Therefore, he levied the rising-out of
> his tuath, not delaying to send the arrow by the hand
> of the slow hireling, but hastening himself from place
> to place, and his people took into their breasts the gen-
> erous wrath of the boy, and with one accord they came
> together (p. 256).

In Emain Macha word of Cuculain's "rising-out" reaches Concobar and his retinue. At a council they decide on the advice of Cathvah to place three naked women on a bridge over which Cuculain must pass on his way to the city. As Cuculain approached the city and saw the three naked women,

> . . . the reins dropped from the hands of the boy, and
> red shame suffused his neck and face; but as he was
> embarrassed and confused with drooped head, Con-
> cobar Mac Nessa himself hastened forward, and took
> Cuculain by the hand and led him into the city to the
> Dun; and after that Cuculain shed many tears (pp. 257-
> 258).

Significantly, Cuculain is a boy at the point that he goes into revolution and a boy who is sexually uninitiated. By having Cuculain demonstrate his immaturity in the act of rebellion, O'Grady is also demonstrating that revolution is an immature act. A boy who can be so flustered by the sight of three naked women is hardly ready to undertake the overthrow of the High King of Ulla.

The original rendering of this story may be found in O'Daly's translation, and there it is part merely of the initiation rite of Cuculain. There are no political overtones to the story at all; it is not part of the aftermath of the Deirdre story. O'Grady's change makes it clear that his *History* must be read with a political consciousness because it is written with one. O'Grady is profoundly anti-revolutionary. Ireland needs only the transforming hero.

O'Grady's treatment of the initiation story in the source[26] is critical for a variety of reasons. Not only does his rendering demonstrate his political consciousness; it also exhibits his sense of literary decorum as well as his distaste for the humorous, the frankly sexual, and the fantastic.

In O'Daly the initiation rite follows the story of Cuculain's taking of arms and his subsequent foray to the South where among other feats he cuts off the heads of three enemies. (In O'Grady's *History* these events are narrated immediately after the Deirdre story). It is on his return from his foray to the South that Cuculain encounters the naked women. This time however, there are not three, but thirty women, "and they active and blushing naked, exposing their persons and their shame before him."[27] They expose themselves to prevent Cuculain from wantonly slaying "the youths of Eamhuin."[28] Cuculain has no political purpose; indeed, he has no purpose at all.

The reduction of the number of women from thirty to three in O'Grady's rendition reveals his sense of literary decorum. This was O'Grady's notion of toning "the heroic tale . . . down to epic proportion and reasonableness" (p. 48). He also completely eliminated the events subsequent to Cuculain's reaction to the women. In O'Daly they are broadly comic:

> Then descended he from the chariot and he was placed
> in a bath of cold water and the first vessel he was placed
> in the hoops and the staves burst like nuts under him and
> the water ran out of the second vessel and the third
> vessel no one could stand at all, then in the long run the
> anger left the youth. . .[29]

A fantastic description of Cuculain follows:

> . . . and his form came back to him and he was changed
> into a crimson pillar from his head to the ground; and
> beauteous was the youth. He had seven toes on each of
> his feet and seven fingers on each of his hands, seven
> pupils in each of his eyes, and a bunch of Eye Bright in
> each separate pupil; and he had four dimples in each of
> his cheeks, viz., a blue dimple, a crimson dimple, a green
> dimple and a yellow dimple. . .[30]

All such lavish and grotesque descriptions O'Grady eliminated in his *History*. His sense of the epic could not brook such superhuman characteristics. In a note to his *History of Ireland: Critical and Philosophical*, O'Grady explained, and partially apologized for, his sense of epic proportion:

> Fergus mac Roy, recovering his sword long lost,
> addresses to it a song of welcome and endearment, and,
> as he wheels it around his head in a frenzy of joy, shears
> off the tops of three mountains. It is evident from this
> that the character of the great champions of the age, at
> least in the eyes of some of the bards, ascends to the
> gigantic. In my own attempt to treat the age epically,
> I have represented the stature as rather greater than
> human, but not gigantic. Otherwise it would be im-
> possible to mould all into a harmonious and reasonable
> form. At the same time, I am aware, that a more Titanic
> treatment, by one having the necessary genius, might
> be more true to the bardic temper and traditions, and
> productive of a greater and more valuable literary re-
> sult.[31]

This passage also reveals O'Grady's blindness to, or at least his refusal to repeat, the humor in O'Daly's rendition. There the tale may be "more Titanic" in terms of the strict physical descriptions, but the humor has the effect of rendering the gigantic grotesque and laughable and therefore reduces the scale of the composition greatly.

Instead, O'Grady wrought his sources into whatever shape best served his purposes. It is fair to say that most of the conceptions of the characters and events in O'Grady's *History* are his own, and only rarely does he allow his sources to control his composition.

Accordingly, after the Deirdre story, when O'Grady tells of Cuculain's "Knighting," his foray to the South and his killing of three warriors, his rendition serves *his* purpose of demonstrating the nature of the true Carlylian hero. Cuculain is not content simply to receive arms: he must act immediately. Indeed, in both volumes of the *History*, Cuculain speaks very little. We come to know some of the principal characteristics, for instance, of Fergus and Maeve in a way we commonly expect to learn about characters in a novel. We see them quarrel, and we know something of their temperament. Almost all we see Cuculain do is act. Indeed, to paraphrase Carlyle, Cuculain's deeds are greater than his words.[32]

And it is in the raid on the North by Maeve's forces that

Cuculain performs his greatest deeds. O'Grady next turns to the story proper of the *"Tan-bo-Cooalney"* or "The Cattle Raid at Cooley." He begins by recounting the peaceful attempt of Maeve to procure the prize bull of the North, the Donn Cooalney. She sends Fergus to ask the king of Cooalney for the loan of the bull. However, Fergus fails in the mission because of *hubris.* He leaves without the bull, having "uttered words [to the king] in which the scoff was thinly veiled" (p. 133).

On his return Maeve levies a "rising-out" of the forces of the four provinces under her control and prepares to raid the North. Before doing so, Maeve is visited by a divine prophetess, Faythleen, who warns Maeve to make " 'no bargain' " with Cuculain, " 'for that bargain thou shalt rue' " (p. 137). Faythleen tells Maeve further that she will " 'spread amazement in the hosts of Ulla. They shall not return to their right mind for a season. And do thou hasten forward the expedition, for thou shalt conquer the province ere they be aware' " (p. 137).

Faythleen, however, provides for Cuculain's absence from the North as the spell descends upon the province. She makes an appointment to meet him in the South but fails to keep it.[33] The spell renders all the warriors in the North mindless of the impending raid by Maeve's forces. This spell, or "enchantment," as O'Grady more often called it in Vol. II, is more than a magic trick. To O'Grady it represents the political state of the North. O'Daly does not use the word "enchantment" in his translation, and it is likely that O'Grady borrowed it from Carlyle, who used it often. For Carlyle, it represented a state in which men found it impossible to act or to work. It was the state of England in the 1840's that Carlyle addressed himself to in *Past and Present.* The rich were idle and cared not to see that the poor should have work to do. Instead the workers were left to sit idle:

> '. . . near by one another; but in a kind of torpor, es-
> pecially in a silence, which was very striking. In silence:
> for, alas, what word was to be said? An Earth all lying
> round, crying, Come and till me, come and reap me;—
> yet we here sit *enchanted*! In the eyes and brows of
> these men hung the gloomiest expression, not of anger,
> distress and weariness; they returned my glance with a
> glance that seemed to say, "Do not look at us. We sit
> *enchanted* here, we know not why. The Sun shines and

> the Earth calls; and, by the governing Powers and Im-
> potence of this England, we are forbidden to obey. It
> is impossible they tell us!. . .'[34] (italics added)

Cuculain had sent his father, Sualtam, to rouse the men
of the North, and Sualtam's detailed explanation, on his return,
of his attempts to alarm the men of the North closely parallels
Carlyle's description of the England of the 1840's. Sualtam reports: "Enchanted are all the warlike clans of Ulla, so that they
are sunk in a mortal stupefaction, or wildly raving like men
whose intelligence has been taken away" (p. 170). Essentially
the aristocracy of the North like the idle English aristocracy of
Carlyle's day has abandoned the responsibilities of rule. They
attack the herds and frighten the common people who, significantly, are unaffected by the enchantment. Indeed, they continue to do their work only to see it wantonly destroyed by the
distracted warriors.

Sualtam reports many telling instances of the dissolution
of the aristocracy. Konal Karna, one of the three greatest
warriors of the North, mistakes Sualtam for a merchant (p. 171)
—an error that is indicative to O'Grady's mind of a very warped
set of values.[35] Folloman, the son of Concobar, stands on the
beach with his warriors in a distracted and misdirected state of
readiness, " 'awaiting some signal, which never came' " (p. 177).
In a disorderly assembly at Emain Macha (which resembles
Carlyle's conception of the English Parliament),[36] Concobar
addresses his chiefs and talks about high-sounding irrelevancies
(p. 172).

This is the state of affairs that Cuculain's heroism must
dispel, and O'Grady believed that it was also the state of affairs
in the Ireland of his time. "Enchanted" became his word to describe the Anglo-Irish aristocracy, and in his *All Ireland Review*
and in *The Peasant* he wrote several essays with the title "The
Great Enchantment."[37] Indeed, in one 1900 essay, a response
to a letter from W. B. Yeats on the subject, his rhetoric reveals
that he still thinks of the antidote to the Enchantment in
Carlylian terms:

> The Enchantment must be assailed from many points,
> and writing is only good as a preparation for action, for
> it is only by action that the power of the Spell can be
> effectually broken. The true deliverers will be the doers
> not the sayers.[38]

In O'Grady's *History* Cuculain is the ultimate doer, and his heroic actions work deliverance for the North. After his father's report, he realizes that it is up to him to fight alone. He begins by harrassing attacks on Maeve's forces in which hundreds of warriors are killed. However, Cuculain does his fighting in the spirit of high chivalry. Before he makes his first attack, he thinks it fit to warn Maeve's men of his presence so as not to " 'fall upon them unawares' " (p. 149). He kills Eiderkool only after the latter forces him into combat. He does not want to show disrespect for Fergus under whose protection Eiderkool approaches him.[39]   Finally, he strikes a compact with Maeve's men which forces them to fight by the rules of strict chivalry—one-to-one combat. Each day Cuculain will face one warrior until he is vanquished. The men of the four provinces will move no farther into the North until Cuculain has been defeated.

Many single combats follow in which Cuculain beats each warrior that faces him. Maeve encounters considerable difficulty in persuading warriors to face Cuculain. Many refuse either because they fear Cuculain or because they have great affection for him. Neither attitude reflects credit on Maeve's cause. She offers rewards to warriors who will defeat Cuculain—even her daughter's hand in marriage. On one occasion she tries to have a warrior killed one day, so that the superior warrior who is pledged to avenge his death will have to fight Cuculain the next day. The superior warrior has too much love for Cuculain to fight him. All such stratagems to trick warriors into combat are ignoble.

However, although that stratagem fails, Maeve is successful in cornering Cuculain's boyhood friend, Fardia, into fighting Cuculain. Fionavar, Maeve's daughter, is the bait which traps Fardia into the duel. Cuculain defeats Fardia in a tragic conflict that neither warrior wanted.[40] Maeve comes off badly because she is responsible for disrupting the sacred bond of friendship.

In his rendering of the fight with Fardia, O'Grady changed the original text considerably.[41]   In O'Daly's translation, the fight ranges over several days, and the narrative dwells on the friendship between Cuculain and Fardia. O'Grady's sense of decorum, however, required him to cut the scene to what he considered to be the proper epic proportion. The scene achieves an intensity that fits with the decorum of the rest of the volume. The original, though quite complete in itself, would have sprawled too much for O'Grady's *History*.[42]

In the duel with Fardia, Cuculain is severely wounded although he triumphs. Maeve's forces believe that he has died, so they are now free to raid the North. At last, however, the North begins to stir. Laeg, Cuculain's charioteer, rouses himself and heads south to aid Cuculain.[43]

On Laeg's way south, an incident occurs which counterpoints the heroism of the preceding duel. Laeg encounters a former slave, Ayha Coelshanig, who in fact owed his freedom to a magnanimous action by Cuculain. The story, completely made up by O'Grady, reveals the mercenary mind at its worst. Coelshanig will not extend hospitality to Laeg without payment first. Laeg deals with this penuriousness summarily, tying Coelshanig up and helping himself to the goods and services of Coelshanig's house.[44] Even while Coelshanig is bound, he can think only of the retribution that will be his under the law. He regrets only that he has not a higher rank since the recompense would be greater. Actually Coelshanig could have attained a higher rank but preferred the lower because at that rank he could exploit the people under him more. The higher rank would have required him to have free men for tenants whose tributes would be prescribed by law. The tributes of the slaves under him

> . . . were voluntary and not under the protection of the
> law, by which means he became wealthy indeed, but
> continued ignoble, not having a generous mind, which
> thing, namely, that he had not taken out his flautship
> [the higher rank] in the tuath, now grieved him in his
> computations (pp. 251-252).

In short, O'Grady makes the relevant point for his time: Coelshanig is a bad landlord, and such people are fundamentally base. Indeed, they are so base that they have no appreciation for heroism like Cuculain's, as the rest of the passage makes clear:

> Moreover, in his churlishness he was not wise, for he
> knew not the usages of war, and the suspension of the
> strict law in the imminence of danger, and the necessities
> of brave warriors, by whose prowess alone might all law
> be sustained, therefore, even in his avaricious mind he was
> not wise (p. 252).

Significantly Coelshanig is contemptuous of bards and
harpers, but he strictly obeys the advice of his druid. The druid
interprets for Coelshanig "dreams and omens and the notes of
wrens and ravens" and teaches him "the observances which were
due to the Shee that they might be favourable to him in his
affairs. . ." (p. 253). It is primarily this side of religion, priestcraft and its relationship to mercenary matters, that disturbs
O'Grady so much. On the other hand, he seems to have
tolerated, even reverenced, some of the notions of the ancient
gods. Since, indeed, the ancient gods were apotheosized heroes,
religious worship was simply the natural culmination of hero
worship. Coelshanig does not reverence heroes, so he could not
possibly reverence the gods in the correct spirit.

After a stay of one night with Coelshanig, Laeg moves on
until he finds the wounded Cuculain. Vol. I closes at this point
with a chapter entitled "Ah Cu!" which is a paean to, and a
virtual apotheosis of, Cuculain. As Cuculain lies wounded, all
the gods of ancient Ireland come invisibly to visit him. The
list of their names covers two pages, and the parallel construction O'Grady uses gives the list the effect of a litany:

> From the Shannon, where the hills are dark above the
> waters of the Red Lake, came Bove Derg, endlessly
> grieving for his grand-children, the cruelly transformed. . .
> Came Lear of the Shee Fionahah, on Slieve Few . . .
> Came Mananan, the son of Lear, from his isle . . . Came
> the warrior queens of the Gaeil Bauv, and Macha, and
> Moreega . . . and the three sweet sisters Eire and Fohla
> and Banba . . . Came Fion, the son of Cool . . . so above
> the mighty Cuculain appeared the blessed Shee, speaking
> words of comfort and of praise, and Cuculain conversed
> with the Tuatha De Danan, being noble of heart like
> themselves (pp. 265-267).

Cuculain alone can see them since he seems to be blessed
with a kind of beatific vision. Laeg can only feel their presence
and fears to see them because he is not blessed with Cuculain's
vision. Laeg fears "lest he should be smitten with blindness or
struck suddenly dead, seeing with his eyes the blessed Shee"
(p. 267).

The rhetorical device of the litany works well in this
chapter, and brings Vol. I to a fit conclusion in the glorification

of Cuculain's heroism.   O'Grady used other rhetorical devices
in the book, but with less success.   For example, he was fond of
constructing Homeric similes, but many of them were ridicu-
lously inapt. A great stone smashing through the shield of Lok
Mac Favash is compared to "the trained rider" breaking "through
the paper hoops held up before her."   Then "the fragments
flutter around, and some of them adhere to her guazy raiment. . ." (p. 209).

If this use of the modern circus was inappropriate in an
ancient context, O'Grady's use of modern phrases was equally
inapt.   He was capable of speaking of the "lavatories" and
"naval stations" of the ancient Irish.   Often such usages occur
when he is introducing "the ancient civilization of the country"
into his text.   In attempting to show the advanced state of that
civilization, his vocabulary sometimes became too modern.

Sometimes also he created problems for himself in his
adaption of the ancient text to his modern rendition. What
makes sense in the original seems misplaced in the *History*. For
example, in Chap. XLIV an old hag tricks Cuculain into blessing
her. This hag had harrassed Cuculain in his single combats, and
he had wounded her.   In O'Grady the blessing seems to be no
more than a nasty trick.   In O'Daly the hag's need for the
blessing is explained, "for no one that was wounded by Cuchullin
could be cured without he had a hand himself in the cure."[45]

Yet all such difficulties aside, O'Grady does achieve in
Vol. I an inspiring portrait of Cuculain as an actualization of
the Carlylian hero. This volume (more than Vol. II) is the book
that inspired Yeats, AE, and the Irish writers who followed.
Apparently sales were slow at first, and the reviews few.   The
reviewer in *The Spectator*, however, did recognize the possibility the book had for arousing interest in the ancient Irish
literature and, indeed, pleaded for wider use of that literature:

> Laying down this volume, it will naturally occur to
> the reader to ask why Irish poets have left so long un-
> wrought this rich mine of the virgin poetry of their
> country. Why does not some one arise among them as-
> piring to do for these legends what Tennyson has done for
> the legends of King Arthur and the Knights of the Round
> Table? . . . Will the Irish Muse sleep on till the foreign in-
> vader pounces upon her treasures? The author of the pre-
> sent work is doing something to bring these beautiful

legends under the notice of the world, and he deserves all honour for an attempt which we sincerely hope may be successful.[46]

Success came, but slowly.

Notes

[1] *History of Ireland: Critical and Philosophical*, pp. 56-57.

[2] *History of Ireland: the Heroic Period*, p. x. Subsequent references to this volume in this chapter will appear as page numbers in parentheses in the text.

[3] Cf., pp. 32-33.

[4] *Early Bardic Literature, Ireland*, p. 38.

[5] Standish James O'Grady, *Toryism and the Tory Democracy* (London: Chapman and Hall, 1886), pp. 137-138.

[6] Thomas Carlyle, *Past and Present* (New York University Press, 1977), p. 162.

[7] Thomas Carlyle, *On Heroes, Hero-Worship and the Heroic in History* (Lincoln, Nebraska: University of Nebraska Press, 1966), p. 162.

[8] *Past and Present*, p. 196.

[9] *Past and Present*, p. 191.

[10] *Past and Present*, p. 192. Perhaps Carlyle's most famous chapter in *Sartor Resartus*, "The Everlasting Yea," is deeply imbued with this military language:

> 'Our Life is compassed round with Necessity; yet is the meaning of Life itself no other than freedom, than Voluntary Force: thus have we a warfare; in the beginning, especially, a hard-fought battle. For the God-given mandate, *Work thou in Welldoing*, lies mysteriously written in Promethean Prophetic Characters, in our hearts; and leaves us no rest, night or day, till it be deciphered and obeyed; till it burn forth, in our conduct, a visible, acted Gospel of Freedom.' *Sartor Resartus*, p. 178.

[11] *Past and Present*, p. 42.

[12]Cf., e. g., Carlyle's essay, "On History Again," in *Critical and Miscellaneous Essays,* Vol. XXVIII of *The Works of Thomas Carlyle* (New York: Scribner's, 1899), p. 167: "History is the Letter of Instructions, which the old generations write and posthumously transmit to the new. . ."

[13]"Enchanted," as I shall explain.

[14]Peter Allan Dale, *The Victorian Critic and the Idea of History* (Cambridge, Mass. and London: Harvard University Press, 1977), p. 75.

[15]*Early Bardic Literature, Ireland,* p. 77.

[16]Thomas Carlyle, "Boswell's Life of Johnson," in *Critical and Miscellaneous Essays,* Vol. XXVIII of *The Works of Thomas Carlyle* (New York: Scribner's, 1899), p. 79.

[17]Thomas Carlyle, "Historic Survey of German Poetry," in *Critical and Miscellaneous Essays,* Vol. XXVII of *The Works of Thomas Carlyle* (New York: Scribner's, 1899), p. 342.

[18]O'Grady's prejudices show in this passage. The Eskimo was on the opposite end of the evolutionary scale from the Aryan for the nineteenth century ethnologist. Intriguingly, the Irish were often given the same characteristics as O'Grady gives the Eskimos here. A favorite device of Victorian caricaturists was to depict the Irish with prognathous jaws. Cf., L. P. Curtis, Jr., *Apes and Angels* (Washington, D. C.: Smithsonian Institution Press, 1971).

[19]Cf., p. 25.

[20]Compare Swinburne's "Thou hast conquered, O pale Gallilean," in his "Hymn to Proserpine."

O'Grady wrote to Swinburne on at least one occasion, and the tone of his letter reveals that O'Grady wished the Irish to resume the traits of the Fianna described here. The letter was probably written in the late 1860's or early 1870's since O'Grady gives Trinity College as his address. It reads in part:

> I am an Irishman Sir, and one who deeply feels the degradation of his country and the baseness, the cap-in-hand servility and paltriness of spirit with which centuries of oppression have stained the Irish character. National independence alone with the public-spirit and self-respect which are its concomitants will redeem the name of Irishman from the contempt into which it has deservedly fallen. . .
>
> The object of this letter is to implore you to add your music and passion to our efforts. . . .

Standish James O'Grady, Letter to Algernon Charles Swinburne, 19 Jan. [n.y.], Henry W. and Albert A. Berg Collection, The New York Public

Library, Astor, Lenox and Tilden Foundations.

In passing it is worth noting that the theme of primitive glory and Christian misery runs through the works of other O'Grady contemporaries, notably Yeats, Hardy, and Lawrence.

[21]William Irwin Thompson has also commented on this section of O'Grady's *History*. He does not point out how O'Grady's rendering realizes Carlyle's *Past and Present,* but he perceives clearly the conjunction of past and present:

> A sequence of events, the present, is set off with its own day-to-day consciousness, then suddenly it intersects with another sequence of events, the past, with a consciousness that understands it even though the present had no knowledge of the other's existence.

The Imagination of an Insurrection (New York: Oxford University Press, 1967), p. 23.

[22]It is very important to remember that disorder and injustice were synonyms in Carlyle's vocabulary, and O'Grady's *History* is informed throughout by the same thinking. Cf. Carlyle's essay, "Chartism," in *Critical and Miscellaneous Essays,* Vol. XXIX of *The Works of Thomas Carlyle* (New York: Scribner's, 1899), p. 145: "What is injustice? Another Name for *dis*order, for unveracity, unreality; a thing which veracious created Nature, even because it is not Chaos and a waste-whirling baseless Phantasm, rejects and disowns." This passage occurs immediately after a chapter on Ireland.

[23]Cf., pp. 64-65.

[24]Cf. p. 67.

[25]Cf. *On Heroes, Hero-Worship, and the Heroic in History,* p. 15:

> In times of unbelief, which soon have to become times of revolution, much down-rushing, sorrowful decay and ruin is visible to everybody. For myself, in these days, I seem to see in this indestructibility of Hero-worship the everlasting adamant lower than which the confused wreck of revolutionary things cannot fall. The confused wreck of things crumbling and even crashing and tumbling all round us in these revolutionary ages, will get down so far; *no* farther. It is an eternal corner-stone, from which they can begin to build themselves up again. That man, in some sense or other, worships Heroes; that we all of us reverence and must ever reverence Great Men: this is, to me, the living rock amid all rushings-down whatsoever;—the one fixed point in modern revolutionary history, other wise as if bottomless and shoreless.

[26]Cf. Appendix C for the entire text of the initiation story in O'Daly's translation.

[27]O'Daly, p. 91.

[28]O'Daly, p. 90.

[29]O'Daly, pp. 91-92.

[30]O'Daly, p. 92.

[31]*History of Ireland: Critical and Philosophical,* p. 202n.

[32]Cf., p. 66.

[33]In O'Daly, Cuculain makes the trip to the South to meet a woman, and sex is strongly hinted to be the purpose of the trip. Cf., p. 55.

[34]*Past and Present,* p. 8.

[35]Cf. p. 50 and pp. 86-87.

[36]Cf., e. g., *Sartor Resartus,* p. 66: Man " 'collects apparently by lot, six hundred and fifty-eight miscellaneous individuals [the House of Commons], and says to them, *Make this nation toil for us, bleed for us, hunger and sorrow and sin for us;* and they do it.' "

[37]Lady Gregory reprinted some of these essays in *Ideals in Ireland* (1901; rpt. New York: Lemma, 1973).

[38]Standish James O'Grady, "The Great Enchantment," *All Ireland Review,* 1 (22 Sept. 1900), p. 4, c. 1-2.

[39]Cf. p. 56 for O'Daly's rendition of this story.

[40]Cf. p. 2.

[41]O'Grady removed Cuculain's unfairness from the fight. Cf. p. 55.

[42]Phillip Marcus disliked O'Grady's cutting of the original story since the original was perhaps the most complete story among the bardic tales. I disagree with Marcus because O'Grady's rendition is consonant with his sense of decorum. Cf. Marcus, pp. 33-35.

[43]In O'Daly's translation Laeg is always with Cuculain. O'Grady had Laeg suffer the enchantment to increase the heroic character of Cuculain by having him stand alone against the invading force.

[44]O'Grady tells a similar story in Part II of *The Masque of Finn* (Dublin: Sealy, Bryers and Walker, 1907).

[45]O'Daly, pp. 167-168.

[46]Rev. of *History of Ireland: the Heroic Period,* by Standish James O'Grady, *The Spectator,* 51 (22 June 1878), 800.

Chapter IV

History of Ireland: Cuculain and his Contemporaries

If Vol. I of the "bardic history" was more favored by succeeding Irish writers than Vol. II, that favor ran contrary to the expressed wish of O'Grady himself. By 1879, he apparently had re-thought his approach to the bardic literature because in *Early Bardic Literature, Ireland* he requested "the reader, when the two volumes may diverge in tone or statement, to attach greater importance to the second, as the result of wider and more careful reading and more matured reflection."[1] He made this statement because he had come to the conclusion that the "characters and chief events" of the bardic literature "are absolutely historic" and he had given his rendition too much the nature of "legend and romance."[2]

It is difficult to judge whether O'Grady's change of mind was stimulated by reactions to his work or simply by his own continued reflection on the bardic subject matter. The reviewer in *The Spectator* did call the "heroic period of the history of Ireland" a "picturesque romance."[3] And a reviewer in *The Celtic Magazine* called Vol. I a "magnificently brilliant historical romance."[4] Perhaps these reviews bothered him because they placed the *History* in a genre which made it possible to regard the bardic literature as the result merely of the poetic imagination and therefore less true. If the bardic literature were not historical fact, then it would not have the capacity to inform the present in the manner that Carlyle prescribed.

O'Grady seems to have been fighting an Irish intellectual current which dismissed the early literature as poetic fancy. Despite this trend O'Grady speaks directly to the inability of the Irish mind to escape the "ineluctable modality" of Irish history:

> Educated Irishmen are ignorant of, and indifferent to, their history; yet from the hold of that history they cannot shake themselves free. It still haunts the imagination, like Mordecai at Haman's gate, a cause of continual

> annoyance and vexation.   An Irishman can no more
> release himself from his history than he can absolve
> himself from social and domestic duties. He may outrage
> it, but he cannot placidly ignore. Hence the uneasy,
> impatient feeling with which the subject is generally
> regarded.[5]

It seems likely, then, that O'Grady's first volume, when it was read, was dismissed with some impatience. But it was probably ignored more than it was dismissed. This reception may explain the insistent note that *Early Bardic Literature, Ireland* strikes.   O'Grady seems to be saying over and over again, "This literature is true. This literature is important."

O'Grady argues, therefore, for the greatness of Ireland because it has, albeit with a defect, precisely what "educated Irish men are ignorant of, and indifferent to":

> To all great nations their history presents itself under
> the aspect of poetry; a drama exciting pity and terror;
> an epic with unbroken continuity, and a wide range of
> thought, when the intellect is satisfied with coherence
> and unity, and the imagination by extent and diversity.
> Such is the bardic history of Ireland, but with this literary
> defect. A perfect epic is only possible when the critical
> spirit begins to be in the ascendant, for with the critical
> spirit comes that distrust and apathy towards the spon-
> taneous literature of early times, which permit some
> great poet so to shape and alter the old materials as to
> construct a harmonious and internally consistent tale,
> observing throughout a sense of proportion and a due
> relation of the parts.[6]

O'Grady saw himself as that epic poet with the critical spirit who would perform the task of creating the perfect epic and therefore assure Ireland's place among the great nations.[7] Then all Irish people would have a model upon which to base their actions, for a "noble moral tone pervades the whole" of the bardic literature.   O'Grady would have played his role in creating a noble people in the mold of their ancestors, " 'the Fianna of Erin' " who " 'never uttered falsehood.' "[8]

After arguing so stridently for the historicity of the bardic literature, O'Grady spends some time describing the restrictions on poetic license the bards observed which kept the literature "unsullied" by poetic invention. He then gives a broad sketch of Irish history starting with the year 2379 B. C. Though he does not claim historicity for the accounts of such a remote period, his method of presenting the information (somewhat analogous to *The Annals of the Four Masters*) does lend an air of verisimilitude to the sketch.

Vol. II proper of the *History* begins with a long chapter which is quite similar to, although more detailed than, the sketch of Irish history in *Early Bardic Literature, Ireland*. O'Grady does make a few points in which he tries to explain how documents such as the bardic tales can contain historic fact despite features that give them the air of pure imagination. He explains, for example, the huge number of warriors that a single champion is able to slay as the "bardic tendency to ascribe to the chief all that the prowess of his warriors under his guidance might achieve."[9] The "marvelous, the weird, the sublime" in the ancient texts he explains as additions to the original historical report caused by "the feelings of the minds through which that history in those centuries passed" (p. 118).

At the end of the first chapter, O'Grady says that he will now return "to that point at which I broke off in the first volume" (p. 119), and it is a welcome return. Chapter I is very dull and contains whole pages with little more than dates and the names of kings which can have little meaning to the reader.[10]

Chapter II resumes the narrative, and despite all O'Grady's talk about historicity, the rest of Vol. II resembles the narrative sections of Vol. I. If anything, O'Grady becomes more proficient at the literary devices which plunge the reader into a story and dull any concern that he or she might have for absolute historic fact. O'Grady uses suspense masterfully in this volume, shifting the point of view often and using flashbacks to achieve dramatic tension. Characters undo themselves by what they say, and a strong sense of fate pervades the atmosphere against which the actions are set.

Chapter II displays this "literary quality" immediately. O'Grady takes up the story at a point after Maeve's forces have raided the North. The chapter opens with a description of a plain on the second day of May:

> When the sun rose over Fremain on the second day of
> the month of Belthinne, his light was reflected only on

> the innumerable drops of glistening dew, with which,
> all over, the immense plain was begemed, and a happy
> silence reigned. . . For this plain . . . was sacred and un-
> tilled from of yore, since within it Uta the Prosperous had
> been interred . . . but the immense plain lay, from age to
> age, a pure and undesecrated soil. . . (pp. 119-120).

By nightfall the plain is changed; O'Grady's parallel construction alone points to the contrast and suggests the dese-
cration involved in the change:

> When the moon rose over Fremain on the night of
> the second day of the month of Belthinne, her beams
> were reflected from the burnished points of innumerable
> spears, the bright faces of shields, and the ornamented
> embroidered banners, that floated over the tent-doors
> of the kings of the four provinces of Eire. And a mighty
> din, a vast confused uproar, resounded where camped
> the great host of the men of Maeve, returning from the
> desolation of Ulla. . . (pp. 120-121).

So Chapter II begins, and much of Vol. II concentrates similarly
on the "confused uproar," the bankruptcy of Maeve's cause, and,
especially, her unfitness for rule. O'Grady uses the same kind
of indirection often. Maeve is subtly contrasted with other
characters; her own speech ironically undoes her.

The Men of Maeve camp on the plain of Uta, and a description of her chief warriors follows. The description of Fergus
is direct, like his characters; he is a "shape gigantic of heroic
mould, holding a joyless majesty and a spirit in ruins" (p. 122).
O'Grady knew the limits of indirection; he wanted to make clear
that Fergus was a man blessed with the capacity for heroism but
unfortunately enlisted in the wrong cause.

As night comes on, the extent and nature of that wrong
cause becomes clear. The bard of the Olnemacta (the Western
tribes) begins to sing and chiefly of the great deeds of Cuculain.
His audience is rapt, and Cuculain's friends (all except Fergus)
weep over his supposed death. This kind of singing does not sit
well with Maeve, who directs "against the bard scornful glances,
and bitter arrows of sharp speech, capricious and fickle, [she]
who formerly caressed and honored the son of Sualtam, living,
but now desired to minish and stain his glory, being dead, and

to gather to herself and her nation all the renown attending that great foray" (p. 131). To this section O'Grady appends a note which shows clearly his attitude toward such treatment of the bard:

> Some time after this a persecution was raised against the bards, who, by their insistence upon law as opposed to force, were the democratic element in the various states. The exiled bards were received at the Court of Concobar (p. 132n).

The center of order and right is in the North, and the bards and warriors of Maeve recognize that fact. Despite Maeve's injunction, the bards continue to sing of Cuculain because he is the most worthy of their singing. Again Maeve is angered, but this time she suggests instead that they sing of Cethern Mac Fiontann. The suggestion reflects great discredit on Maeve. She herself had wounded Cethern in battle, but O'Grady precludes any honor accruing to her from that fact. He tells us that before wounding Cethern "she had first insulted [him], for the dazed [from the enchantment] hero had come naked, hastening to the relief of Cuculain, and the great Queen, unqueenly, had diverted herself with his state, uttering jests among her captains" (p. 136). In O'Daly's translation Maeve is often capable of such bawdiness. In the age of Victoria O'Grady could hardly deem it proper conduct for a queen.

Again Maeve is refused, and the bard sings of Cuculain, not Cethern. The warriors are delighted, but Maeve is "indignant." She attacks the bards directly and undoes herself by comparing them to women:

> "Effeminate, unwarlike, resembling women, whose weapon is their intemperate tongue; worse than women, for they give birth to warriors, but you, laws to impoverish noble clans, lying tales, and pedigrees. Forsooth, you chronicle the past" (p. 140).

The last charge is a serious breach of the code of values that O'Grady believed the ancient Irish held sacred. History writing, he believed, was one of the most important activities of the ancients. The great heroes of the past inspired the warriors of the present. A rebuke to Maeve is not long in coming. Queen Fleeas of the Gamanradians, a tribe allied with Maeve in the raid, takes Maeve to task and clearly delineates the bards' function:

> "Thee to asperse the singing men of Eire! who guard with rhymed tuneful words the wisdom of all the wizards of ancient times, together with the heroic deeds of our ancestors, and the ramifications of the tribes and noble clans, who inflame with heroic thoughts the minds of youthful warriors. . . Rightly too, O thou most unjust Queen, have they this night praised the heroic son of Sualtam, who perished nobly on the borders of Ulla, contending singly against the whole host of the Tan" (p. 141).

Immediately after this rebuke from Fleeas, who is a model queen, the assembly of Maeve's forces breaks up in an uproar. The Mor Reega, on of the war goddesses, appears to the assembly, and complete chaos takes over as Maeve's forces flee in all directions. The Mor Reega's appearance is a bad omen for the men of Maeve, and it also reveals the latter's cowardice—a quality that makes her unfit for rule. Though she always boasted of her military prowess, she "fled through the host like a timid hare" (p. 148) at the sight of the Mor Reega.

The war goddess actually only inflames the disorder already smoldering among Maeve's forces, and Fergus has his hands full to keep them together. Maeve decides to pacify them by announcing the dispersion of the force and the division of the booty. She does this despite Fergus's warning that the North has arisen and that an attack is imminent. She tells a herald who comes with news of the North's approach: " 'Tell me not thy tidings, for I will not hear' " (p. 152). Despite Maeve's attitude Fergus manages to hold the troops together.

A quiet evening affords Maeve the opportunity for pleasant conversation with her knights and Queen Fleeas. O'Grady uses the conversation to make important points about queenship and aesthetics. The conversation begins with Maeve expressing homesickness to Fleeas. Maeve's feeling is generalized; Fleeas makes clear that home is the place for a queen:

> ". . . there is a young ollav out of the kingdom of Luhar Dega, who for me has been collecting the history of the

> noble clans of the Partree and the achievements of their
> ancient heroes and heroines.   Truly for many causes
> would I that I were now in my greenan [women's
> quarter], having around me those wise men with whom I
> love to converse, regulating the affairs of my palace, and
> enjoying the society of my husband.   Me too now, my
> dear child is doubtless anxiously awaiting" (pp. 172-173).

Fleeas has the correct Victorian notion of the province in
which she should rule—the home. O'Grady believed firmly that
a woman's place was in the home. In the O'Daly translation,
Maeve is scorned because she is a woman,[11] but O'Grady gives
the scorn a particular Victorian context.

Perhaps the clearest Victorian delineation of the roles of
man and woman was given by another Carlyle disciple whom
O'Grady also praised highly—John Ruskin. In *Sesame and Lilies*
Ruskin expounded his theory of the appropriate male-female
relationship. He believed that both sexes had distinct qualities,
and therefore a man could not assume a woman's role or vice-
versa.

> Each [sex] has what the other has not: each completes
> the other, and is completed by the other: they are in
> nothing alike, and the happiness and perfection of both
> depends on each asking and receiving from the other what
> the other only can give.
>
>   Now their separate characters are briefly these. The
> man's power is active, progressive, defensive. He is
> eminently the doer, the creator, the discoverer, the
> defender. His intellect is for speculation and invention;
> his energy for adventure, for war, and for conquest,
> wherever war is just, wherever conquest necessary. But
> the woman's power is for rule, not for battle,—and her
> intellect is not for invention or creation, but for sweet
> ordering, arrangement and decision.[12]

Ruskin makes clear in the following sentences that the
appropriate realm for a woman's rule is the home. Maeve, however, is married to an ineffectual husband, Aileel, who is now
too old to fight and perform the manly functions. He holds
"the silver staff of his ancient sovereignty," but "at all times the
little finger of the Queen was stronger to govern men than the

sceptre of her lord" (p. 210). This is an unnatural situation, which Maeve's homesickness subconsciously recognizes. The North must win to reestablish kingship.

Fleeas follows her expression of homesickness with a plea to the bards that they sing of more than war. To them "the blackbird . . . is . . . but the symbol of martial courage" (p. 175). It is only natural for a Victorian woman to feel this way, for her function in creating the home is to create a "place of Peace," to use Ruskin's words. It "ceases to be home," in "so far as the anxieties of the outer life penetrate into it, and the inconsistently-minded, unknown, unloved, or hostile society of the outer world is allowed by either husband or wife to cross the threshold."[13]

Maeve, however, quickly takes up Fleeas' idea and transforms it into a suggestion that the bards concern themselves with irrelevancies. She wants to be a law unto herself, and it would be better for her if art had less to do with life, or, at least, human life. She answers Fleeas:

> "Much indeed, I desire . . . that the bards of Eire would sing only of these things, and relinquish to their betters that which concerns princes. But now they must needs be heard in the making and administration of the laws, with close-inspecting and jealous eyes observing all that we do. Let them sing of the wars of cats and rats, and chronicle the wisdom of the black-bird in making his nest, and glorifying the brightness of his eyes and the redness of his legs, rather than concern themselves with laws" (p. 176).

The discussion is now joined by two warriors and a bard. Cailitin, whose sons are fated to be the undoing of Cuculain, echoes and extends Maeve's idea. O'Grady makes perfectly clear that a vile character has appeared on the scene, and Cailitin's agreement with Maeve serves only to reflect great discredit on her. Cailitin is "an admirer of himself, and a contemner of ancient times." "Moreover, where he went he attracted to himself honour, and he lessened the honour of dignities, such a spell did he cast over the minds of men" (p. 176). He foresees a utopia ruled by bards who " 'will forget the works of war.' " Heroes will no longer be necessary, so " 'the fierce race of savage heroes shall expire.' " Then the bards will " 'hymn the mild and beautiful . . . . and chiefly the pleasures of love' " (pp. 176-177).

The other warrior and the bard respond immediately with what must have been O'Grady's attitude toward decadence. Mainey Ahrimail, the warrior, calls Cailitin's thoughts base and defiantly rejects Cailitin's vision of the future, " '. . . for out of Eire the race of heroes shall not, at any time, expire' " (p. 178). Bricne, the bard, addresses Fleas and tries to explain to her the reasons why the bards sing of heroes. They " 'need a chronicler and a historian' " because " 'deeds of heroic breath' " are seen " 'only at times' " while the beauties of nature are there always to be seen and heard.

To this common-sense explanation Bricne adds more substantive reasoning. The nation needs the heroic spirit, for it

> ". . . is impossible, that one whose soul is immersed in the soft beauty of the world should sustain, unimpaired, the high heroic ardour, the daring and fearlessness and contempt of death which have given to every nation its heroes, and to every clan its divine names, both in old times and now also, men excelling in stature and beauty, and in heroic bearing and words, the tame small tillers of the soil, the slaves and fudirs of Fohla [Ireland], who, if they eat and sleep and gender in peace, and die a bloodless death, think that the gods have been most gracious" (pp. 178-179).

To this speech, Mainey Ahrimail adds the last word. He dispenses with any distinction between the heroic and the beautiful. He finds beauty in the warrior doing battle:

> "When I see Cormac Conlingas . . . spring, all armed, into his chariot on the edge of battle, with his gleaming cathbarr and broad shield, that, indeed, appears a beautiful sight to me, and his battle-shout seems, to me, beautiful, and beautiful his magic spear levelled, when his arm is drawn back to hurl, and the firm muscle of his upper arm stands out from the glistening purple bratta" (p. 180).

In short, the heroic is the beautiful.

The aesthetic discussion ends, but Maeve changes the sub-

ject and speaks of her admiration for Cailitin. This speech begins
a new chapter, entitled "The Enchanter," which is O'Grady's
word for Cailitin.   In so labeling him, O'Grady connects him
with the enchantment of the North, and indeed, Cailitin says,
" 'I deepened the stupefaction of the Ultionians' " (p. 184).
Cailitin is a master of the " 'wizard arts' " (p. 181), and so
O'Grady connects him with the negative characteristics that
he has given to the druids.

Cailitin becomes the embodiment of all that O'Grady
detests.   He is the vision of the future ruler who will keep Ireland
in an "enchanted" state.   To a slight extent he mitigates the
evil of Maeve because she too is enchanted by him.   This evil
behind the evil represents some change on O'Grady's part in
Vol. II.   Cailitin does not figure at all in Vol. I, while in Vol.
II Cuculain's primary struggle is with him and his posterity.
O'Grady seems to have been influenced even more by Carlyle
in Vol. II than he was in Vol. I, and the Carlylian code word,
"enchantment," is used more frequently than it was there.

Cailitin has all the attributes to which O'Grady has attached negative connotations in Vol. I and in Vol. II up to this
point.[14]   Like Ayha Coelshanig, the tightfisted freedman in
Vol. I,[15] Cailitin is of plebian stock in Ireland and has close
associations with the merchant class, his father having been
" 'honoured highly by the merchants and burgesses' " (p. 186).
Cailitin is not a bad warrior, but "his strength" lies "in his
magic power" (pp. 182-183).   He has twenty-seven sons, "not
sprung from the same mother, for he wandered in his affections,
and many women had he led to his house as concubines, some by
compulsion and in tears, having gained, with bribes, the consent
of their parents, and some willingly for he was very rich" (p.
182).

O'Grady draws the lines of conflict between Cailitin and
Cuculain very carefully.   It is an eternal war between good and
evil, or to use Carlyle's terms, between "Belief" and "Unbelief,"
between truth and sham.[16]   Cailitin reports that his father's
dying words warned him that Cuculain, " 'and such as he, were
the deadly enemy of all our race, and that between him and
us there could be no truce, any more than between the fierce
forest-roaming wolf and the gentle and fleece-producing sheep,
and that it was fated that I should destroy him, or he me' "
(p. 186).

The conversation of Maeve, Cailitin, and Cormac Conlingas

ends abruptly after this announcement of eternal enmity between Cuculain and Cailitin. The cause of the interruption is very significant, and O'Grady expects his reader to catch the significance without any overt indication on his part. A warrior simply states, " 'Methinks I see Fergus Mac Roy afar off, approaching.' " The effect of that heroic figure's presence on Cailitin and his Clan is immediate: "Thereat Cailitin and the Clan Cailitin arose, and went away to where was their own quarter. . ." (p. 187). O'Grady leaves it to his reader to infer that the vile cannot stand the presence of the heroic.

And Fergus's role throughout much of the rest of the volume is to dispel Maeve's blindness which is caused by her association with the vile. The scene next shifts to a plain beyond which the Ultonians can be seen approaching. Fergus forces Maeve to look out across it. Instead of the troops of the North, Maeve sees mystical visions:

> "I hear a vast confused hum like the murmur of some gigantic hive, when in the spring-time there is a noise of preparation amongst its populous youth, . . . and I hear, or hardly hear, voices as of gods or giant heroes, and a faint ringing as of brass amid that mysterious mist, and now more clearly I distinguish the flashings and the stars, and the rapid fires. Amid the mist there is the beckoning of a gigantic hand, blood-red, and around it, as it were, lightnings. It is the Fomoroh, or the people of Mac Erc, raised by sorcerers from their tombs, or the high gods of Erin descending visibly out of Tir-na-n-og, and the realms of the dead" (pp. 190-191).

After this speech Maeve screams and tries to run away, but Fergus prohibits her and rebukes her for her " 'unwarlike panic' " (p. 191). He then explains the mystical vision to her in real terms.[17] The " 'white fairy mist' " is " 'the breath of the valiant, and the steam of the breathing of the mighty men of Ulla. . .' " (p. 192). The " 'lights like quick-glancing stars' " are " 'the shining of innumerable helmets. . .' " (pp. 192-193).

In that manner Fergus forces Maeve to see the truth of the situation. He has the heroic vision which enables him to see things as they really are. A chapter in which the heroes of the North are highly praised follows this unmasking of Maeve's delusions. The chapter uses the same form as the preceding—a

conversation between Maeve and Fergus, this time with Cormac
Conlingas, the son of Concobar, joining in. As previously, the
worthiness of the Ultonian chieftains is emphasized. Maeve
loses "her fear . . . in wonder and awe" (p. 201) at the great
warriors she beholds. She disparages Concobar, but her words
serve only to demonstrate his greatness, even from his youth:

> "At him [Concobar as a boy] the farcoming kings won-
> dered, because he loved not our pleasures, but went to
> and fro among the cairns and the tombs of the men of
> old, and the armour and weapons of ancient heroes
> preserved in our halls, listening greedily to every lying
> tale of the bards and antiquaries of Temair [Tara]"
> (p. 198).

On the next day the two armies contend, and Maeve's men
have much the better of the fighting. O'Grady, however, reports
only the scenes in the respective camps after the day's fighting.
The North is downcast, while the four provinces are jubilant.
Their jubilance, however, is disrupted by a great roar from the
camp of the North. The roar is the North's reaction to what
appears to be the return of Cuculain from the dead. Maeve's
forces do not know the cause of the great joy in the Northern
camp, and O'Grady does not reveal it to the reader either, although the probable cause can be easily conjectured. O'Grady
deliberately heightens the reader's anticipation by this preparation for the grand entrance of Cuculain.

Indeed, O'Grady's narrative technique throughout the
ensuing chapters serves to move the action slowly toward a grand
climax in which the great feats of Cuculain will transform the
entire situation. Dividing the battle up into two days was
O'Grady's invention, and it serves to accentuate the transforming presence of Cuculain. With his arrival, the gloom of
the North is transformed into joy; the joy of the four provinces
is dissipated.

The battle of the second day is described in the next
chapter, and O'Grady shifts the point of view. The battle is
seen from the perspective of Aileel Mor, Maeve's husband and
the ineffectual Western king. He, however, is nearly blind, so
he relies on the eyes of his charioteer, Fer-loga, to learn how the
battle is faring. The chapter reports the conversation of the two:
it covers first the almost complete rout of the Ultonians and

then gradually builds to Aileel's recognition that the great warrior who belatedly enters the battle is Cuculain. Aileel then recognizes that the battle is lost for his side: " 'It is the Hound of Murthemney, O Fer-loga, returning again to battle unsubdued. It is Cuculain, the invincible, son of Sualtam' " (p. 218).

Having brought his narrative to Cuculain's entrance onto the battlefield, O'Grady again shifts the point of view and backtracks to the point where he left Cuculain at the end of Vol. I. Laeg has been nursing Cuculain with some success, but Cuculain is "debilitated" by "some unseen evil power" (p. 219). However, Cuculain regains enough strength to return to the battle, so he and Laeg set out for Emain Macha.

They rest one night at a liss, or noble's residence, and much of the chapter centers on their stay there. What follows is probably O'Grady's invention. He provides a picture of the sorry state of a land without its heroes. The nobleman of the liss has gone off to the war, so the servants take unaccustomed liberties which the lady of the house and her daughter are unable to control. Cuculain is greeted at the door of the house by a servant who stands "straddling in the entrance with an uncouth dignity of demeanour, and, with much authority," demands Cuculain's "name and purpose" (p. 222). Similarly Laeg is treated insolently by a steward, but the lady of the house apologizes, pointing out the need for a man to control such base persons. She tells Laeg, " '. . . when he who is the head of a household is departed, a woman cannot restrain the insolence of intemperate minds. . .' " (p. 230). She has the same problem Maeve has with the Clan Cailitin. Disorder takes over when those who are incapable of rule possess power, and in the Carlylian scheme of things injustice is the inevitable concommitant of disorder.[18] O'Grady pointedly demonstrates the unfitness of the servants and tenants in their response to Laeg's query about the extent of the plundering of Maeve's men. They "answered, as is the custom of their race, with many voices, and contradiction, and mutual recrimination" (p. 229).

The day after this visit to the liss, Cuculain and Laeg journey on to the camp of the men of the North, having realized that the men had already left Emain Macha. As Cuculain nears the camp, the spell upon him increases and weakens him. Nevertheless, his appearance in the camp is a great joy to his compatriots, and O'Grady again tells of Cuculain's arrival, this time from the perspective of the warriors inside the Northern camp.

The next four chapters retell the story of the second day of the battle, also from a point of view inside the Northern camp. O'Grady is clearly promoting the epic and dramatic interest in this scene contrary to his intention expressed in *Early Bardic Literature, Ireland* to downplay these elements. Again, he slowly builds to the climactic moment of Cuculain's entrance onto the battlefield. The battle commences without Cuculain, who lies asleep overcome by the spell that is plaguing him. The forays of the heroes, especially Fergus, are described in great detail. O'Grady dwells on Fergus's heroism, and in a chapter significantly entitled "Deirdre Remembered" Fergus contends with Concobar.

O'Grady once more makes clear that Fergus has a great deal of right on his side. Concobar answers Fergus's challenge to identify himself with a denunciation in which he boldly admits his own perfidy:

> "[I am] One who cheated thee out of thy sovereignty when thou wast captain of the Red Branch, who slew the sons of Usna, surrounded by thy vain protection, who conquered thy rebel hosts in battle, who expelled thee like a wolf out of Ulla, and made thee an exile and a roamer, till thou hast become the servant of a woman, receiving unmanly wages from a lewd termagant" (p. 249).

Fergus, also, is hardly blameless, and indeed he admits that his exile with Maeve hardly brings credit to him since he has been " 'receiving from a woman unmanly wages' " (p. 250). Furthermore, he condemns Concobar for the latter's respect for druids and poets, and disrespect to the latter, at least, is a flaw to O'Grady's mind. Fergus tells Concobar that the latter went wrong when he strayed from Fergus's tutelage: " '. . . thy mind wandered from me, going after druids with their idle lore, and poets and lying chroniclers, and thou wast familiar with the base man and the coward, and talked wild unprincely words' " (p. 249).

Concobar, however, has the last word in the argument, and the question he asks is very significant: " 'To whom clave the son of Sualtam, O Fergus—to me or to thee?' " (p. 250). In short: I am right because Cuculain is on my side. And that illogicality is the fundamental Carlylian logic of O'Grady's *History:* the

heroic is the right. Cuculain transforms all. The balancing of
rights and wrongs between Concobar and Fergus has meaning
only up to a certain point: the appearance of the hero, Cuculain,
to whom the correct response is hero-worship.

As if to give added meaning and reality to Concobar's
statement, Fergus is defeating Concobar in the ensuing battle
until Cuculain appears on the scene. O'Grady makes very clear
that Cuculain appearance is akin to a divine apparition, and, in
so doing, he fulfills a basic Carlylian requirement for the hero:
that he be the manifestation of the divine in the world. Therefore, O'Grady describes Concobar as reeling from the blows of
Fergus until "it seemed that not even a *god* could be his
salvation, or deliver him from the vengeful exile" (p. 252 [italics
added]). This sentence is followed by a single line:

Then rang Cuculain's battle-cry across the plain (p. 252).

When Cuculain appears on the scene, Fergus withdraws
because of a prior agreement with him, but O'Grady again delays
that fateful moment of Cuculain's appearance. Instead, he backtracks once more, this time to a point earlier in the day. The
scene is the tent where Cuculain is sleeping under the influence
of the spell. Despite Laeg's anxiety, Cuculain sleeps on until
Lu Lam-fada, his tutelary deity, appears to him in a vision. Lu
tells Cuculain to arise and fight, and he, Lu, will dissipate the
spell of the Clan Cailitin and the Mor Reega. Cuculain, then,
has received his mandate directly from the divine, and, intriguingly, the divine in this case, Lu Lam-fada, had once
"delivered the gods from Fomorian tyranny" (p. 257n) as
O'Grady tells us in a footnote. Cuculain's deliverance of Concobar and Ulla will follow the Carlylian pattern of *Past and
Present,* the future in relation to the past being "the *same* fact
in new dress and development."[19] Cuculain hears the call of
Lu Lam-fada, and no thought, but "a fell rage grew to madness
within him" (p. 260). He is immediately impelled into action.

Cuculain works his deliverance in a chapter appropriately
entitled " *'Αριστεία Conculain.*"[20] O'Grady finally allows
all the heroism of Cuculain to show forth. Although Fergus's
withdrawal is explained as part of a previous agreement with
Cuculain, O'Grady seems only to have made a bow to his sources
in so presenting it. At the voice of Cuculain, Fergus stands
"in amazement" (p. 262) and withdraws, awestruck by

Cuculain's greatness.   Cuculain then commences to turn the
tide of battle and puts on a great (and entertaining) show of
military prowess.   Finally, it comes time to fight the Clan
Cailitin.   Again Lu Lam-fada speaks to Cuculain and impresses
upon him the historical importance of his fight with them.
At stake is the very survival of the Irish as a noble people:

> "Not alone for the Red Branch shalt thou now fight,
> but for all the nations of Eire, who, thee beaten, will
> no longer yield men and heroes, and fair peaceful fields,
> but her fens shall be enlarged, and dragons shall dwell
> there, and slimy unnameable monsters, and all manner
> of foul creeping things, and few and base shall her people
> be" (p. 278).

Cuculain's action in the present, then, will profoundly
influence the future course of Irish history.   So Cuculain engages
the Clan Cailitin who shroud themselves in the darkness, and
the past and the future come together with the present in
Cuculain's heroic action.   Carlyle's notion of the *"Life-tree
Igdrasil"*[21] is realized in O'Grady's description of that historical confluence:

> From their tombs brake forth the ancient dead at the
> noise of that strife like the shock of worlds, for the earth
> stirred herself, and the dead arose out of their sleep of
> ages.   Then time gave up her secrets and births to be, and
> her veiled nations and generations arose rank behind rank.
> Like a torrent's fall their voices sounded from afar, sum-
> moning him [Cuculain] to their deliverance, their thin
> voices unheard in the crash and roar of that awful strife
> (p. 281).

At last, the magic darkness clears, and Cailitin and his
twenty-seven sons lie dead.   The men of Maeve then flee, and
Cuculain allows Maeve to retreat unimpeded—a chivalrous
action to which O'Grady draws attention.   Cuculain's victory is
complete.
       The remainder of Vol. II is concerned with Cuculain's
death and the events that lead up to it.   O'Grady makes considerable use of foreshadowing in building to yet another climax
in the same volume.   In his first apparition to Cuculain, Lu

Lam-fada had told him the omens by which he would know that his death was approaching. Most importantly, he would perish at the hand of " 'the remnant of the Clan Cailitin' " (p. 258). To the warriors who are close to Cuculain, the day of fulfillment of that prophecy seems imminent. In the chapter immediately following the " *'Αριστεία Conculain,'* " these warriors are preparing to depart from Dublin for an expedition to Scotland. Cuculain will not accompany them on the expedition, and the warriors' anxiety for his safety foreshadows the coming events.

O'Grady, however, brings Cuculain's death to pass very slowly, and in the meantime he uses the Dublin setting for even more exposition of points that he has hammered home since the start of Vol. I. Now that he has invested Cuculain with the glory of the greatest hero of the Irish, he has him sit in judgment of the Dubliners. (A variation from his previous presentation of Cuculain's character: Cuculain *thinks* in this chapter). Dublin is the city of merchants, and they and Cuculain react to each other as complete strangers. The temper of the merchant has little in common with the heroic temper. As Laeg and Cuculain walked through the city,

> . . . Cuculain was dejected when he looked upon the people, so small were they, and so pale and ignoble, both in appearance and behaviour; and also when he saw the extreme poverty of the poor, and the hurrying eager crowds seeking what he knew not. But they, on the other hand, were astonished at the heroes, the greatness of their stature, the majesty of their bearing, and their tranquility. . . For, amongst the citizens of Ath-a-Cliah [Dublin], they seemed like scions of some mighty and divine race long since passed away (p. 292).

This is the Standish O'Grady of 1880 speaking to the Dublin of 1880. O'Grady regarded the city as an inherently bad place, and he maintained his antagonism towards it for most of his life.[22] As in the Dublin of 1880, the judicial apparatus of the Dublin of Cuculain's time is hardly worthy of praise. Unlike the wise and learned judges whom Lara found at Slieve Mish in Vol. I,[23] Cuculain finds courts where "many alterations and innovations" have been made in the ancient laws, and the proceedings are carried on in an atmosphere of "unseemly dispute and much bickering and clamour" (p. 293). Laeg and Cuculain are disgusted by the scene in a courtroom, so they leave. Many of the people follow them, drawn by their heroic presences—a comment on the absence of the heroic virtues in the court.

Cuculain returns to his home, and O'Grady takes the opportunity to present Cuculain's wife, Emer, as a model of queenship. After a feast some "of the warriors . . . played at chess, but others, and these the best, conversed with the queen. For pure and good was the wife of Cuculain; her mind eager concerning the noble and the true, and those who conversed with her were happy for many days" (p. 296).

Having thus reiterated once more the heroic values, O'Grady now slowly brings the death of Cuculain to pass. There are omens at Emain Macha, and once more there is a hosting of Maeve's troops under the instigation of the remnant of the Clan Cailitin. Before the hosting Maeve and her compatriots discuss the idea of rebelling, and once more Maeve shows the worthlessness of her enterprise. This time her words are more ironic than ever before. One king, Erc, hesitates to join the rebellion because his sister told him to be faithful to the Red Branch of King Concobar (a poor reason for faithfulness). Maeve scornfully replies:

> "Who is Acaill [Erc's sister] that she should govern the thoughts of men? It is not right that a woman should take upon herself authority and rule. Thou didst well to obey her when thou wast a child; but a king governs himself, and is guided by his own counsel" (p. 303).

Maeve succeeds in enlisting Erc with this taunting speech, and they prepare to attack the North while most of the Northern warriors are in Scotland—hardly the honorable time for an attack.

Meanwhile, Concobar and his ruling council, having received the omens of Cuculain's impending death, summon him to Emain Macha and place him under the protection of the druid, Cathvah. They guard Cuculain from knowledge of the hosting of Maeve's forces because they know that his immediate response will be to take action. Cuculain, however, has visions of the hosting, and he points out how foolish it is to try to avoid one's fate: " '. . . if the gods permit the Clan Cailitin to slay me, they will slay me in Emain Macha as well as on the frontier' " (p. 313). In short, impending death is no reason for heroic action to cease. The hero meets his fate head-on.

Cuculain's visions seem to be more apparitions of Lu Lam-fada, but the Northern druids dismiss them as the enchantments of the Clan Cailitin. Lu criticizes Cuculain for not taking action, and eventually Cuculain realizes that there is a battle to be fought—impending death and enchantments notwithstanding.

So Cuculain abandons the protection of the druids and goes off to fight. For seven days he attacks and beats Maeve's forces. On the eighth day, however, the spells of Cailitin's descendants finally catch up with Cuculain. His death comes, and, in O'Grady's rendering, it bears strong resemblance to Christ's death. Cuculain dies for his people as Christ did. As the hour of death approaches, Cuculain believes that his gods have " 'forsaken' " him (p. 338). The Clan Cailitin have taken upon themselves the forms of his patron deities, and the false gods laugh at Cuculain, inducing his moment of Christ-like despair. Significantly also, Cuculain's final agony comes upon him at "two hours after noon" which also suggest that he is a type of Christ since the traditional understanding of the Gospels holds that Christ hung on the cross from noon to three o'clock. As Christ died upright on the cross, so too Cuculain, having tied himself to a pillar, dies in a standing position.

The Clan Cailitin exults, but in death Cuculain is greeted by a child who strongly suggests the Christ-child. The child takes Cuculain by the hand, saying, " 'Regard not these children of evil, O my brother, their dominion is but for a time' " (p. 346). The words are similar to Christ's own utterances on many occasions, and O'Grady is suggesting that the torch has passed from Cuculain to Christ.[24]

Vol. II closes, then, with the hoeric temper succeeded by the saintly temper.[25] O'Grady has worked out his *History* so that it follows the course he believed the actual history followed. Cuculain's life and death are the zenith as well as the denouement of the heroic period of Irish history. To paraphrase Carlyle, O'Grady has completed two volumes of the "History of the World" by providing the biography of one of its great men—Cuculain.[26]

Notes

[1] *Early Bardic Literature, Ireland,* p. 32. Since *Early Bardic Literature, Ireland* was reprinted in Vol. II of the "bardic history," all references to the former work may be found on the same numbered pages of the latter work.

[2] *Early Bardic Literature, Ireland,* p. 31.

[3] Rev. of *History of Ireland: the Heroic Period,* by Standish James O'Grady, *The Spectator,* 51 (22 June 1878), 799.

[4] Rev. of *History of Ireland: the Heroic Period,* by Standish James O'Grady, *The Celtic Magazine,* 3 (1878), 399.

[5] *Early Bardic Literature, Ireland,* p. 33.

[6] *Early Bardic Literature, Ireland,* pp. 40-41.

[7] That O'Grady's *History* is written in prose did not mean that it was not also poetry. Cf. pp. 20-21.

[8] *Early Bardic Literature, Ireland,* p. 43.

[9] *History of Ireland: Cuculain and his Contemporaries,* p. 116. Subsequent references in this chapter to this volume will appear as page numbers in parentheses in the text.

[10] Significantly *Cuculain: an Epic,* O'Grady's compilation of the narrative sections of Volumes I and II, begins with the second full page of Chap. II (p. 121).

[11] Fergus rails at Maeve often in the O'Daly translation. He blames the final defeat of their forces on her with the strong imputation that they lost because they were following a woman. Cf. O'Daly, pp. 271-372: " 'We were equal to them this day' says Fergus, 'but there is woe to that woman by whom this host has been wounded and betrayed (or led astray) and as an horseman that emerges out of a mist-covered district and knows neither the road nor what he ought to do so is this host now.' "

[12] John Ruskin, *Sesame and Lilies,* in *Sesame and Lilies, The Two Paths,* and *The King of the Golden River* (London: and Toronto: J. M. Dent; New York: E. P. Dutton, 1907), pp. 58-59. Compare also the similar delineation of male and female roles in Book VII of Tennyson's *The Princess.*

[13] Ruskin, p. 59.

[14] In O'Daly's translation, Cuculain contends with the Clan Cailitin, but they have none of the vileness O'Grady attributes to them. They do use

poison, however, to which O'Grady would attach vile significance. Cf. O'Daly, pp. 205-212.

[15] Cf. pp. 86-87.

[16] Cf. Carlyle, *On Heroes, Hero-Worship and the Heroic in History,* p. 204: ". . . I will call it [the war of the Puritans] a section once more of that great universal war which alone makes up the true History of the World,—the war of Belief against Unbelief! The struggle of men intent on the real essence of things, against men intent on the semblances and forms of things."

[17] In O'Daly, the approach of the North is also described by Fergus to Maeve, but, unlike O'Grady's version, Maeve does not see mystically what Fergus sees clearly. Cf. O'Daly, pp. 310-313.

[18] Cf. p. 91, n. 22.

[19] Cf. p. 69.

[20] "Ἀριστεία excellence or prowess. *Conculain* is O'Grady's Irish spelling of the genitive case of Cuculain.

[21] Cf. p. 69.

[22] In a series of open letters to Dublin clerks published in *The Peasant* in 1908 and in *The Irish Nation* in 1909, O'Grady attacked the city life and encouraged the Dublin clerks to escape the city by forming communes in the country.

[23] Cf. pp. 75-76.

[24] This introduction of Christ into the story of Cuculain's death is not O'Grady's invention, but he probably is responsible for the extensive parallels drawn between Cuculain and Christ and for the final scene with the child. O'Grady was probably aware of the excerpts from the Old Irish tale which had appeared in translation in the *Revue Celtique.* After his death Cuculain appeared to "the fifty queens who had loved him, and they saw him floating in his spirit-chariot over Emain Macha, and they heard him chant a mystic song of the coming of Christ and the Day of Doom." Whitley Stokes, "Cuchulainn's Death," *Revue Celtique,* 3 (1876-78), 185.

I cannot find the child's words in the same form in the Bible, but the parable of the tares (Matthew 13: 24-30; 36-43) is close in spirit to them.

[25] In a later (post-1900), unpublished TS in my possession, O'Grady inserted Finn and the Fianna Eireen between Cuculain and his contemporaries and the Irish Christian "heroes"—the monks. In that writing he used the word "heroic" in a more general sense and delineated six historic groups of Irish heroes:

> 1) "the superhuman and semi-divine Heroes of the 'Heroic Period' ";

2) Finn and the Fianna Eireen;

3) "the founders of the great monastic communities conventionally known as 'the Saints' ";

4) the "mediaeval chieftainry and their martial clansmen";

5) "the Protestant Irish landed gentry of Ireland of the 18th century";

6) the Irish peasant.

Of these, O'Grady regarded the "Saints" as the manifestation of the heroic most worthy of emulation. This attitude seems to differ from the extreme praise he lavished on the ancient heroes in both volumes of the "bardic history."   In this later writing he still condemns the later Irish Christians who made "gods and goddesses" out of their predecessors and told "silly stories about them." O'Grady wants Young Ireland, to whom his essay is addressed, to emulate the original "Saints," not worship them:

> The Hero-Saints, save and except that we cannot all be cele-
> bates, are for ever and for us all a grand pattern exemplar and
> realised Ideal. They lived mainly in the open air and the light
> working there with their hands at noble and useful and beautiful
> occupations. Otherwise they worked indoors in their workshops,
> and on such manly labour outdoor and indoor they erected this
> great spiritual intellectual scholarly and artistic life.

"Chap. 3: Air & Light & the Heroic." TS, p. 53 (so numbered), The Standish De Courcey O'Grady Collection.
   [26]Cf. p. 67.

Chapter V

History of Ireland: Critical and Philosophical

It is difficult to determine how Vol. II of O'Grady's "bardic history" was received,[1] but his next book may give some inkling of the probable nature of the reception. That book, *History of Ireland: Critical and Philosophical,* published in 1881—a year after Vol. II, is a very different kind of history. It is consciously "scientific" in method throughout, and O'Grady struggles hard to keep his penchant for the "good story" in check. The difference in approach is probably an attempt to validate his previous work, for throughout this volume he argues for the historicity of the bardic literature. Perhaps Vol. II of the "bardic history," like Vol. I, was received as a work of mere fancy.

Regardless of the reception of the "bardic history," however, O'Grady's need to prove the historicity of the bardic literature is evident in each of the *Critical and Philosophical History's* thirteen parts, which cover classical and bardic accounts of Ireland from the earliest times to the time of St. Patrick. This need had been bothering O'Grady for some time: it had led him to mix "archaeological," "scientific" chapters with his narrative chapters in Vol. I of the "bardic history." Now, in 1881 he decided to satisfy this need fully, and, in fact, he repeated the first six "scientific" chapters of Vol. I *verbatim* in the *Cricital and Philosophical History* with only a short addition to the fifth chapter. Other passages were repeated as well, and they fit better in the later work than in Vol. I.

O'Grady does argue his case well in general, but the *Critical and Philosophical History* would not bear his trademark if it were not outlandish at times. Throughout the volume, he writes with absolute assurance concerning matters that no one else would dare to be so categorical about. There are many of his familiar declarative sentences which state opinions as bald and absolute facts.[2] For example, he begins a paragraph (his favorite place for such sentences) by declaring, "Prehistoric narrative is of two kinds—in one the imagination is at work consciously, in the other unconsciously."[3]   I suspect that he would not have been at all timid about providing detailed descriptions of the mating habits of dinosaurs.

This *History* is pervaded by many such "factual assertions," and it is important to realize that they express more than O'Grady's desire to secure popular respect for the bardic literature.   For, to his mind, all great art was rooted in historical fact.[4]   Indeed, art was the natural culmination of history (pp. 56-57).   Therefore, the bardic literature could only become great art if it could be proven that it was rooted in history.

This aesthetic principle informs all thirteen sections of the *Critical and Philosophical History*—sometimes in uneasy association with other aesthetic principles, which he has asserted categorically.   Following Niebuhr, for example, he asserts that the bardic literature is based on a "metrical original" (p. 238). He finds evidence for this earlier form in the "strange ideas" in the bardic literature which suggest "the existence of a deeper and stranger literature upon which that we know has been formed."   Presumably that literature was closer to the historical facts, so for O'Grady this presumption is reason enough to pass judgment on a literature that he never read and never could read.   He declares with his usual lack of timidity: "This I regard as certain, that the more ancient the literature the better, and the more modern the worse.   What it gains in polish it loses in depth and sublimity" (p. 214n).   By this standard an epic—the result of the late-arriving critical spirit—would be less praiseworthy than the "metrical original."   Yet he previously had described the "defect"[5] in the early Irish literature as its failure to achieve the more modern form of the epic.

The excess of O'Grady's statement on the relative merits of ancient and modern literature may result from his dislike of modern renditions of the ancient literature.   He singles out the eighteenth century Scottish poet Macpherson for criticism (as indeed did Dr. Johnson and other of Macpherson's contemporaries). Macpherson had found "traces" of the early Ossianic literature "in the debased and floating ballads of the Highlands," but "in Scotland, in the eighteenth century, the historical origin of the ballads, their epic continuity and coherence, and the position in time and place of the heroes whom they praised had been long lost.   Thus, released from the *curb of history,* he gave free rein to the imagination. . ."   The results he achieved, therefore, partook of the "false sublime" (p. 293 [italics added]).

A similar feeling, though not exactly the same principle, led O'Grady to compare Shelley's poetry unfavorably to the ancient bardic literature. O'Grady believed that the ancient bards lived in very close association with the forces of nature. They, therefore, developed a personal relationship with those forces which far transcended the conventional personifications used by modern poets. O'Grady notes how the forces of nature were real presences, even personalities, to the ancient bards and then compares their strong perceptions to Shelley's expression of "the sympathy of Nature with the fortunes of men:—

> 'Pale Ocean in unquiet slumber lay,
> And the wild winds flew round sobbing in their
>   dismay.'

O'Grady finds Shelley's lines too impersonal, too whimsical, so he concludes: "On this side, modern poetry is mere fancy; ancient poetry is strong undoubting belief" (p. 141). He seems to suspect that Shelley only half believes in his lines. They are merely a pretty conceit.

O'Grady disliked such mere aestheticism and points out that where the bards praised the beauties of nature they did so in the context of history and from the vantage point of personal acquaintance. The bards'

> . . . knowledge [was] not . . . merely aesthetic, but [mingled] . . . vitally with what they believed to be the history of the island. Every spot had its tutelary genius, a being powerful, immortal and invisible dwelling there, or was connected with some remarkable event in the history of some well-known monarch or hero (p. 136).

O'Grady's emphasis in this *History* on the necessary historical basis of poetry might lead his readers to think that he had no place for invention in his aesthetics. On the contrary, he believed firmly in the importance of the imagination. Properly educated and focused, the imagination was an instrument for seeing the true relationships of characters and events. In fact, history is not history without the imagination; it is pure chronology:

> The legends represent the imagination of the country;

> they are the kind of history which a nation desires to
> possess. They betray the ambition and ideals of the
> people, and, in this respect, have a value far beyond the
> tale of actual events and duly recorded deeds, which are
> no more history than a skeleton is a man (p. 41).

O'Grady further believed that the reader was far more likely to find history properly so conceived in the ancient literature of the country than in "times like these, when the treatment of the past has fallen altogether into the hands of critical persons and archaeologians, men whose labours are indeed indispensable, but who certainly do not fire the heart of youth with generous emotions, rouse the passions and educate the imagination" (p. 288).

Though O'Grady criticizes Shelley in this book for his failure to produce literature which would be so inspiring, it was Shelley whom he praised in an 1874 article for his repugnance to the so-called "progress" which civilization had wrought.[6] That attitude informs the *Critical and Philosophical History* throughout: the ancient and the primitive are better than the modern and the civilized. O'Grady extends that notion here by arguing that civilization is merely the art of making the primitive "beneficent" and permanent:

> . . . we must remember that civilization, like culture, is
> by no means so great or all-important as we have been
> taught to believe. Civilization indeed seems to be nothing
> else than the art or faculty of directing into beneficent
> and lasting results those forces of human nature which
> have been generated by causes with which civilization has
> nothing in common, primal spontaneous energies of the
> human soul (p. 14).

Significantly, this passage is part of the only two paragraphs that he added to the first six chapters which he repeated from Vol. I of the "bardic history." And the virtues of the primitive are reiterated many times throughout the *Critical and Philosophical History* and reveal that his thinking on the primitive has not changed since he wrote his periodical articles in the 1870's. For example, he argues once more[7] for the superiority of the primitive religious sensibility, for to his mind modern religious thinking is only now "catching up" to primitive religious thought:

> All these rude primitive beliefs, seem to be an instinctive
> expression of that faith to which the higher religious
> thought of the present century is steadily inclining, that
> the sensible world is a manifestation of God inseparable
> from and one with Him (P. 317).

O'Grady probably believed seriously that the primitive
was superior on intellectual grounds, but he also found it a
convenient argument to justify contemporary Ireland's
undeveloped state. Instead of refuting the charges of endemic
backwardness often leveled at the Irish, O'Grady made a virtue
out of primitivism. He even found residues of the ancient
practices amongst the people. He considered it "remarkable,
that even to the present day, the druidic healer, termed fairy-
doctor, is extensively patronized by the Irish peasantry" (p.
111).[8]

O'Grady must have felt a strong need to justify his claims
of greatness for the Irish because he even evolved a theory to
explain their ostensibly backward current state. He believed
that "in the cyclic progress of ages . . . changes of relation, and
reversions of mutual power and dignity, arise from no inherent
superiority of one race or nation of this great Aryan or Indo-
European family" (p. 390). In short, if the English dominate
the Irish now, they will not do so forever, nor have they always
done so.

In fact, O'Grady makes the present domination of the
English no sign of superiority. Indeed "it may be, I see clearly
in the case of neighbouring nations it is, that the period of fame
and worldly greatness is not the age of the most signal virtue;
such periods being rather a spending and dissipation of virtues
accumulated in ages of depression" (p. 391).

O'Grady is so carried away by his desire to show the lack
of "signal virtue" in Ireland's closest neighbor that he violates
his own logic. If the "races" and nations of the "Aryan or
Indo-European family" are all equal, then the following sentence
makes an impossible assertion: "But this I know, that the assumption by one nation of a radical and race-superiority over
another, tends rather to establish its own inferiority" (p.
391).[9] By O'Grady's own tenets, one member of the Aryan
family cannot "establish its own inferiority" to other members,

but he was too anxious to defend Ireland to worry about such inconsistency.

This kind of inconsistency—the result of emotion—may seem incongruous in a *History* that calls itself *Critical and Philosophical*. But O'Grady's writing was colored by more than his antagonism to English attitudes. He seems also to have been annoyed by the behavior of his own class—the Anglo-Irish Ascendancy—in the Land War that was disrupting Ireland in the 1880's. The *Critical and Philosophical History* is filled with criticisms of the ancient aristocracy both in theory and in practice—an unusual stance for O'Grady.

The explanation of O'Grady's attitude may lie in his political activity about the time this book was published. In 1881, he was involved in the political struggle between the tenants and the landlords. He served as the Honorary Secretary of a landlords' meeting in Dublin in December of 1881, and in 1882 he published a political tract on the subject—an address to the landlords calling them to an awareness of their extreme circumstances.

The tract criticizes the landlords severly for their past profligacy, cleverly putting the criticism in the mouth of a fictional British Premier:

> "But you [landlords], having entered into the lordship of the isle, not through your own might but through ours, took to yourselves the absolute and irresponsible dominion over the soil. You imposed what rents you pleased upon a people whom we laid prostrate before you, you swallowed up in rent every improvement which the labour of your serfs might effect, and you took to yourselves the whole of the enhanced value of the soil which accrued to it during the present century, owing to the growth here in England, and through English genius, of a great industrial population, a result to which in no way directly or indirectly did you contribute. With rent you stripped your country to the bone, failing not to extract, too, the marrow."[10]

In the *Critical and Philosophical History* O'Grady criticized a much earlier aristocracy, the Fianna Eireen, in similar fashion. They "failed, as all such military aristocracies must fail, by ignoring the common rights of humanity, and regarding their inferiours as made only to minister to themselves" (p. 319). The problem with the Fianna was that "the soil of Erin, not the people of Erin . . . inflamed their patriotism. Before charging they lay down and kissed the ground. This also is true universally of the aristocratic temper. It will easily love the land, while it despises the people" (p. 321).

While O'Grady did not support the Land League, the tenants' organization, he frankly admired its discipline, and he suggested that the landlords look to it for a model of organization:

> Look rather at the Land League, the iron discipline, the organisation, the self-reliance, the marvellous astuteness and courage of its chiefs, the never-failing plan, always the pursuit of a definite line of action marked out by the leaders endorsed by the rest.[11]

The Land League had the qualities which marked the ancient heroic temper, and O'Grady believed that such qualities would always triumph. In his *Critical and Philosophical History* he makes this point:

> Such [Northern] nations retaining the heroic temper, and having aggregated themselves into large combinations, necessarily and with ease overran regions where settled law encouraged private irresponsible wealth, and private irresponsible wealth had, as it everywhere does, degraded and impoverished the mass of the population (p. 375).

O'Grady's parenthetical phrase—"as it everywhere does"— is typical of the kind of generalizing he continually undertakes in this *History*. O'Grady found in Ireland the data for making universal judgments. His political consciousness was thoroughgoing, and there was small difference between the political and the critical and philosophical in his mind. It makes sense, therefore, to read his *Critical and Philosophical History* with the same sensitivity to his political consciousness as his "bardic history" requires.

As the only new material in Part I of this *History* serves O'Grady's purpose of legitimating the primitive, and, especially, primitive Ireland, Part II, "Classical References to Ireland," also serves that purpose by showing the association of Ireland with two of the world's earliest civilizations. After he had so praised the primitive, the fact that Rome and Greece were *civilized* ought to have caused him some difficulty, but he was simply interested in gaining respectability for Ireland by showing its associations with the best the ancient world had known.

His use of the classical references to Ireland is similarly idiosyncratic: he affirms those that he prefers and denies the others. Ancient Ireland gains further legitimacy, for example, by being identified as the Ogygia of Homer's *Odyssey* (pp. 22-24), for even the noble Greeks knew of Ireland. However, O'Grady quickly dismisses the classical writer who attributed cannibalism to the Irish.[12] His dismissal is very intriguing: not only does he use Caesar and Tacitus to refute Diodorus Siculus, but he also expounds a rationale for Diodorus Siculus's statement that clearly has a modern equivalent—the comments of British writers on the Irish. Diodorus Siculus made the charge of cannibalism because about his time:

> . . . classical writers began to express an inordinate contempt and aversion for all peoples outside the bounds of conventional civilization. . .
>
> The Britons as well as the Irish were the subject of various slanders of this kind, which, from the authoritative, positive, and negative testimony of Caesar and Tacitus, we know to be untrue. This intellectual vice is always engendered under an Imperialism (p. 26).

Having thus used Caesar to refute Diodorus Siculus, O'Grady turns right around and uses the heroic literature of Ireland to show that the ancient Irish were good, chaste Victorians contrary to Caesar's testimony. The heroic literature "breathes . . . the antique German spirit of heroic chastity" while the "community of wives ascribed by Caesar to the Britons is quite repugnant" to the spirit of the literature (pp. 31-32).

Part III, "Introduction to the Bardic History of Ireland," presents O'Grady's theory of art most explicitly[13] and justifies, in particular, the study of early Irish literature. O'Grady emphasizes the value of Irish literature to Aryan studies. After having made his point about the Basque and Celtic origins of the Irish in Part I, thereafter he seems to emphasize only the Celtic or Aryan part of the Irish racial mixture. One can only presume that he felt a strong need to insist that the Irish were Aryans. He argues that early Irish literature is important because its study will reveal a stage in the development of Aryan culture that has become submerged in other countries. "The stream of the Irish bardic literature still lingers in the mountains which gave it birth. It is near the well-head" (p. 53).

Parts IV and V discuss the Irish gods, and O'Grady immediately puts his theory of the importance of the Irish to work. He uses his notion of the development of the Irish gods to make generalizations about the development of mythologies elsewhere. Accordingly, the fact that the Irish perceived the forces of nature as personal gods leads O'Grady to the conclusion that "the strife between Achilles and the river gods, indicates the late origin of that portion of the *Iliad*. In the primal imagination, the gods would not have been so vague and elemental. They would have risen in armour out of the waters, and resisted the hero" (p. 133). Similarly O'Grady argues

> . . . that the Olympians arrived at deity by the same means as our Tuatha De Danan, viz., by magic. . . . The Irish gods effect all their great work by spells, incantations, and the use of the druidic wand. It is therefore, probable, that an idea so fundamental, holding such an influence over the mind of one branch of the Aryan race, affected all equally in the same stage of civilization (p. 102).

O'Grady believed that the gods were the apotheosized heroes of an earlier age. As memory of the actual hero grew dim, his deeds grew in magnitude in the popular imagination until only a god using magic could have performed them. On this basis O'Grady rejected the view that the cycles of the Irish gods, of which there were several, could be explained as different races sweeping over Ireland at different epochs. O'Grady called this view "absurd" (p. 122) because it is impossible to know the exact history of the development of the gods. We do know that one cycle of gods would replace an earlier one, and we can only accept the bardic theory that the new gods were heroes who were able to raise themselves "above nature by druidic skill" (p. 123) and, therefore, above the preceding gods.

The "classical gods" of Ireland, the Tuatha De Danan, for example, win their sovereignty over Ireland by defeating the

Fir-bolgs, their predecessors. The Tuatha De Danan are eventually defeated by the Milesians and retreat into invisibility. The Tuatha, however, had defeated the Fir-bolgs by superior magic. They "dried up all the streams and lakes" "by their weird power" when the Fir-bolg king sought to quench his thirst after six days of battle.

During their reign the Tuatha were not always supreme, and O'Grady takes the opportunity to use the story of their temporary enslavement as a prototype of more modern events. At one point the Fomorians succeeded in enslaving the Tuatha. O'Grady makes the Fomorians sound like the absentee landlords of his own day:

> The Tuatha De Danan sink down into hopeless slavery. The Fomorians do not even live in the land they oppress. From some far off region their insolent tax-gatherers annually appear, and sweep away all the produce of the island (p. 116).

Salvation comes in the form of Lu Lam-fada, the son of a Fomorian mother and a De Danan father and later the tutelary deity of Cuculain. O'Grady sees Lu as the progenitor of a long Irish tradition:

> On reaching man's estate, the choice is presented to him of ruling over his own people as a member of the dominant Fomorian nation, or of allying himself with the enslaved and trampled De Danans. To many at all times in all nations that choice has been given, and the hero's alternative often accepted, viz., by Moses in Hebrew history, by Gaudama in Indian, by the Gracchi at Rome: nor is the character unknown in the modern history of the nation whose progenitors worshipped the Ioldana [Lu] (p. 117).

It is hard to tell if O'Grady had a specific person in mind as the successor to Lu, "the genius of patriotism and heroic loyalty to the cause of the downtrodden" (p. 117). But O'Grady might well have been thinking of himself or a person like him, one of both Anglo-Irish and Celtic Irish blood. While he aligned himself with the landlords in the Land War, he expended more effort in reminding them of their responsibilities to the tenants than in defending their rights.

In Part VI O'Grady finishes his discussion of the gods and points out that no Irish "world-mythus" or myth of the origin of the world has come down to us. This time he reverses his method of reasoning and argues that the Irish must have had a "world-mythus" because the Greeks, the Norse and the Hebrews all had their own.[14]

The absence of a "world-mythus" is a crucial defect in a nation's mythology, and perhaps that fact explains O'Grady's desire to suppose that one did exist. Typically, he blames Christian redactors for the absence of the "world-mythus" from the bardic literature. O'Grady was fond of the notion that Ireland as a nation was stillborn, but he did not want the development to be cut off so far back as the times of the gods.

The development of the Irish nation is also O'Grady's concern in Part VII and the first Part VIII.[15] In these parts O'Grady traces the Irish kingship from prehistory down to the time of Cuculain. He finds evidence in the fact of the kingship for seeing the Irish as a nation—an idea that many of O'Grady's contemporaries hotly debated. The bardic literature gives evidence of incipient nationhood, for it provides "this dominant conception of the Irish race, as forming a single homogeneous nation, owing allegiance to a single sovereign, and governed by edicts issuing from one centre of rightful authority, namely, Tara" (p. 147).

O'Grady's concern in these parts is similar to his concern in Vol. I of the "bardic history" to establish the grounds of legitimate kingship. Much of the same material is covered, and the difference in style between the two books can be seen most clearly. As in Vol. I of the "bardic history" O'Grady here dwells on the reign of Conairey Mor after sketching the reigns of the kings up to that time. He repeats the description of the fruitfulness of Conairey's reign from Vol. I,[16] but the rest of the story does not have the same quality because it is narrated by a third person and has been therefore stripped of the dialogue that marked the "bardic history" version. For example the story ends on a flat note with a simple factual sentence: "Ferrogane stabbed himself rather than share in the impious deed" (p. 198). Yet although the story lacks the dialogue of Vol. I, O'Grady is not capable of destroying a good story. The death of Conairey Mor is still fairly lively, and many of the other stories in this volume are written with similar verve. O'Grady preferred to be

Livy, not Niebuhr.

This last being the case, O'Grady had to restrain himself severely in the second Part VIII, which treats principally of Cuculain and his contemporaries. O'Grady's enthusiasm for Cuculain is still unbridled, but there is a changed emphasis in this *History*. O'Grady emphasizes Cuculain's humanity more than his heroism:

> Through his whole career, in war and peace, in the world and out of it, in spite of all the cold dictates of reason and logic, the heart of the reader is stirred and his imagination inflamed by the contemplation of all that terrible and superhuman heroism, and the knowledge of those deep wells of pity, tenderness, and love, whence sprang those gentle deeds and words which, even more than his heroism, go to the formation of the noblest character ever presented in literature (p. 208).

The explanation for this changed emphasis probably lies in O'Grady's desire to provide a model of humanity for the aristocracy of his own day. The emphasis on Cuculain's humanity is consonant with O'Grady's criticism of the Fianna in this volume for their lack of concern about the people.[17]

Curiously, however, though O'Grady shows great concern for the people in this *History*, he is even more anti-revolutionary. He does not even allow Cuculain the momentary uprising against Concobar in the aftermath of the Deirdre story that he allowed in Vol. I of the "bardic history." Instead, he states categorically that Cuculain "never faltered in his allegiance to his uncle, Concobar mac Nessa" (p. 210). Indeed, O'Grady even excuses Concobar's perfidy: "The chief stain on his [Concobar's] character is the treacherous slaughter of the sons of Usna, but then Concobar loved Deirdre, and it was one of his own Knights who had so wronged him" (p. 217).

This kind of anti-revolutionary thinking seems to be behind some of O'Grady's supposed scholarship in Part IX. This part, "Tara and her Kings," traces the High Kings down to the time of the extermination of the Fianna. It begins with an account of a plebeian revolution called the Atticottic Revolution. O'Grady, however, dismisses it as not genuine history. His reasoning is unconvincing:

> The revolution of the Aithech Tuatha is so minutely
> described, and seems so historical, that I at once felt a
> suspicion of its genuineness, knowing the obscure char-
> actor of the centuries in which it is placed. In fact, it is
> too historical to be history (p. 249).

There may be a perceptive scholarly mind behind this
reasoning, but it is hard to believe that O'Grady would dismiss
another story because it was "so minutely described." Indeed,
he might well point to it as evidence of the extreme concern of
the bards for exact detail.[18] The explanation for the rejection
of this story probably lies in O'Grady's dislike of revolution and
especially his desire not to provide a model of a successful
plebeian revolution.[19] Perhaps he wished to counter-balance
his criticism of the aristocracy by keeping the plebeians in their
place.

When he does present a plebeian rebellion, it hardly provides incentive for a modern attempt. The last chapter of this
part describes the revolt of the people against the Fianna whom
O'Grady has characterized as an irresponsible aristocracy.
O'Grady's conception of the revolution follows closely Carlyle's
ideas on revolutions, especially the French Revolution. Carlyle
regarded the French Revolution as a horror, but an inevitable
horror, necessitated by the failure of the aristocracy to care
for the people. When such a revolution takes place, nobody
wins.

And in the uprising against the Fianna, the people and
their leader are defeated, but it is a Pyrrhic victory for the
Fianna. Only a handful of them survive the battle. O'Grady
believed that this revolution clearly followed the Carlylian
pattern:

> There is in human nature a *satanic* element of revolt
> which will suffer for ever no ruler who despises those
> he governs. Thus this fine mythus, if, indeed, it be a
> myth, of the glory and greatness of the Fianna Eireen
> and their final overthrow, is a type and symbol of many
> a more authentic revolution (p. 323 [italics added]).

Carlyle believed that the hero made such revolutions unnecessary, and that a civilization could be judged by its manner
of welcoming its great men. The conditions that produced the

revolt against the Fianna did not always exist, for at one time the heros of the Fianna were held in very high regard. By Carlyle's standard then, the time preceding the demise of the Fianna must have been very great, for O'Grady says that "hero-worship, in the sense that men were perpetually immersed in the thought of the great characters of ancient times, seems to have been the chief religion of these ages" (p. 315). Indeed, O'Grady adds that "belief in gods" by itself evidences, "a comparatively advanced stage of civilization and mental power" (p. 315). Presumably this religion had broken down when the plebians revolted against the Fianna.

In Parts XI and XII O'Grady further demonstrates the advanced state of the ancient Irish by reference to the Fianna. In Part XI, "Ossian and the Ossianic Cycle," he compares the joyful humanity of Ossian to the somber otherworldliness of Patrick and thereby suggests that Patrick's Christianity was no improvement.[20] In addition, he finds in the bardic tales "the precursors of the romantic literature of mediaeval Europe." There may be some truth to this assertion, but O'Grady matter-of-factly states:

> The heroic and knightly temper once common over the whole of the north of Europe, produced in Ireland its earliest and perhaps noblest expression. Afterwards blending with Christianity, it gave birth to the chivalrous literature of the Continent, and the real ideal knights of the fourteenth century (p. 356).

Part VII is entitled "Irish Military Predominance," and O'Grady points to the superior Irish military strength that complements the intellectual prowess which he believed to be an influence on Europe as late as the fourteenth century. In refutation of Gibbon, he states unequivocally "that Britannia was overrun and made tributary by the Irish" (p. 390). He conjectures that the Irish participated in battles in Gaul as the Romans' power in their provinces receded.

O'Grady's adulation for the great strength of the Irish in those centuries leads him to drop all pretense of a "critical and philosophical" attitude. The following paragraph is a virtual paean to those halcyon days:

> Such and so dimly seen [in the surviving historical

records] the shipborne warriors of Ireland row and sail
from Irish ports in the track of the Romans' retreating
steps, with behind and beyond that illuminated bard-
created world, a glorified background ever present to
the mind and spirit of these men, significant gestures
and looks of gods and heroes, voices monitory or inspiring, the mighty and the brave of yore, whose flesh
was now dust, urn-sheltered beneath many a massive
carn, many a wall-encircled rath, but whose memory
sent blood quicker through the veins, inflamed many
a mind, and gave strength and fire to many a heroic
appeal and indignant or approving word.   The body
of their past was dead, but its soul was alive and strong
(p. 396).

In Part XIII, the final section, O'Grady discusses the
question of his own credibility. Perhaps he was somewhat aware
that paragraphs like the preceding were not likely to satisfy the
requirements of "scientific" history.   Indeed, the reviewer in
Hibernia took O'Grady to task on precisely those grounds:

> . . . we would impress upon the author that if his suc-
> ceeding volumes are to become the standard work on
> Irish History, they must deal less with the imagination
> and more with facts; he must not forget his historical
> power in his fresh and original views and vividness of
> narration—eminent   characteristics   of   this   volume.[21]

O'Grady anticipated such criticisms in Part XIII and suggested that those who did not believe in the historicity of his
volume ought to find it "interesting, even from a severely critical
point of view, for, so considered, it will, at all events, be a
notable phenomenon and a portion at least of the history of the
Irish mind" (p. 463).

The *Critical and Philosophical History* is interesting and
probably even strictly historical in parts, but its greatest value
probably lies in the view it gives of a portion of the history of
O'Grady's mind.

Notes

[1] I have yet to find a single review of Vol. II.

[2] Cf. p. 25.

[3] *History of Ireland: Critical and Philosophical*, p. 50. Subsequent references in this chapter to this volume will appear as page numbers in parentheses in the text.

[4] Of necessity, I have discussed O'Grady's aesthetic theory as propounded in this volume previously, especially in Chapters I and IV. Carlyle also believed in the necessity of an historical basis for art; cf. pp. 69-70.

[5] Cf. p. 94.

[6] Cf. pp. 17-18.

[7] Cf. pp. 22-23.

[8] The Irish writers who followed O'Grady, especially W. B. Yeats, were fond of this idea.

[9] O'Grady appended the following note to this sentence: "See *passim* Macaulay, Carlyle, Froude" (p. 391n). O'Grady's allegiance to Carlyle was sorely tested on the subject of Ireland.

[10] Standish James O'Grady, *The Crisis in Ireland* (Dublin: E. Ponsonby; London: Simpkin & Marshall, 1882), pp. 39-40.

[11] *The Crisis in Ireland*, pp. 54-55.

[12] Compare Keating's treatment of cannibalism. Cf. pp. 54-55.

[13] His theory of art has been explained earlier in this chapter and in the Introduction and Chapter III.

[14] O'Grady used the non-Aryan Hebrews whenever it suited him.

[15] There are two Parts VIIIs and no Part X in this *History*.

[16] Cf. pp. 64-65.

[17] O'Grady makes several favorable allusions to Celestius the Pelagian, a fifth century Christian heretic. According to the *Dictionary of Sects, Heresies, Ecclesiastical Parites, and Schools of Religious Thought*, ed. John Henry Blunt (1874; rpt. Detroit: Gale Research Co., 1974), p. 103, Celestius was accused of teaching "various false doctrines, especially the four subjoined: [1] that Adam was created mortal, and that whether he sinned or not he would have died; [2] that the sin of Adam hurt himself only and not mankind; [3] that infants new born are in the same state that Adam was before his fall; [4] that a man may be without sin and keep the commandments easily if he will."

Celestius may have been an Irishman, and O'Grady believed that he had been. Most importantly, O'Grady liked the humanity of the doctrines of Celestius and found them to be the result of the amalgam of the old bardic tradition and the new Christian teaching: "The doctrines of Celestius are exactly those we would expect to find arise in Ireland where men could not ignore, in the face of the bardic literature, the inherent nobleness of humanity" (p. 35 n).

[18] To give O'Grady his due, he does discuss the sources of the story of the Atticottic Revolution and tries to contruct a plausible explanation for the story's existence.

[19] The Atticotti do succeed in overthrowing the king and ruling for a time.

[20] O'Grady's dislike for Christianity permeates this *History*. Consider the following passage:

> In the Christian ages, though we may be certain that actual ferocity decreased from what it had been, yet a sort of imaginative and intellectual love of the terrible and the cruel widely prevailed, which may be clearly seen in the lives of the saints. . . . In the genuine and indubitable bardic literature, issuing out of the pre-Christian ages, there is no parallel to this. Though there is much fierceness there is no cruelty (p. 405).

[21] Rev. of *History of Ireland: Critical and Philosophical,* by Standish James O'Grady, *Hibernia,* (2 Jan. 1882), 14.

Chapter VI

O'Grady's Later Versions of the Bardic Literature

O'Grady maintained his interest in early Irish literature throughout the rest of his life and published four novelistic renderings of the ancient tales and one masque. After the publication of *Cuculain: an Epic* in 1882, ten years elapsed before *Finn and His Companions* appeared in 1892. The first volume of his Cuculain trilogy, *The Coming of Cuculain*, was published two years later in 1894, but the second volume, *In the Gates of the North*, did not appear in book form until 1901. The third volume, *The Triumph and Passing of Cuculain*, took even longer. It was published by the Talbot Press in 1919 along with new editions of the first two volumes and a highly laudatory introduction by AE. *The Masque of Finn* was published in 1907, but it was written and performed several years earlier, probably between 1898 and 1901.[1]

The novelistic books were probably an attempt on O'Grady's part to secure that popularity for the early literature that his "bardic history" had failed to earn, but he also continued to use the early literature to promulgate his constantly evolving social and political views. In particular, he seems to have been anxious to attract a young audience since the novelistic renderings appeal more obviously to the imagination of boys than his "bardic history" does. In the 1890's O'Grady wrote several boys' stories, and the atmosphere of "boydom" in them also permeates the novelistic renderings of the bardic literature. However, he was more successful in selling his boys' stories,[2] and by 1919 when the trilogy was at last completely published in book form, there were better renditions in English of the bardic tales—notably Lady Gregory's *Cuculain of Muirthemne* and *Gods and Fighting Men*.

The novelistic books are interesting primarily for the changes in O'Grady's attitudes towards the bardic tales as the years passed. He became no less enthusiastic about the tales, but his renditions of them changed with his political and social concerns. Most notably, he became less interested in the military virtues of his heroes and more concerned with their service to their people. He found this latter ideal embodied in the Christian virtues, and his ancient heroes accordingly possess both Christian as well as the old, manly, heroic virtues. In short, his notion of the heroic expanded.

An O'Grady typescript written after 1900 reveals this synthesis of values more directly than any of the later renditions of the bardic literature does. In it, he discusses the continuing need for the heroic in the world and then interprets one of the beatitudes in the light of the love of the outdoors engendered by the old, heroic warrior values:

> So, Peace is eternally good: "Blessed are the peace-makers." But the peaceful must be men who are alive and well, not men who are corrupting. Therefore when a Nation cries "Pax! Pax! War is horrible," and goes indoors it is not long for this world.[3]

Although written much earlier than this typescript, *Finn and His Companions* expresses a similar reconciliation between the saintly and the heroic and also represents a considerable change in attitude toward the Fianna from that expressed in O'Grady's *Critical and Philosophical History*. The Fianna are given more positive traits than in the earlier book, and I suspect that O'Grady was trying to influence the modern Fenian movement, which was named, and supposedly patterned, after the ancient Fianna.

Finn and His Companions is divided into four parts, and each part tells a story that is unconnected to the other parts. Part I, significantly entitled "Saint and Hero," recounts the visit of the survivors of the last battle of the Fians to St. Patrick centuries after the battle. Caelta and his warriors had been enchanted by a prophetess and had stayed in her house for hundreds of years. They come to Patrick's house in search of Ossian, their lost leader, unaware that so much time has passed. Patrick is a very gracious host, and in this version he and Caelta learn to respect each other. O'Grady works the story out so that there is divine approbation for this reconciliation of the heroic and the saintly. Patrick is troubled by his enjoyment of the Pagans' company, so he asks the angels

> . . . whether it was displeasing to God that he should feel

so much delight in the profane conversation of the great Pagans. And the angels said that it was not, but pleasing, and that Finn, though a Gentile, was nevertheless a prophet without full knowledge, and had prepared the minds of the Gael for the preaching of Christ's gospel, and they also bade him write in a book such things as Caelta might tell him, for the instruction of future generations.[4]

Part II, "Finn and the Curmudgeon," resembles closely the story of Ayha Coelshanig and Laeg in Vol. I of the "bardic history."[5]   Here, Finn asks Nod (which means "stinginess") for hospitality after a day of hunting in the vicinity of Nod's house. Nod refuses, and Finn ties up Nod and hangs him from the ceiling of his house. After an appeal from Nod's beautiful wife, Finn relents and lets Nod down. Finn cures Nod of the disease of penuriousness, and Nod becomes a happy warrior.

Part III, "Finn and the Historian," tells of the visit of Finn to an aged historian's house. There is not much action in the story, but it allows for exposition of the characteristics of the Fians.

Part IV, "The Coming of Finn," would actually belong first in any chronological account of the exploits of Finn. O'Grady probably put it last here because it is the dramatic highpoint of the book. The story tells of Finn's coming to power among the Fianna. There had been a conflict between two branches of the Fianna: the Clan Morna under the leadership of Goll MacMorna had defeated the Clan Basna and killed its leader, Cool—Finn's father. The story opens with the remant of the Clan Basna sitting around a fire. It is the last day in which the prophecy of the coming of a saviour for the Clan Basna can be fulfilled. The faith of the men around the fire has been incredible, and their leader is very noble. Finn comes into their circle at the last possible moment for the fulfillment of the prophecy and carries with him the tokens of his revenge— including the head of his father's slayer. Afterwards he goes to Tara, defeats an enchanter who had been stealing the king's children, and receives pledges of fealty from the Clan Morna.

Throughout the book, O'Grady goes to great lengths to show the humane values of the Fians. Unlike the Fians in the *Critical and Philosophical History* whose "aristocratic temper . . . despises the people,"[6] Finn says: " '. . . I do not surround myself with guards and royal state, but live simply in the midst of my people, like one of themselves, for I love them well, and well they love me.' "[7]   The democratic idealism of Whitman here finds an embodiment in Finn, and O'Grady reveals a sensibility that is developing the confidence in the people necessary for his later adherence to "communism."

Furthermore, O'Grady makes Finn into a type of Christ. In addition to curing Nod, Finn cures the historian's son in a miraculous, Christ-like manner:

> Finn looked upon the lad and asked whether there was a well of pure water in the neighbourhood, and when they answered him "Yes," he bade them lead him to it.
>
> There he scooped up the sparkling water in the hollow of his right hand, and when he had spoken some poetry in a strange tongue, he gave to the young man to drink. From that day the youth steadily recovered.[8]

Thus, instead of Ossian's complaint to St. Patrick in Vol. I of the "bardic history"—" 'How then hast thou conquered, O son of Calpurn,' "[9] Part I of *Finn and His Companions* presents the saintly so that it no longer puts a dead stop to the heroic: now the former temper flows naturally from the more ancient temper.[10]

In order to make this flow possible, O'Grady had to mitigate somewhat his glorification of the military manifestations of the heroic temper. In the opening paragraph of Part IV, O'Grady states explicitly the lessons the life of Finn should teach. There is a biblical ring to some of his phrases:

> Now that you are sufficiently acquainted with Finn as he appeared in the fulness of his power and glory, I desire to let you see him in his youth, while he was struggling upwards out of obscurity, when he was friendless, solitary, and surrounded by enemies. The lesson taught by Finn in his power is the lesson of flowing goodwill towards men. From his youth we learn the lesson of cheerfulness and courage.[11]

That Finn's "power" should be manifested in "flowing goodwill towards men' represents a considerable change from the manifestation of Cuculain's power in his battle-feats described in the "*Ἀριστεία Conculain*" chapter of Vol. II of the "bardic history."[12]   And indeed O'Grady seems to have backed off from the notion of the proper subject matter for the bard that was affirmed in that volume. There in the discussion of aesthetics among Maeve, Fleeas, and others, O'Grady gave the last word to Mainey Ahrimail, who proclaimed the superior beauty of the battlefield.[13]   Here, Finn's instructions to the historian strike quite a different chord. The historian

> ". . . should not, in making his histories, concern him-
> self exclusively with wars and things horrible, but should
> tell also of the common daily life of men and women;
> let women and children . . . be frequent in your stories,
> for they are the light of life, nor let the sun be long
> absent from your tale, seeing that he himself is never
> long absent from us."[14]

Perhaps O'Grady felt that he had provided models for emulation in the "bardic history" that were too warlike, so now he wished to give a less martial character to the leader the modern Fenians wished to emulate. Such an attitude would fit well with the abhorrence of violent revolutionary upheaval that he expressed in his later life even when he advocated drastic social change. He believed that violence, as a practical matter, would do the most harm to those who supported his "communist" program.

Yet it is very difficult to explain these changes in O'Grady's attitudes without recalling the contradictions in his character from the very beginning of his life. Lady Gregory called O'Grady a " 'Fenian Unionist,' "[15] and the label describes well the careful balancing act O'Grady performed between his allegiance to the traditional Protestant cause of Unionism and his strong sense of Irish nationalism.

At any rate, if O'Grady wished to keep the modern Fenians less militant and therefore, within the Union, he was also careful to provide them with a cause of grievance against the British— even as far back as the time of Finn. In Part II O'Grady "tacks on" a story to the cure of Nod which must have been his own invention in great part.[16]   The fabled King Arthur of "Briton-land" steals three of Finn's dogs while on a hunt in Ireland at Finn's invitation. Nine of Finn's warriors go to Briton and re-take the dogs by force. They slay all of Arthur's men and take

him captive back to Ireland. He and Finn, however, are reconciled—an important fact as O'Grady's authorial intrusion,
which prefaces the story, points out:

> The following story will not be pleasing to those who
> think that the famous King Arthur could do nothing
> wrong. It is pleasant, however, to find that two such
> illustrious men as Finn and Arthur, though they had their
> quarrel, finally became good friends.[17]

To O'Grady's mind the note of reconciliation was probably
an important curb to any model of retribution he was setting
up, but it is almost comically childish in expression and, therefore, not likely to have made a more profound impression than
the fact of Arthur's thievery. This is the Arthur who was so
celebrated earlier in the century in Tennyson's *Idylls of the
King* as a model of perfect kingship. Arthur and, by extension,
British rule are hardly so perfect when O'Grady is finished with
them.

The story is not repeated in *The Masque of Finn*, but Parts
I and II of that play closely resemble Parts IV and II respectively
of *Finn and His Companions*. Only Part III, "The Transformation of Finn," is new. O'Grady wrote only one other play,
Hugh Roe O'Donnell, besides this one, and his attitude towards
the drama was at best ambiguous.[18] Both plays were performed
outdoors initially, and O'Grady seems to have felt that the open-
air was the appropriate place for drama, as well as all life-giving
human activity.[19] He seems to have fully developed this attitude
towards the open air after 1900, and it informed his politics as
well as his attitude towards the drama. The strong distaste he
held for the city's confined spaces extended also to is theaters
and its audiences, for whom, he believed, culture was dead.[20]

In his "Prefatory Note" to *The Masque of Finn*, he finds
precedence in his sources for his liking for the open-air:

> I am not sure what is the exact definition of a Masque,
> but it meant a play having supernatural elements and of
> a generally open air character. Like many others, I never
> hear the word without thinking of Milton's *Comus*. Finn
> and his Fians are certainly very open-air personages: we
> seldom hear of them except in connection with field and
> forest, lake and hillside, with the cry of the hounds and

the sound of the horn heard or just waiting to be heard.[21]

The Masque of Finn does bear some slight resemblance to Comus in that O'Grady does present the supernatural forces so that their appearance has a rational, common-sense explanation as it so often does in his "bardic history." Just as the lady encounters the evil spirit Comus in Milton's masque, actual encounters with spirits are responsible for Nod's enchantment in Part II and Finn's transformation in Part III. O'Grady seems to have lost his repugnance to the magical: at the least he accepts it metaphorically and indeed may have found it useful as a dramatic "short-cut."[22]

As in Finn and His Companions, the masque emphasizes the humanity, not the martial ardour, of the Fians. The old men in Part I who await the arrival of the promised one are represented as exceedingly fair and generous to each other despite their poverty. In Part II, Nod goes through the enchantment of penury in order to learn the lesson of generosity and good-will to all—a necessary lesson for all those who are to live in a grand democratic and communal society. Part III presents Finn going through an experience similar to Nod's, and thus, O'Grady suggests that leaders must be prepared, to use an American expression, to mingle with the "great unwashed." Finn experiences 2,000 years of life in a moment and returns to earth a very old man having "trodden all the depths / Where the sons of Man defeated / Wander broken and oppressed."[23] Nod, alone of Finn's companions, recognizes him because Nod has undergone a similar transformation. The Fairy restores Finn's youth, but Finn keeps his silver hair as a reminder of his bath in the "Ocean of Humanity." The Fairy tells Finn the purpose of his experience:

> It is thine to hunt the red deer,
> 　　Thine to lead victorious hosts,
> 　Thine to scatter joy around thee
> 　　　Life and light and pride and hope.
>
> Be it thine, henceforth, my hero,
> 　　To uphold the weak and frail,
> 　To be kind and just and gentle
> 　　　To the lowliest of the Gael.[24]

In so transforming Finn, O'Grady seems to have achieved a balance between his attitude toward the Fians in the *Critical and Philosophical History* and his attitude towards them in *Finn and His Companions.* The latter book simply presents Finn as full of "glowing goodwill towards men," while the former speaks of the Fians' "private irresponsible wealth."[25] The Fairy teaches Finn the former attitude, but his faults prior to the transformation are hardly as bad as those attributed to him in the *Critical and Philosophical History.* He seems only to be fun-loving and careless of responsibility to the common people—sins of omission rather than commission.

O'Grady's Cuculain trilogy also gives evidence of similar attitude changes on O'Grady's part. The first volume, *The Coming of Cuculain,* tells the story of Cuculain's life up to the time of his "knighting." The description of the events is considerably expanded from that in Vol. I of the "bardic history," and O'Grady changes Cuculain's character considerably. For example, Concobar predicts that Cuculain the man, like O'Grady's later Finn, will have " 'more of love in his heart than war.' "[26]

In addition to O'Grady's new-found distaste for violence, the change in Cuculain's character may relate to the book's intended audience. He seems to have aimed this volume at boys, and indeed the boyhood of Cuculain is a logical choice for a boys' story.[27] He may have desired to provide a less war-like story for them and so diminished Cuculain's keenness for battle. (Cuculain still likes to fight, however). Yet it is hard to know what audience O'Grady had in mind. There is an atmosphere of boyish charm that runs throughout the book, but on the other hand Concobar, Fergus, and company feast and make merry with the corpses of their enemies suspended from the ceiling above them. The description hardly seems to be intended for the enjoyment, or even the edification, of boys:

> Aloft, suspended from the dim rafters, hung the naked forms of great men clear against the dark dome, having the cords of their slaughter around their necks and their white limbs splashed with blood.[28]

This passage seems out of place in a story that describes the friendship struck up by Concobar and Cuculain shortly after Cuculain's arrival at Emain Macha as "like that of a great boy and a small boy when such, as often happens, become attached to one another."[29]   Such descriptions are complemented by the plot of the story which O'Grady simplified considerably from Vol. I of the "bardic history." The events are clear-cut and un-complicated as might be expected in a boys' story although the absence of complication is less satisfying to the mature reader.

Whatever his reasons, O'Grady reduced the conflict be-tween Concobar and Fergus to a simple matter of right and wrong. Concobar does not usurp Fergus's throne; instead he assumes it reluctantly:

> ". . . I, newly come to this throne, having been but as it were yesterday your comrade and equal, till Fergus, to my grief, resigned the sovereignty, and caused me, a boy, to be made king of Ulla. . ."[30]

The narrator makes clear that the change in kings is for the good:

> . . . for in royal wisdom the king [Concobar] far excelled his foster-father [Fergus], and that was the reason why Fergus had abdicated the supreme captainship of the Red Branch in favour of Concobar, for though his heart was great his understanding was not fine and acute like the understanding of his foster-son.[31]

Concobar is the right man for the kingship, and he always upholds the right in this book. O'Grady tells the Deirdre story so as to cast blame on Fergus and on the sons of Usna. In this version Concobar makes no guarantees to Fergus that he will not harm the sons of Usna on their return to the North. Fergus alone makes the decision to have them return, and Concobar kills them on their return. In doing so, Concobar upholds the law. Fergus's defiance is based on logic that has unchaste implications:

> "All laws in restraint of true love and affection are un-just . . . and the law by which Deirdre was consigned to virginity was the unrighteous enactment of cold-hearted and unrighteous men."[32]

Fergus's revolt, therefore, becomes the willful act of an individual in defiance of the law. Concobar is presented as the supreme upholder of the rule of law,[33] and there is no doubt but that Fergus is wrong. O'Grady even increases Concobar's rectitude by making the sons of Usna more violent in their abduction of Deirdre and, therefore, more culpable.

With the moral choice between Concobar and Fergus so clear-cut, O'Grady has no need to have Cuculain react to the Deirdre story. Instead, the story of the naked women on the bridge is restored to Cuculain's initiation rite.[34] This time also O'Grady restores the number of women to thirty as it was in the original. O'Grady's description of the incident is subdued and emphasizes that the women's act saves the community. In O'Daly's rendition the communal spirit of the women is not so much in the forefront, and their act is more unabashed. Here the women are careful to minimize the display:

> They bade all the men retire into the dun after they had lowered the bridge; and when that was done three tens of them, such as were the most illustrious in the rank and famous for accomplishments, and they all in the prime of their youth and beauty, and clad only in the pure raiment of their womanhood, came forth out of the quarters of the women, and in that order, in spite of shame they went to meet him. When Cuculain saw them advancing towards him in lowly wise, with exposed bosoms and hands crossed on their breast, his weapons fell from his hands and the war-demons fled out of him. . .[35]

This last line is also indicative of a change in an O'Grady attitude: he is much more accepting of spirits such as war-demons in all of the novelistic renderings of the ancient tales. He seems to have reached a point where he no longer needed to have a common-sense explanation for phenomena like the Enchantment. A note explains it simply as a curse:

> At Tailteen a man boasted that his wife could outrun Concobar's victorious chariot-steeds. Concobar compelled the woman to run against his horses. She won the race, but died at the goal leaving her curse upon the Red Branch.[36]

Examples of O'Grady's new attitude towards divine intervention abound. Though Cuculain is guided by Lu Lam-fada in the "bardic history," the sense of the divine acting through the hero is more keenly felt here. Cuculain is also more obviously a type of Christ: he is "the child who had been promised to the Ultonians."[37]   On his initial approach to Emain Macha "it came to him that he was urged forwards, by whom he knew not."[38]

O'Grady himself provides the explanation for this difference: these books are written without the concern for historicity that dominates the *Histories*.   In his "Preface," he writes:

> I will therefore ask the reader, remembering the large manner of the antique literature from which our tale is drawn, to forget for a while that there is such a thing as scientific history, to give his imagination a holiday, and follow with kindly interest the singular story of the boyhood of Cuculain. . .[39]

Apparently, O'Grady no longer believed it necessary always to find a "scientific" explanation for the events in the tales. They could have value simply as tales—a shift in attitude that reflects some turning away from the "curb of history."[40] Indeed, it was during the 1890's that O'Grady first wrote stories strictly of his own invention. The fact that he did so then suggests a change in his attitude toward the imagination. However, he hardly wandered far from his allegiance to history. It is significant that O'Grady was concerned enough about "scientific history" to make the above explanation in *The Coming of Cuculain*.   It demonstrates that he was aware that he was departing from the "curb of history."

Yet, the average reader would hardly be so concerned about historicity. The characterization of Cuculain fits well with an increased sense of divine intervention. He is drawn on a much less grand scale than in the "bardic history," and therefore his incredible deeds are appropriately accomplished only with divine assistance. We know Cuculain more intimately and thus his heroic stature is lessened. We see his boredom at his life with his mother and father. He cries when no one welcomes him to Emain Macha. He discusses his attack on the Southern enemies at length with Laeg before he undertakes it. Cuculain is a character whom we feel with and whose mind we see into. We come to know him in much the same way that we usually come to know characters in a novel.[41]

The next volume in the trilogy, *In the Gates of the North,* is written more in the manner of the "bardic history" than either of the other two volumes. This volume relates the events from the time of the "rising-out" of the four provinces to the events immediately subsequent to the duel between Cuculain and Fardia. It repeats much of the second half of Vol. I of the "bardic history" *verbatim.* Unlike *The Coming of Cuculain,* the narration in this volume allows us to see into Cuculain's head very little; for the most part we see only his actions.

The similarity of *In the Gates of the North* to the "bardic history" creates a problem in interpreting the character of Fergus. In this book, Fergus is bitter about the loss of the High Kingship of Ulla as he was in the "bardic history." He claims that he was driven from the throne; he did not abdicate as he says he did in *The Coming of Cuculain.* He does not directly blame Concobar, however:

> ". . . I was once Captain of the Red Branch and high King of all the Ultonians till the rhymers and historians and cunning lawyers drove me from my high seat, for I could not endure their stale and bygone wisdom, nor understand it. . ."[42]

Wrath against these people hardly lends credit to Fergus, and O'Grady probably wants us to think badly of him. But the issue is not clear-cut as it is in *The Coming of Cuculain.* Since Fergus claims to have been driven from his throne here, is he lying, as a reading of the first volume of the trilogy would suggest? Or has O'Grady struck a middle-ground between Fergus's righteous grievance against Concobar in the "bardic history" and Fergus's absolute wrong-doing in *The Coming of Cuculain?*

It is impossible to know how O'Grady meant *In the Gates of the North* to be read in relation to the other books, but the fact that it takes up the story of Cuculain at the point where *The Coming of Cuculain* leaves off should suggest some continuity. Yet *In the Gates of the North* is quite different from its predecessor. It does not at all seem to have been aimed at a young audience. In fact, O'Grady warns his readers in his introduction that "they must be prepared, in the beginning, to read it like a task, and pursue it, at least through some initial chapters, as if it were a severe mental exercise. . ."[43] O'Grady's estimate of his work is quite accurate: the first few chapters of his work make for slow reading. Boys would not be likely to read them with joy.

Despite these confusions, however, O'Grady did make some changes which should have tightened the structure of the Cuculain story. He connects Maeve with the Fomorians, and Caelshanig, the penurious freedman, with the Clan Cailitin.

Though he aligns Maeve with the Fomorians, the significance of his alliance is unfortunately lost on readers who are not acquainted with O'Grady's *Critical and Philosophical History*. In that *History* O'Grady explains the Fomorians as the counter-force to the ruling gods. The Fomorians are a constant threat to the legitimate authority. At times they do rule, but then they do so "by force, not by acknowledged right."[44] When in the present volume Maeve goes to visit a druid before her forces invade the North, she visits "not one of the known and honoured druids of the province, but one who held commerce with forgotten posers and dread unworshipped sovereignties of old, Fomorian principalities shorn of all glory and might by the younger gods of the Gael."[45]

This Fomorain druid encourages Maeve to attack the North because the enchantment has descended on its warriors. In the "bardic history" Maeve received a propitious, though qualified, prophecy from Faythleen,[46] but now O'Grady casts Faithleen in the role of a good druidess who accurately predicts destruction for the four provinces. After the Fomorian druid has encouraged Maeve to attack, Faithleen says that Maeve's forces will be "bloodied all and crimson,"[47] while in the "bardic history" she used the same words to describe the future state of the Ultonians.[48]

Maeve rejects Faithleen's prophecy in the later book and, in doing so, aligns herself with the perennial forces of revolution. O'Grady has now made the present even more "the *same* fact"[49] as the past, for as Lu Lam-fada, Cuculain's tutelary deity, defeated the Fomorians,[50] so too, Cuculain defeats the Fomorians of his time—Maeve and her men.[51]

O'Grady's connection of Caelshanig to the Clan Cailitin creates a similar unity in the story of Cuculain. Whereas in the "bardic history," the story of Ayha Coelshanig seems to be tangential to the main action, O'Grady here has Laeg recognize Caelshanig[52] as "a northern kinsman . . . of Cailitin, the mighty mage and enchanter of the East."[53] In so connecting Caelshanig to Cailitin, O'Grady should have been able to increase the reader's sense that the enchantment of the North is more than a mystical spell. Mammon, as well as magic, has the capacity to enchant.   Unfortunately, however, O'Grady makes the connection only once, and then he makes it before the full significance of Cailitin is known.

The last volume of the trilogy is similarly marred by O'Grady's failure to knit all his plot elements together. *The Triumph and Passing of Cuculain* presents the same story of Cuculain as Vol. II of the "bardic history" only in greatly reduced length.   In cutting the story, O'Grady seems to have forgotten to account for Fergus's withdrawal from his duel with Concobar.[54]   Since Fergus is pressing Concobar hard at the moment of Cuculain's entrance onto the battlefield, the reader can only surmise that Cuculain has some effect on the duel.

It is difficult to believe that O'Grady deliberately left out the explanation of Fergus's withdrawal, but there can be no mistake that he intended Dublin to be the home of Danes eight centuries before the actual Danish invasions.   When Cuculain and Laeg wander through Athaclia (or Dublin) in the days surrounding the departure of the Northern warriors for the invasion of Scotland, they are affronted by a pub keeper's exacting of payment for food.   After Laeg breaks the man's hand and Cuculain heals it, the man prays to the Danish god, " 'Thor, the Thunderer, to protect' " him " 'against ever again' " meeting Cuculain or his like.[55]   O'Grady was exercising considerable license in so importing the Danes into the Dublin of Cuculain's time, and it is a mark of his lack of interest in historicity that he does so. The point he makes in so connecting the Danes to mercenary interests is a bit peculiar, but he probably felt that such interests were not native Irish traits.[56]

This volume is peculiar also for two other odd vignettes. One is more anti-female than O'Grady ever has been previously. The other presents Cuculain in less than absolute approval of the bards.

The first vignette occurs while Cuculain and Laeg are on their way home from Athaclia.   Laeg speaks of a beautiful stream that he has known since childhood.   He tells of one particular occasion when the stream was very inhospitable:

"Long since in the boyish days I sought to gather a

sheaf of those very bulrushes. They were in flower at
the time and very beautiful. Soon I found myself in
what was neither water nor land but a mingling of both,
so that I could not swim nor find a footing on which to
stand, and thence hardly did I escape with my life."[57]

Cuculain surmises the motivation for Laeg's quest, and he
reveals a mind deeply suspicious of the value of going on a
quest for a woman. That the quest in this case is so minor reveals O'Grady in a very mean-spirited moment: if Laeg once
was caught in quicksand, Cuculain is only right to surmise that
he went there at a woman's behest:

"It is in my mind, Laeg," said Cuculain, smiling, "that
it was for some woman thou didst go upon that quest."

"Thou art in the right," said Laeg. "It was for Acaill
. . . She desired them [the bulrushes] as an ornament for
her greenan [woman's quarter].[58]

The second vignette is not so remarkable as the first. It
represents only a slight change in O'Grady's previous attitudes
toward the bards. As Cuculain heads south for his final con-
frontation with Maeve's forces and the Clan Cailitin, there are
no signs of life ahead of Laeg and him. But behind him there
is evidence of life everywhere. The people go about their chores
confidently because they believe Cuculain will protect them. Of
this exhibition of confidence, Cuculain remarks:

"Truly, O Laeg, we are well praised in these sights and
sounds [of the people]. Many a time, as thou knowest,
have I been the recipient of laudatory poems such as the
bards make with ease, yet have I heard them with a
mingling of pain and shame, but this praise which is in
act and deed toucheth me nearly."[59]

Cuculain's attitude here fulfills the Carlylian *dictum* that
"Deeds are greater than Words,"[60] but O'Grady has changed
his usual method of fulfilling that *dictum*. In the "bardic his-
tory" Cuculain is a man of few words: his deeds do his talking.
Here we see right into Cuculain's mind and listen to his words.
Cuculain's words do serve to lessen the value of the bards,

whose work O'Grady never previously allowed a completely good character to diminish in importance. It is remarkable that in his last published work O'Grady should allow Cuculain to speak this way.

The work is noteworthy also for several other differences between it and Vol. II of the "bardic history." As in *The Coming of Cuculain*, O'Grady's changes simplify the plot. Here, Maeve and Queen Fleeas conflict more directly with each other, and Fleeas is no model of queenship. Perhaps O'Grady decided to make Fleeas more similar to Fergus, whose virtue is also considerably less than it was in the "bardic history." Taking away Fleeas' goodness allows for a more clear-cut battle between good and evil since the four provinces now have less good to stand on.

O'Grady replaced the long discussions between Fleeas and Maeve, which revealed the latter's unfitness for rule, with a simple action. Maeve's troops sense her unfitness and disobey her orders. They follow Fergus instead, and their action says it all.

Having cut the long discussions which reveal Maeve's character, O'Grady focuses *The Triumph and Passing of Cuculain* on Cuculain to an even greater extent than Vol. II of the "bardic history." Though much of that latter work is simply repeated, O'Grady increased the extent to which Cuculain is a type of Christ—a change which may reflect his increased respect for the Hero-Saint. For example, on the occasion on which Laeg breaks the "Danish" pub keeper's hand, Cuculain's healing of the hand recalls Christ's healing of the soldier's ear which had been cut off by Peter when the soldiers came to take Christ away from the Garden of Gethsemane.[61] Immediately following this incident a young poet accosts Cuculain and recites a poem to him. Cuculain invites the poet to be his "honoured guest" at his home in Dun Dalgan and to " 'preside over my poetic school there.' "[62] The young poet immediately drops everything and joins Cuculain's "retinue" in an action strongly reminiscent of the response of the apostles to Christ's summons, "Follow me."[63] Finally, the actual death scene repeats the Christ-like resemblances of the "bardic history" and even heightens them. As Cuculain receives his fatal wound, "the sun darkened, and the earth trembled. . ."—celestial actions which resemble those that are reported to have occurred when Christ died.[64]

In so depicting Cuculain, O'Grady effects a reconciliation

between the heroic and the saintly, the Pagan and the Christian, much as he did in *Finn and His Companions.* The Christ typology in Vol. II of the "bardic history" serves to place Cuculain simply in the role of redeemer. The later additions to this typology, in the cases of both Finn and Cuculain, serve to make those characters more Christ-like in their personal attitudes—in their "flowing goodwill towards men." Thus, O'Grady tempered his previous antagonism to Christianity, broadened his notion of the heroic, and found in Cuculain intimations of the Christ-like qualities that were to produce the "Hero-Saints," whom he regarded as "for ever and for us all a grand exemplar and realized ideal."[65]

Ironically, in so rendering the bardic literature, O'Grady was following in the traces of monkish redactors, who had often tried to "Christianize" the literature and had thus reduced its "historicity." But even their work could be made to serve O'Grady's purpose of reconciling all elements of the Irish puzzle.

Notes

[1] In his introduction to the play, O'Grady says it was written and performed in Kilkenny. He was the editor of the *Kilkenny Moderator* from 1898 to 1900, and his *All Ireland Review* began publication there in 1900. A crippling libel suit forced O'Grady to return to Dublin probably sometime in 1901.

[2] Vivian Mercier writes: "During the 1890's O'Grady wrote several books quite frankly for boys. Two of these, *Lost on Du-Corrig* and *The Chain of Gold,* were the only works which ever earned him significant amounts of money." "Standish James O'Grady," *Colby Library Quarterly,* 4 (1958), 288.

[3] Standish James O'Grady, "Chap. 3; Air & Light & the Heroic: To Young Ireland," TS, with corrections in O'Grady's hand, p. 46, The Standish De Courcey O'Grady Collection.

[4] Standish James O'Grady, *Finn and His Companions* (Dublin: Talbot; London: T. Fisher Unwin, 1921), p. 24.

[5] Cf. pp. 86-87.

[6]Cf. pp. 120-121.

[7]*Finn and His Companions*, p. 97.

[8]*Finn and His Companions*, pp. 98-99.

[9]Cf. p. 72.

[10]Cf. pp. 113-114.

[11]*Finn and His Companions*, p. 103.

[12]Cf. pp. 107-108.

[13]Cf. p. 101.

[14]*Finn and His Companions*, p. 98.

[15]Ernest A. Boyd attributes this remark to Lady Gregory in his "Introduction" to Standish James O'Grady, *Selected Essays and Passages* (New York: Frederick A. Stokes, 1918), p. 17

[16]There is some basis for the kind of actions that occur in the story of Finn and Arthur, but I can find no mention of Arthur in connection with Finn anywhere. Two stories in John Gregorson Campbell's book, *The Fians* (1891; rpt. New York: AMS Press, 1973) have some slight similarity to O'Grady's story. In one, "How Fin Went to the Kingdom of the Big Men" (pp. 176-184), Fin has trouble with invaders from the overseas Kingdom of the Big Men. He goes to their country and succeeds in alleviating the oppression. His dog, Bran, figures prominently in his success. In the other story, "How Fionn Found Bran" (pp. 204-207), Fionn performs a service for a foreign king and procures Bran as the result of his exploits.

The resemblance between these stories and O'Grady's story is only slight, but perhaps O'Grady envisaged the Kingdom of the Big Men as Britain. His imagination might have filled in the rest of the story.

[17]*Finn and His Companions*, p. 72.

[18]In 1900, O'Grady, delivered the following blast against the Irish theater:

> . . . I am constitutionally averse to seeing things or people that I love subjected to public exposure in any form. Now Finn is one of my heroes. . . Then I go to "the Gaiety," and I find Finn personated by a burly person with a wooden manner and a hoarse voice; but even if the hero was very well personated by a first-class actor, I don't think I should like it. . . . In fact I feel towards the whole Irish literary movement, except the Language movement, something of the same feeling, though, of course, on a very different plane, that I feel to the tourist movement. I don't like the introduction of the general public into the places where Solitude and Beauty now reign, or the exposure of our hitherto withdrawn and veiled heroic and romantic cycles to the idle and careless eyes of the habitues of theatres. . . . I read with great

> pleasure Miss Mulligan's drama about the fairy maid from Tir-
> nanogue, but cannot help perceiving too that its effect upon the
> general public when acted was the result of stage scenery. I
> thought the Irish dramatic movement would abolish stage scenery,
> and trust unreservedly to the mighty and all-compelling power
> of Sound and not at all to light and colour, and here my loquacity
> must end and my dumbness prevail.

"Current Events," *All Ireland Review,* 1 (24 Feb. 1900), p. 5. AE responded to O'Grady's attacks on the dramatic movement in "The Dramatic
Treatment of Heroic Literature," *Samhain* (Oct. 1902), 11-13.

[19] In an essay suitably entitled "Sun and Wind," O'Grady raged against
"the great industrial English giant" which sent men indoors to work in un-
healthy environments. His essay expresses his strong belief in the Sun as the
source of life:

> Here, out of Ireland, in the light of the great ascending Sun, I
> declare that the civilization which drives men to do such things
> [as work indoors], and, which blinds them as to their horror,
> is impious, unnatural and accurst; I say that this civilization is
> going to perish: surely. I say that Nature meant Man to live in
> the Light, that he ought to live in the Light, and that he knows
> that he ought. He knows that when the Sun rises and he himself
> leaves his couch, refreshed with slumber and when he crosses
> the threshold of his home, Nature never meant him to go indoors
> again into an office or a shop or a factory, or down into a mine,
> and spend the bright day there.

"Sun and Wind; Chapter I: An Irish Sunrise," TS, with corrections in
O'Grady's hand, p. 5, The Standish De Courcey O'Grady Collection.

[20] In his "Prefatory Note" to *The Masque of Finn,* O'Grady praised
the simple and direct reaction of his rural audience to the initial performance of his play:

> A girl sitting near me cried out in intense excitement: "O Glory,
> but sure they're coming down to kill him." It is a pleasant char-
> acteristic of our Irish rural audiences that they always come to
> enjoy an entertainment and never to criticize.

Standish James O'Grady, *The Masque of Finn,* in *Finn and His Companions*
(Dublin: Talbot; London: T. Fisher Unwin, 1921), p. 6 [separate pagination
from *Finn and His Companions*].

[21] *The Masque of Finn*, p. 5.

[22] O'Grady's acceptance of the magical may also reflect a growing acceptance of spirits and demons as psychological realities. *The Chain of Gold*, published in 1895, suggests O'Grady was interested in psychology. Cf. pp. 164-169.

[23] *The Masque of Finn*, p. 82.

[24] *The Masque of Finn*, p. 82.

[25] Cf. pp. 135-136 and p. 121.

[26] Standish James O'Grady, *The Coming of Cuculain* (New York: Frederick A. Stokes, [n.d.]), p. 103.

[27] O'Grady's first boys' story, *Lost on Du-Corrig*, was published in the same year as *The Coming of Cuculain*—1894.

[28] *The Coming of Cuculain*, pp. 3-4.

[29] *The Coming of Cuculain*, p. 13.

[30] *The Coming of Cuculain*, p. 13.

Several years after the publication of *The Coming of Cuculain*, O'Grady offered an explanation for his changed attitude towards Concobar.

> The same objection lately urged by me against the play which Mr. Yeats and Mr. Moore made out of the degenerate pseudo-Ossianic story of "Diarmid and Graine" applies, too, to the assumption that the true and actual Concobar of heroic history is presented to us in the tale of "The Children of Uisnech." It is the one tale out of the whole mass of Red Branch literature in which his character is vilified. Elsewhere he is always the hero-king; of divine origin; a god, or the incarnation of a god. . . .
>
> Now, the story of "The Children of Uisnech" does not properly belong to the cycle at all. It is an invention of the decadence and of plebeian and late origin. . . . It is late traditional, derived from beaten, subject, and ignoble races.

All Ireland Review, 2 (30 Nov. 1901), p. 311, col. 2. O'Grady seems to have forgotten that he told of Concobar's perfidy in his "bardic history."

[31] *The Coming of Cuculain*, p. 12.

[32] *The Coming of Cuculain*, p. 70.

Some might find this emphasis on chastity Victorian in origin, and indeed O'Grady's comment on *The Coming of Cuculain* in the *All Ireland Review* suggests that he was aware of his own nineteenth century prejudices:

> "The Coming of Cuculain" is not a translation and yet is not original. The first five centuries of Irish History are in it, and also the nineteenth century, and I can say no more.

"Dear E.B.," *All Ireland Review*, 1 (29 Dec. 1900), p. 6, col. 2.

[33]Concobar connects chastity with the heroic code, which is what he is upholding when he upholds the law: " 'Without chastity there is no enduring valour in a nation.' " *The Coming of Cuculain*, p. 94.

[34]Cf. pp. 79-81.

[35] *The Coming of Cuculain*, p. 167.

[36] *The Coming of Cuculain*, p. 104n. O'Grady leaves out the pertinent fact that the woman was pregnant, and so the men of the North undergo a debility similar to that experienced by a pregnant woman. Kinsella uses the word "pangs" where O'Grady uses "enchantment," and Kinsella's word is more suggestive of the origin of the problem.

[37] *The Coming of Cuculain*, p. 15.

[38] *The Coming of Cuculain*, p. 31.

[39] *The Coming of Cuculain*, pp. v-vi.

[40]Cf. p. 116.

[41]The Cuculain we come to know, however, is almost trite: he is a good, affecting, little boy who only wants to love and be loved.

[42]Standish James O'Grady, *In the Gates of the North* (Kilkenny: Standish O'Grady, 1901), p. 19.

[43] *In the Gates of the North*, p. 11.

[44] *History of Ireland: Critical and Philosophical*, p. 85.

[45] *In the Gates of the North*, p. 23.

[46]Cf. p. 83. Note that O'Grady change the spelling of the prophetess Faythleen's name to the druidess Faithleen.

[47] *In the Gates of the North*, p. 28.

[48] *History of Ireland: the Heroic Period*, p. 137.

[49]Cf. p. 69.

[50]Cf. p. 124.

[51]This action takes place in *The Triumph and Passing of Cuculain*, so this explanation is predicated on the assumption that O'Grady intended the connection of Maeve with the Fomorians to achieve its full meaning in the third volume of the trilogy. This is debatable as is the succeeding assertion about Caelshanig and the Clan Cailitin, but these changes from the "bardic history" only reach therir full resonance in the succeeding volume.

[52]O'Grady dropped the first name and changed the spelling of the freedman's name in the later book.

[53] *In the Gates of the North*, p. 117.

[54]Cf. p. 107.

[55]Standish James O'Grady, *The Triumph and Passing of Cuculain* (Dublin: Talbot, 1919), p. 96.

[56]Cf. p. 50.

[57] *The Triumph and Passing of Cuculain*, p. 103.

[58] *The Triumph and Passing of Cuculain*, pp. 103-104.

[59] *The Triumph and Passing of Cuculain*, p. 145.

[60] Cf. p. 66.

[61] Cf. Luke 22:50-51 for the story of the cutting off and healing of the ear. John 18:10 identifies Peter as the man who cut off the ear.

[62] *The Triumph and Passing of Cuculain*, p. 98.

[63] Matthew 4:18-22; 9:9.

[64] Cf. Luke 23:44-45; Matthew 27:45, 51-52.

[65] Cf. p. 114.

Chapter VII

O'Grady's Other Works and His Influence

While O'Grady's renditions of the bardic literature reflect the flux of his political attitudes, his newspaper writing
and political tracts provide a direct, albeit similarly confusing,
record of his evolving views over a period of about 40 years.
Though his first political tract did not appear until 1882,
O'Grady had been a leading article writer for the conservative
Dublin newspaper, the *Daily Express,* since 1873. He kept
this job until 1898 and presumably was a strong voice for
responsible Unionism if his other political writings are any
clue[1] to the kind of leading articles he is likely to have written
in the *Daily Express.* Those political writings, as well as two
other interests that seized him in the 1890's and that reflect
his political thinking in those years—Elizabethan Ireland and
the writing of boys' stories—are worthy of notice because they
may indeed represent O'Grady's best writing despite the fact
that he is known primarily for his renditions of the bardic
literature. They also reveal O'Grady engaged in his most characteristic activity—seeking to influence other people's actions
and the course of events.

Since O'Grady began as both a leading article writer for
a conservative newspaper and Honorary Secretary of a landlords' meeting and then became a communist and advocate of
A. R. Orage's "Guild Socialism," it may seem on the surface at
least this movement represents a drastic change in his attitude
over the years. While there is a significant difference between
speaking for the rights of private property and asserting that all
property should be held communally, the difference is not so
great as might be imagined. O'Grady was always looking to
reestablish feudalism as he imagined it had existed in primitive
times and to some extent during the Middle Ages. While his
idea of feudalism did evolve somewhat, he simply changed his
mind about how to implement it. It took him some time to
realize that the classes with power could not be persuaded to
return to feudal ways.

He came to believe that the ruling classes were unshakable because their power was vested in private property.   He formulated this opinion under the influence of writers who advocated the more democratic idea of communal ownership. After 1900 especially, he was influenced by Charles Fourier, the French utopian writer, who argued that civilization had produced an unnatural accumulation of wealth among the rich and had forced the mass of people to undertake enslaving work. O'Grady found similar arguments in Prince Kropotkin's *Fields, Factories and Workshops,* Henry George's *Progress and Poverty,* and Sir Henry Maine's *Lectures on the Early History of Institutions.*   All of these argued that "progress" and historical change had conspired to place the rich and the poor in an unnatural adversarial relationship.   They confirmed O'Grady in the dislike of civilization that can be found even in his earliest writings—a dislike that is expressed in terms similar to Fourier's right from the start although I can find no evidence that he had read Fourier before 1902.

O'Grady regarded the commercialization of land and thus of the relationship of the serf to the lord as the great enslaver that had brought about so-called "civilization." That civilization was the "big lie" that had destroyed a previous age of innocence and virtue.   Ironically, at the last he finds himself at war with history, the handmaiden of civilization, and reveals his real interest lay always in pre-history.   In an unpublished typescript which was probably part of his last work, *Arcadia,* a utopian treatise, he writes:

> Strong crime emerges, the robber Kings of Assyria, the tyrant empire of Athens, the man-slaying power of Rome and, with the robber thief and murderer, their applauder and kept flatterer, History emerges too and announces, not the end of the reign of innocence, but the beginning of Civilization!
>
> Happy the Nations that have no History. Unhappy and thrice unhappy the Nations concerning whom History is eloquent, for she is only eloquent and can by her nature be only eloquent concerning crime.[2]

Holding such a view of history and the ruling classes, O'Grady could hardly continue to try to arouse the latter to assume a leadership role in bringing about a change so inimical to their interests. Once he saw the futility of trying to restore a sense of responsibility to the ruling classes, he began to speak almost exclusively to the laboring classes.

A survey of his political writings and his other later work reveals the most noteworthy shift in his work over the years—the changing nature of his intended audience. O'Grady's first tract, *The Crisis in Ireland* (1882), was an address to the land-lords of Ireland. His next tract, *Toryism and the Tory Democracy,* appeared in 1886 and appealed to the landlords and the laboring classes although it was addressed primarily to the former group. He sought to heal the breach between the two groups by adding his voice to a movement within the British Conservative party.

Tory Democracy was initiated within that party in response to the extension of the franchise under the second Reform Act of 1867. The Tories, the party of the landed classes, were faced with a severe erosion of strength by this extended franchise, and in the elections of 1868 they suffered severe reverses. Thereafter a party faction, led by Lord Randolph Churchill among others, started the Tory Democracy movement in order to broaden the base of popular support for the party. The name of the movement is suggestive: in theory, at least, the movement sought to reconcile the ideals of the old Toryism with the new Democracy. (It is easy to see why the movement would appeal to O'Grady). In practice, it seems to have been little more than a device for securing the support of newly enfranchised voters. This view, at least, is the well-argued opinion of Francis H. Merrick whose article traces the movement between 1867 and 1885. He quotes the opinion of an earlier commentator on the movement, Lord Roseberry, and calls the latter's opinion "cruel, but worth quoting." It is worth repeating:

> "Tory Democracy was a good catch word for recon-ciling Toryism and Democracy, if that were possible. But Toryism means something which Democracy cannot recognize, and Democracy means something which Toryism cannot supply. . . . Tory Democracy was an imposture, an honest and unconscious imposture, no doubt, but none the less an imposture. It was in reality a useful denomination or resource for anyone who found himself with Radical opinions inside the Tory party, and

who did not wish to leave it."[4]

O'Grady seems to have had no sense at all of the strictly political purposes of this movement, and indeed he even dedicated *Toryism and the Tory Democracy* to Lord Randolph Churchill. If O'Grady was seriously interested in bringing the landed and laboring classes together in 1886, he must have been either incredibly naive or extraordinarily pigheaded because Churchill did more in that year to divide Ireland than any single person may have done since. Churchill coined the slogan—"Ulster shall fight and Ulster shall be right"—which is still used by Ulster Protestants. Churchill, for his own political purposes, advocated the theory of the "two Irelands," and in 1886 he played his celebrated "Orange card" which permanently aroused Protestant opposition to the Home Rule bills which were discussed in Parliament on and off for the next 30 years.[5]

Though Churchill was a demagogue, O'Grady was absolutely sincere in his appeal for reconciliation between the landed and laboring classes. *Toryism and the Tory Democracy* is a virulent attack on capitalism and the mere pecuniary relationship that O'Grady believed capitalism established between the high and the low. He, therefore, sought to bring the laboring and landed classes together in a campaign against the bourgeoisie.

In essence, he was attacking the "cash-nexus" society that Carlyle had so denounced. He was particularly influenced in this regard by Carlyle's close disciple, John Ruskin, and O'Grady's political thinking for the remainder of his life shows the strong influence of Ruskin's words, especially *Fors Clavigera*.[6] In *Toryism and the Tory Democracy*, O'Grady wrote:

> The Tory Democracy would be on this side reinforced not only by many votes but by some noble and patriotic natures; men, for example, of the type of the late Charles Kingsley, who called himself a Christian Socialist, Mr. William Morris, Mr. Ruskin and his whole school. I do not merely guess that Mr. Ruskin is a Tory Democrat, as I understand the word, I know it. But for Mr. Ruskin and his books I should probably not have written this work.[7]

In *Unto This Last,* for example, Ruskin insisted on the

essential brotherhood of all peoples—using Christ's words, "I choose to give unto this last even as to thee" (Matthew 20:14), as his inspiration. This recognization of the essential relationship among men had been lost in the modern capitalist state, or so both Ruskin and O'Grady believed. O'Grady held that this loss troubled the lower classes more than even their poverty: "It is not poverty that the poor suffer from, not hardship, nor unintermittent toil, it is the sense of isolation, the sense that no one cares for them—that they are in no human relation with other classes."[8]   This problem is easy enough to solve; they knew the solution in less "civilized" times: "This dark, waste, mutinous proletariat has in it the old heroic stuff, the old loyalty, obedience, and love which our ancestors, in the ages called dark, knew how to evoke."[9]

The main purpose of this tract, then, is to inspire a similar sense of responsibility in the landed classes. O'Grady firmly believed that the laboring classes would rally to them if they would only reassume their natural functions. O'Grady's plea is eloquent, and his description of the probable career of the landed classes if they fail to reassume their natural functions has a rolling cadence that is dead-ended appropriately. He tells the present aristocracy:

> Your career is like some uncouth epic begun by a true poet, continued by a newspaper man, and ended by a buffoon; heroic verse, followed by prose, and closed in a disgusting farce.[10]

O'Grady's next political tract, *All Ireland,* did not appear until 1898, and in the intervening years his politics became somewhat more democratic as the side of him that Whitman had touched gained the ascendancy. He did display some bad temper, however, in the 1890's when he seems to have been upset by the attempts of Nationalists to view all Irish history as one long saga of British oppression. Consequently, in 1894 he wrote *The Story of Ireland,* a brief sketch of Irish history from the earliest times right up to his own time.[11]   Despite the respect for Christianity expressed in *Finn and His Companions,* O'Grady is harder than ever on it, especially on Christian monasticism, and the hallmarks of Christianity (like monasticism) that he chooses to attack are more often associated with Roman Catholicism—the religion of the majority of the

Nationalists—rather than any form of Protestantism. He suggests most explicitly that Christianity was responsible for the deterioration of the Irish habit of truth-telling.[12]   He even goes so far as to attack the most famous art work produced by Irish monks:

> The Book of Kells which visitors may see to-day in
> Trinity College, Dublin was their most wonderful work
> in this sphere of industry, and is certainly an appalling
> monument of misdirected and too ingenious toil.[13]

O'Grady also dwells at length on Elizabethan Ireland—a subject that absorbed his interest during the 1890's and one that he had immediate political purposes in exploring. The reign of Elizabeth saw the breakup of the Old Irish aristocracy and the arrival of centralized authority.   Though the Irish chiefs had pledged fealty to the British monarch for centuries, it was only during the time of Elizabeth that the authority of the Crown began to affect the Irish to any great extent. O'Grady saw this extention of British authority as a natural process: it was time for the nation-state to replace the decentralized authority of the petty chiefdoms, or monocracies as he called them.[14]   Indeed, he believed that it was the wish of the majority of the people that this change come about. Such a view runs strongly counter to the strict Nationalist viewpoint, which always regards the imposition of British rule as an unwanted and malicious intrusion.   Indeed, to the Nationalist mind, O'Grady's attitude is downright sacrilegious.

On the other hand, O'Grady did temper his view of the period by pointing to the high nobility of some of the Irish chiefs in their last stand against the encroachments of the Crown. To their nobility he contrasted the ignobility of the current aristocracy—the Anglo-Irish Ascendancy.[15]

During the 90's, O'Grady wrote extensively on the nobility of the Irish chiefs, and his books on the subject merit discussion here because his intention in writing them was even more directly political than any of his treatments of the bardic literature. He wrote three novelistic accounts or romances of the period—*Red Hugh's Captivity* (1889), *The Bog of Stars* (1893), and *The Flight of the Eagle* (1897)—and one play—*Hugh Roe O'Donnell* (1902).   He also edited in 1896 a new edition of the *Pacata Hibernia,* an account of the battle of Kinsale written (O'Grady

believed) by Sir Thomas Stafford and first published in 1636.
Stafford was an aide to the commander of the Royalist forces
in the battles between the chiefs and the Crown fought between
1600 and 1603.

O'Grady wrote a lengthy preface to this edition to the
Pacata Hibernia in which he tried to explain the actual state of
affairs at the time of the battle. His primary purpose was to
show that the Elizabethan age was fond of skullduggery and
there existed almost no code of honor. Thus, it is possible to
see the consistency in his attitude towards "civilization." The
latest manifestation of the civilizing process has less virtue
than the previous. Elizabeth and her lieutenants would use any
form of deceit to achieve their purposes, and the Irish chiefs
were no better, with the exception of Hugh Roe O'Donnell
and Hugh O'Neill, the Earl of Tyrone. To O'Grady's mind,
then, no particular goodness attached to the Crown (except
strong central authority which, in a different sense, he regarded
as a virtue). The time had simply come for the chiefs to go, and
he insists that their departure was the will of the people:

> . . . The Crown, in all its struggles with the great dynastic
> houses, always had the majority of the Irish nation on its
> side. For the controversy was not at all England *versus*
> Ireland, but the Crown, plus the majority of the [Irish]
> nation, *versus* the great lords.[16]

To this notion of the division of sides, O'Grady adds
another idea that must have displeased the Nationalists:

> For myself I can say truly that I have been only too
> anxious to discovery a chieftain animated by patriotism
> or religion. If there are any such I fear they will be rare
> ones, swimming desperately in the vast welter of con-
> flicting personal and dynastic interests.[17]

In short, most of the chiefs were motivated by their own
personal interests and had little interest in the idea of Ireland as
a nation and therefore a separate entity from Britain.

O'Grady, however, did choose to single out one chief who
was motivated by the old heroic code—Red Hugh O'Donnell.
The Flight of the Eagle—the best of the Elizabethan "novels" or
romances—tells the story of Red Hugh's early life. O'Grady

told the same story in an earlier version—*Red Hugh's Captivity,* but *The Flight of the Eagle* is more polished and therefore more worthy of attention.

This book dramatizes the attitudes that O'Grady had expressed in his preface to the *Pacata Hibernia.* Red Hugh is seen but as an imprisoned teenage boy for the most part, yet a sense that the old heroic blood runs strongly in his veins arises from O'Grady's description of his character and perseverance during his escapes from jail. The story is, on one side, an affecting adventure of a young boy; on another side, it offers O'Grady the opportunity to present his many theories concerning the age.[18]

The story tells of the capture of Red Hugh in 1587 from his home in the North by agents of the Viceroy of Ireland, Sir John Perrott. Red Hugh is to be held hostage to insure the loyalty of the O'Donnells in the expected battle with the Spanish Armada. Perrott uses a stratagem to capture Red Hugh— according to O'Grady, a method typical of Elizabethan state-craft. The remainder of the story concerns the escapes of Red Hugh from prison and his return to the North where he assumes his role as the O'Donnell, the leader of his clan.

O'Grady's depiction of Perrott is very positive[19] despite the fact that Perrott was responsible for the stratagem that so knavishly brought about Red Hugh's capture. He liked especially the fact that Perrott was a very strong ruler and, in fact, commanded the respect and even the love of the Irish chiefs. Under his rule, Ireland was united in its loyalty to the Crown. It was O'Grady's belief that Ireland has suffered its worst mistreatment whenever English rule has been weak. He further believed that it was English policy not to give Ireland a strong ruler because of fear of the consequences of giving such a leader to a warlike nation. He did think that the English were in fact justified in their fears, for he believed that a strong and united Ireland would be able to force England to act in Ireland's best interests.[20] England, accordingly, preferred to have Ireland badly ruled and therefore weak.

Consequently, Perrott is removed as viceroy soon after he has consolidated the country behind the Crown. He is replaced by the weak Fitzwilliam—"a gouty old gentleman and 'of a moist habit,' known to hate the flashing of stript steel, and to love craftiness and double-dealing, a Lord Deputy who could not even ride, 'such were his impediments,' and who was

extremely partial to—gifts."[21]   Fitzwilliam's misrule precipitates
disaffection with the Crown amongst the old Irish aristocrats,
and O'Grady implies that the battles described in *The Bog of
Stars* and the *Pacata Hibernia* resulted in good part from Fitzwilliam's weakness.

O'Grady's story proper opens with this change of command
from Perrott to Fitzwilliam.   From his prison, Dublin Castle,
Red Hugh watches the departure of Perrott.   A great deal of
exposition follows: O'Grady relates the story of Red Hugh's
capture and reiterates the points about the political state of
Ireland that he had made in *Pacata Hibernia*—especially the fact
that most of the Irish were loyal to the Crown and accordingly
had no feeling of sympathy with their co-religionists in Spain.
The action of the narrative resumes with Red Hugh's first escape
attempt, which fails because he trusts a temporizing noble.

To escape, Red Hugh must reach the southern stronghold
of Feagh Mac Hugh O'Byrne—a maverick whom Fitzwilliam
could not control though Perrott had obtained his allegiance.
Unfortunately Red Hugh's feet give out because he does not have
proper shoes.   He decides to seek the help of Felim O'Toole—a
former fellow-prisoner who had promised to help him if he
escaped.   O'Toole lives between the Pale—the center of the
Crown's strength—and Feagh O'Byrne's lands.   O'Toole fears to
defy the Crown, so he decides to send a slow messenger to
Dublin and a fast one to Feagh with the news that Red Hugh
is with him.   However, a flood blocks the passage of Feagh's men
on their way north to rescue Red Hugh, so the Crown authorities
arrive first and take Hugh back to Dublin.

This action enables O'Grady to make a crucial point about
nobility.   He has no respect at all for O'Toole, and his message
to the modern Anglo-Irish Ascendancy is clear: your time is
passing; either move with it or uphold the values that once made
you great.   Don't sit on the fence like Felim O'Toole.   O'Grady
writes:

> The monocracies and the State could no longer co-exist.
> One or the other had to go, and Fate had determined
> that it should be the former.   For the monocracies—the
> reguli and chieftainry of the island—nothing remained
> but to cooperate loyally with the State, and accept
> frankly the terms offered, that is to say, continuity of
> existence as wealthy, influential, and honoured subjects;

or, accepting the other alternative, to fight bravely and
fall gloriously in defence of ancient rights and the semi-
kingly power which they had inherited from afar. . . .
Felim made no figure on either side. . . . Had Felim now
mustered his clan and conveyed the boy [Hugh] to
Glenmalure, regardless of consequences; had he and his
brother and his ill-starred son Gerald died for their friend
and suppliant, and the O'Tooles so vanished from history,
how glorious would have been that final flash of generous
antique chivalry!   How dear and memorable for ever!
But Sir Felim was not made so.   The lion of his house
passed, not, as on his seal, with head erect and brandished
tail, but in a much more ignoble fashion.[22]

Thus, Red Hugh is brought back to Dublin Castle from
which he escapes on another occasion. Then he nearly perishes
from hunger and cold—a story that O'Grady tells affectingly.
This time, however, Hugh makes it to Feagh's stronghold, from
which he subsequently travels to the North. O'Grady gives us
some inkling of the kind of leader who has arrived by showing
the decisiveness with which Hugh acts to assert his authority
once he arrives in the North. He dispatches the Crown's sheriff
and lays claim to the O'Donnell title. A true hero has arisen
who will breathe nobly the last gasp of his dying breed.

O'Grady clearly identifies Red Hugh as that last hero of
the old breed: he is the heir of the greatness of Cuculain and
Finn. As Red Hugh travels into the North from Feagh's stronghold, he passes Slieve Gullion or Slieve Fuad—a mountain full
of associations with the old heroes. O'Grady's description of
the associations becomes a virtual litany of those heroes:

Here lived and reigned Fuad, the far-off Milesian druid
king, till his glory faded, as all things will. The mountain
was Cuculain's sign-post, when, a little boy driven forth
by the war spirits, he secretly left his home and his dear
mother, seeking Emain Macha. Here the sentinels of the
Red Branch from the mearings of Ulster. Here Ossian's
sire slew the enchanter Almain, son of Midna, who once
every year, to the sound of unearthly music consumed
Tara with magic flames.   On this mountain Cuculain
seized the wild fairy steed, the Liath Macha. . . Here,
steeped in Lough Liath's waters, Finn's golden tresses

took on the hue and glitter of radiant snow. . .[23]

O'Grady follows this passage with a paragraph that points the litany's relevance to Red Hugh:

> Of that mythus, all that it meant, all that to which it tended, the last great secular champion, rides today round Slieve Gullion's base, soon to reappear, how differently! at the head of his armies, the eagle of the North, the swift leopard of Tir-Connall, vainly too, despite all his bravery. Such is the power of the weaving stars![24]

The story of the youth of "the last great secular champion" of the old Irish aristocracy ends, and O'Grady has accomplished his careful balancing act between repudiating Nationalist versions of the history and rebuking the modern Ascendancy for not acting up to the example of Red Hugh. O'Grady's "Postscript" indicates that he had immediate political purposes in mind when he wrote the story: "I believe that the history of Ireland in this century has been profoundly misunderstood both by English and Irish writers, and that a true understanding of it would be of great political benefit to both peoples, especially to the people of Ireland."[25]

O'Grady's notion of that "great practical benefit" seems to have included the idea that his tale would help the Irish to accept that strong English rule which would inevitably result in a strong Ireland. That notion, too, seems to have been the underlying idea of a boys' story that he also wrote in the mid-1890's. *The Chain of Gold* was published in 1895, and it is quite unlike O'Grady's earlier works. Besides the interest it reveals in psychic phenomena, the story is not dependent on sources as all but one of his prior books are. (The one previous completely invented story, *Lost on Du-Corrig*, appeared in 1894 and is very similar to *The Chain of Gold*).

These differences aside, *The Chain of Gold* is perhaps most fascinating when viewed as subtle propaganda. The story is written for boys, and O'Grady is seeking to instill in them the spirit and principles he thinks proper. O'Grady's didacticism is evident once more.

The story is part mystery, part adventure and is told by narrators who were themselves participants in the events they recount—a method O'Grady learned from Wilkie Collins.[26] The

story concerns the absence of two brothers for several months
from their homes.   They were fishing in the Atlantic off the
west coast of Ireland when a hurricane suddenly blew up. They
were presumed to be dead when search-parties turned up no
trace of them.

The story opens with the narrative of Frank Furbisher,
an insomniac, well-to-do boy who finds a note from the two
boys floating in a bottle in the sea off the French coast. Frank
is seized by the mystery and eventually traces the note to its
origin in the cliffs on the west coast of Ireland. In the process
he loses his insomnia as he gains a purpose in life—a transformation with Carlylian overtones: he is cured because he has
found his work. His initial reaction to the note, however, was
to dismiss it. Only a visionary dream prompts him to action:

> As I dreamed now, the jar which I had been handling
> just before continued to appear and reappear in my
> dreams, greatly increased in size. Then it seemed to me
> that there were people in it, who passionately cried to
> me to liberate them. The voice that cried out seemed to
> me to be the voices of boys. I awoke with a start and
> sprang to my feet, trembling violently.[27]

The finding of the bottle and the subsequent dream set
the pattern for the events in the story. The discovery of the
bottle propels Frank Furbisher into action in much the same way
that O'Grady himself was propelled into his study of Irish history by his discovery of Sylvester O'Halloran's *History.*
O'Grady's description of that "wet day" is worth recalling:

> It looks like an accident, a mere chance, and yet I don't
> think it was quite such. If the fall of a sparrow is pro-
> vided for, possible so was that wet day in the West of
> Ireland.[28]

The Chain of Gold may be inspired partially by that "wet
day," for there are other autobiographical elements in it.[29] In
any event, O'Grady changes narrators after Frank Furbisher
comes almost to the point of solving the mystery of the two
boys' absence. The story then becomes more of an adventure
story and is narrated by the older of the two brothers, Jack Freeman.   Both he and his brother Ned discover themselves in the

course of their adventure in much the same way that Frank does and O'Grady himself did in the 1870's.

Jack and Ned were marooned in a cave on a cliff high above the water by the hurricane. As their boat was about to be smashed against the rocks, by a combination of skill and luck they were able to steer it to a point where the boat would be wedged against the rocks and they would thus be able to enter the cave. The combination of skill and luck is important: they had learned their boating skills from the Gaelic Irish fishermen in their neighborhood, and their luck has something of the character of O'Grady's "fall of a sparrow."

The events that follow their marooning have a similar pattern. The boys work hard in order to survive, but their efforts are accompanied by fortuitous discoveries that have indeed been "provided for." The major survival problem is the procurement of fresh water. Initially they discover a running stream outside the cave, but eventually it runs dry. As the boys become almost delirious with thirst, Ned has a vision of a hermit who tells him to dig deeper in the rear of the cave. Jack does so and finds a stream of fresh water. The discovery of the water leads the boys to the recognition that the cave was previously inhabited. After searching the cave carefully, they find a very important item: an old Gaelic manuscript.

The fortuitous "accidents" now come together in a rush. On the day they were marooned, Jack had with him a Gaelic grammar book. He had thought that he was taking a history of Henry V's French wars and only discovered the Gaelic book after they were marooned. He had studied the book to some extent before the discovery of the Gaelic manuscript and is now able to translate it. He discovers that the hermit was an old Irish warrior who had become a monk (though still with a mind imbued with drudic lore). The hermit predicted that the boys would one day come to the cave. Furthermore Jack reports:

> He also said that, by his art, he had been able to project an image or resemblance of himself into the future, so that it would be perceptible to us. For time, he said, had no real existence, and all its barriers might be overleaped by one who has been instructed in the *ars magica*.[30]

Ned's dream, then, was not pure coincidence; the past (as so often happens in O'Grady) had "provided for" the present.

Jack, however, now becomes completely enthralled by the psychic and the magical. The hermit tells in his manuscript what happened to him when he became immersed in magical concerns. The state is familiar to O'Grady's readers:

> Age, he said, came suddenly, and like a robber, upon him here; and one day he discovered that, owing to the weight of years, he was cut off from the life of warriors and kings. Moreover, the fascinations of the Druidic art *enchanted* him in a wonderful m͡ar ͡r[31] [italics added].

Jack is similarly "enchanted," and Ned later tells him that he "had become so fierce and terrible as if he had been under the dominion of some evil spell."[32] Eventually Ned seizes the manuscript and throws it into the sea. The spell on Jack is broken, but he has learned one crucial fact from the manuscript which turns out to have immense practical value. The hermit wrote that he kept his treasure in a rock in the rear of the cave. Jack digs for it and uncovers a pile of old Irish ring-type coins. Ned eventually discovers that the coins are capable of being joined together to make a chain. The boys hammer them together, and by that means effect their escape.

The meaning of these events is very suggestive: knowledge of the old language and religion is tremendously useful, but extremely dangerous when it becomes an obsession. The result is enchantment—the state in which men do not work.[33] The things of primitive Ireland must be combined with the true civilizing values of modern Ireland—the values of the Anglo-Irish Protestant Ascendancy. Yet O'Grady would not necessarily have regarded the civilizing values as modern in origin. Actually, he would probably have seen them as residues of primitive values. Thus the positive synthesis of the primitive and the civilized here might well be seen as a dramatization of the definition of civilization that he proposed in his *Critical and Philosophical History:*

> Civilization seems to be nothing else than the art or faculty of directing into beneficent and lasting results those forces of human nature which have been generated by causes with which civilization has nothing in common, primal spontaneous energies of the human soul.[34]

The boys are Protestants and have the work ethic by inheritance from their forebears, although like O'Grady himself, they come from mixed English and "pure Milesian" blood.[35] O'Grady compares them to Robinson Crusoe, for their efforts in the cave bespeak the same Protestant industriousness, inventive skill, and civilizing capacity that Defoe's Crusoe has.[36] In the cave, however, they learn respect for the other Ireland, and they learn to integrate it into their lives. Respect for old Gaelic Ireland is inculcated in every way possible. They survive the storm because their boat is of an old type and they have an old pot on board which is better for bailing than modern bailers. Indeed, Jack reports that if the old pot "had not been such a truly rural vessel, affording me such an excellent purchase for effective work, I am certain the inpour of water would have gained on us."[37] Jack has to learn that the old language is valuable and indeed beautiful. At first, he dismisses the old Gaelic grammar, but afterwards the consciousness of his "Gaelic side" leads him to study the language which later proves to be the key to the escape.

The escape itself reinforces O'Grady's integration of Anglo-Irish and Gaelic Irish qualities. After the boys descend from the cliff, they float to an off-shore island on a raft they have constructed from the remains of their old boat. No one is on the island, but the fields are tilled and sheep are grazing. Apparently, the men who work the land live on a nearby island and only visit this island in order to do the necessary work. The boys help themselves to the food available in a small cabin and kill and eat a sheep. After several days on the island the winds become favorable for the trip home. After they have set out, however, a boatload of angry Islanders[38] bears down on them. The Islanders have discovered the killing of the sheep and have assumed that the boys were mere marauders. They speak no English and are about to do violence to the boys when a coastguard boat manned by *English* sailors appears on the scene. The detective work of Frank Furbisher and another Freeman brother who are aboard the boat are responsible for the coastguard's appearance in that vicinity. A combination of a warning shot from the coastguard—the local representatives of the English Crown—and Jack's acquaintance with the Gaelic language succeeds in quelling the Islanders' anger. As Jack reports it, the combination of those qualities brings out the best in the primitive Islanders:

> Presently I perceive with heart-felt satisfaction that
> their wrath was giving place to curiosity, and the amiable
> and humane feelings so common amongst these islanders
> getting into the ascendant. But certain I am that, but for
> my slight knowledge of Gaelic and the intervention of the
> coastguards on this occasion, such was their fury that
> they would have beaten us to death as pirates and sea-
> thieves, taken red-handed in the act.[39]

The chain of gold has become the symbolic link between ancient and modern Ireland, for it has literally as well as figuratively linked the past which was hidden in the cave and the present outside the cave where the knowledge of the past enables the boys to survive in the present. In order to become reconciled with their neighbors whose lives are still so much in the past, Jack and Ned had to know that past. Thus, O'Grady presents a strong practical reason for learning Irish history: that past shapes the present. By knowledge of it, all the disparate elements in the modern Irish character can be reconciled with one another.

So O'Grady wrote in 1895; by the following year he had found a political issue which he believed capable of reconciling all elements on the Irish scene. In 1896, a report of a Royal Commission on the financial relations between Britain and Ireland revealed that Ireland had probably been seriously over-taxed since the Act of Union. A storm of protest arose after this report, and by 1897 an All-Ireland Committee had been formed to discuss actions that might be taken to insure redress.[40]   O'Grady seized upon the issue because the over-taxation affected all classes in Ireland. In 1898, he published a tract on the subject, *All Ireland,* which is an eloquent (and somewhat romantic[41]) plea for unity on the subject of the financial relations with Britain.

In a chapter entitled "The Veiled Player," O'Grady penned his most virulent criticism of Britain up to that time. Comparing the relations between England and Ireland to a chess game at which England sits as a "veiled player," O'Grady warns the Irish what will happen if England ever loses a game:

> Men of Ireland! gentry and people, high and low, wise
> and simple, leaders and led, what are you prepared to do
> when the veiled figure seeing the game lost, rends the

rules, upsets the table, spills the gold, and shouts for his guards?" And he will do it; trust me he will.[42]

It is especially noteworthy that O'Grady is now talking to all Irishmen, and the note he sounds is very ominous. The principles he lays down for the All-Ireland movement make him sound like a Fenian radical:

> The All-Ireland movement is governed by two laws: they are these:—
>
> 1) *The Imperial Parliament, in its dealings with Ireland, never yields to Justice but always to Force.*
>
> 2) *Ireland united is Ireland irresistible.*[43]

O'Grady is not necessarily advocating the use of physical force here, but he does leave the notion of force tantalizingly vague. Yet, he never seems to have been aware of the effect he was having on people who were given to revolutionary violence. After O'Grady's death in 1928, AE wrote an obituary notice which credits O'Grady with inspiration that he did not intend:

> His work was an inspiration to many Irish Nationalists, for, although in a superficial sense his politics were opposed to theirs, the moment he ceased to think with the conscious mind and surrendered himself to his imagination, he became the noblest Irishman of them all. I think the deep respect men like Arthur Griffith and Padraic Pearse had for O'Grady was because the Ireland they stood for was meditating a deed, and O'Grady was the only Irish writer who exalted the hero or the doer. I think he was sure in his soul that the heroic life was the highest, and it was beyond the contemplative or the aesthetic consciousness. Those who were beginning to contemplate a deed which needed the sacrificial spirit found in his hero tales spiritual companions who went with them into the lonely places of the soul. O'Grady said of the ancient legends of Ireland that they were less history than prophecy, and I who knew how deep was Pearse's love for the Cuculain whom O'Grady discovered

or invented, remembered after Easter Week that he had
been solitary against a great host in imagination with
Cuculain long before circumstances permitted him to
stand for his nation with so few companions against so
great a power.[44]

Although leaders like Griffith and Pearse were not exactly
what O'Grady wanted, he did begin in *All Ireland* to prepare the
way for new leaders. He was pleased that the All-Ireland movement had succeeded in propelling some members of the Anglo-
Irish ascendancy into action and that the people were looking
to them as their natural leaders. However, he added a previously
uncharacteristic word of caution:

And yet we must avoid the error of trusting too much
in leaders. We are now a democracy, and every man must
try to be himself somewhat of a statesman, and accustom
himself to regard public affairs from a statesmanlike
point of view—that is to say, not with an eye to his own
feelings or his class interests, but, as much as he can, from
the point of the interests of all Ireland and the whole
Irish nation—all classes. . .[45]

With this notion of democratic leadership, he coupled
advocacy of a policy that would make that democracy more
real:

. . . I say now that though politically a member of a
decided minority, I support Irish manhood suffrage from
this day forward, believing that every rightful interest
and just cause will be safe in the hands of the least for-
tunate of my fellow-countrymen. The right was always
clear, but the expediency of conceding the right was not.
We shall certainly get on to the All-Ireland track *via* the
finance question. . .[46]

From this point on, O'Grady reposes more and more confidence in the lower classes and begins to see them more and
more as the probable progenitors of his Utopian Ireland. In
1900, he started his *All Ireland Review*, and the title reflects his
continued concern for the reconcilation of all Irish interests.
This weekly review ran for a little more than seven years, and

during those years O'Grady gradually weaned himself from his allegiances to his class.

Such weaning did not come easily as he interspersed his more democratic remarks with comments on the glories of the "Anglo-Irish Empire" and the Crown. He even justified inconsistency at one point:

> With consistency a great soul has simply nothing to do. . . . Speak what you think now in hard words and to-morrow speak what to-morrow thinks in hard words again, though it contradict everything you said to-day.[47]

Thus, in 1902 he tempered his previous anti-merchant rhetoric and renamed his publication *The All Ireland Review and Irish Manufacturers' and Traders' Gazette* in an attempt to spiritualize the merchant class, which he had so long despised. This attempt shows the influence of Prince Kropotkin's *Fields, Factories and Workshops.* The subtitle of that book—*Industry Combined with Agriculture and Brain Work with Manual Work*—suggests its thesis. Kropotkin argued for self-sufficiency in industry and agriculture for each nation and thus opposed separate industrial and agricultural sectors. (His argument for requiring individuals to perform both mental and physical work appealed to O'Grady but does not concern us now). Persuaded by Kropotkin's theory, O'Grady saw a self-sufficient Ireland as a necessity and in 1902 tried to ally the Land Leaguers with the manufacturers and traders against the landlords. He saw that alliance as the best means of diversifying both Irish industry and agriculture.

In a poorly written paragraph, O'Grady bemoans the manufacturers' and traders' lack of awareness of the relationship between agriculture and industry:

> . . . I see nowhere amongst them [the manufacturers and traders] any perception of the fact that their interests are vitally connected with a just solution of the great land problem, or of the importance to them of the creation here, at home, of a great, prosperous, progressive, and expanding rural population, the sole source and spring of our manufacturing and commercial activities. I see amongst them no perception of the fact that those areas of Ireland which they have made so valuable—the

> ground upon which our towns stand are owned and
> commercially exploited by those [the landlords] who
> contribute nothing at all to the enormous value inherent
> in it now, and mainly, through their [the manufacturers'
> and traders'] exertions; people [the landlords] who are
> mere passengers in the boat [sic].[48]

Such words sound like a call for unity in a revolution against the class that O'Grady had allied himself with for much of his life, yet he disavowed any "revolutionary disturbing purposes."[49]   In this attitude O'Grady follows Fourier who similarly forswore revolution as an instrument of change, but it is more important to note how thoroughly O'Grady was divorcing himself from his class. The former secretary of the Landlords' Convention could hardly be regarded as loyal to the interests of the landlords.

By 1906, he had abandoned all hope of the old aristocracy resuming its natural functions. A letter to John Quinn in that year reveals the lasting power Walt Whitman had to temper O'Grady's enthusiasm for Carlyle:

> I have   a no. [of the *All Ireland Review*] coming
> out not bad I think, only I should say very Anarchical
> & too much of the New Order to please most of my
> friends; who go with me mainly because they think of
> themselves as Captains of Industry & Chiefs, High Chiefs
> of Industrial Clans, re-establishing their Aristocracy on
> a new & more rational basis.
>
> This, as you know, is the Carlyle doctrine & theory:
> not mine; for I see that nothing short of freedom &
> equality & the sovereignty of the Individual will satisfy
> the soul of man, our times.[50]

By 1908, O'Grady had ceased to talk to the Ascendancy class. By then he was directly addressing the laboring classes in a publication clearly aimed at them. From 1908 through 1910, O'Grady published several series of articles in a newspaper, *The Peasant*, which changed its name to *The Irish Nation* in 1909.[51] In these articles, O'Grady advocated a return to the communism which he regarded as the primitive form of human organization and the only cure for the evils of "civilization." One series of articles, "Life and Liberty: Letters to a Dublin

Clerk," started in September 1908 and ran continuously to March 1909. They bear some resemblance to Ruskin's *Fors Clavigera* which also advocated communism[52] and which was also directly addressed to the laboring classes. *Fors Clavigera* is subtitled *Letters to the Workmen and Labourers of Great Britain.*

Eight years earlier in a letter published in the *All Ireland Review*, W. B. Yeats had suggested that O'Grady undertake the writing of a similar work for Ireland. The letter is also interesting for its suggestion that the salvation of the Ascendancy is a hopeless task:

> What we want from you is a kind of Irish "Fors Cla-vigera." You are about the best fighter we have against that Death whose most manifest expression in this coun-try is Trinity College (should we not add Alexandra College?) and which has already turned our once in-telligent gentry into readers of the "Irish Times."
>
> I fear that you cannot awake the dying mind of a dying class; but people like you can keep it from dying right out till another class is ready to take its place.[53]

O'Grady's articles in *The Peasant* and *The Irish Nation* attempt to prepare the new class "to take its place." The "Letters to a Dublin Clerk" are typical O'Grady documents: part "philosophical," part practical. For example, on the one hand, he compares socialism and communism; on the other hand, he concocts a scheme for the formation of a commune in which Dublin clerks will pool their resources to buy land in the country.

The difference between socialism and communism is a crucial point in all his contributions to *The Peasant* and *The Irish Nation.* O'Grady was strongly opposed to socialism because it is a system based on money—the root of all evil, to his mind. He wished to return to the primitive system of barter which he believed to be the natural system. Capitalism had un-naturally commercialized the source of money—property—with a view to gain. This "gave a pecuniary aspect to life in general and in a manner compelled all industries and activities, in a word all social human life, to become less human and more sordid."[54] Socialism, because it builds on this commerciali-zation, is not capable of making life more human and less sordid.

Furthermore, because socialism wishes to change the benefactors of the commercialization of property, O'Grady saw in it the threat of violent revolution. His attitude towards revolution has not changed much from the days in which he described the plebeian rebellion against the Fianna[55]:

> A word as to Socialism, whose exponents and leaders imagine such a transformation by law, that is by force, of our existing social system as will permit the emergence of social justice and the re-establishment of right relations between men. I am convinced that the Socialists, however well-meaning they may be and however intelligent and understanding (there is perhaps no one more well-meaning and intelligent in our part of the world than Bernard Shaw), I am, I say, convinced, that, sooner or later, they will come into deadly collision with the champions and representatives of the existing order—in England with the Tories—and provoke a fearful explosion in which all interests, those of poor and rich alike will be swallowed up in a common destruction.[56]

O'Grady did not argue with the correctness of socialism as an economic system, for indeed he had "not one word to say in derogation of its claim to be the only form of political economy which can withstand destructive criticisms, or satisfy at the same time our natural sense of right and justice. . ."[57] He did, however, have a strong sense of its irrelevance to the people it would supposedly benefit the most. He tells them:

> Be a Socialist, if you please. I don't mind. It won't make much practical difference whether you are, or are not, provided you don't join the militant fighting section, or give your hearts to it and inflame yourselves with the fierce revolutionary passions that emanate from it. It won't make any practical difference whether you are a Socialist or not. I was once in an English town where all the rich people were professing Socialists. They lived in nice villa houses, and enjoyed their rents and dividends like other people—Socialism not having yet arrived.[58]

O'Grady's solution called for the laboring classes to return to the countryside and form communes because such organizations would not directly confront the powerful monied classes:

> So I have been driven to the conclusion that the saviours of mankind, as they arise, will be men and women who will deliberately pass out from this money-governed social system and beyond its precincts; and with more of compassion in their hearts for it than either hatred or contempt, create there a new and sane life, founded upon the eternal principles and dictated by Reason and Conscience and by Man's essentially social nature.
>
> Now, such societies will be distinctly communal, and cannot be anything else. If you remember Man as he essentially is, and forget the rapacious creature whom he has been compelled to become, you will see that that is so.
>
> I am against waging war upon this all but almighty power of money, which is the way of the socialists. War means violence, and however seemingly justifiable violence is, still violence. Now there is no promise that the violent shall inherit the earth, but a clear promise that the gentle shall inherit the earth.[59]

O'Grady realized that the formation of communes would be no easy task for Dublin clerks; he had an historical precedent for their state:

> I look around me to see where are the descendants of the men and women of the ages of heroism and romance, where to day are the seed of the giants of the North and the mighty hunters of the South; and hear a cry feeble as that of the bat flitting through the twilight, and which emits the thinnest little voice heard from any animal. It seems to say:—
>
> "We are all here, indoors, chained and in durance, at desks and counters. We are thin-shanked and flat-breasted, anaemic and clammy-handed, sallow and consumptive, strengthless and hopeless, and dying by inches in our dungeons. And we know it is all an *enchantment*, and we can't help it; for our Will is gone from us"[60] [italics added].

Although O'Grady's writing decreased in volume after 1910, the available evidence suggests that he remained interested in the welfare of the laboring classes for the rest of his life. He became a contributor to A. R. Orage's *The New Age* wherein, according to Ernest Boyd, he advocated "the abolition of wagery and the restoration of National Guilds, as the only alternative to the Servile State, that apotheosis of profiteering."[61] To these utopian plans O'Grady added strong interests in the personal health of the people and in the protection of the environment.[62] The preceding passage reflects this concern, and the following prescribes part of the antidote to the enchantment:

> . . . All enchantments may be overcome and all night-mares do come to an end. Get all the sunshine and fresh air that you possible can into your lives, and all the physical activity that you possibly can. . . .[63]

Seventeen years later in 1926, he was still concerned with the personal health of the people. In a letter to W. B. Yeats he raves about the poor sanitary conditions in Ireland and asks Yeats to use his political influence to improve the situation. O'Grady writes:

> Glad to note you are out for cleansing the National Schools.
> I know them. The children ease themselves in a field, making a horror for all who pass.
> But all, high & low, are offenders as to Sanitation, Civilization is quite criminal here.
> The rich have privies & get them cleansed at night by men whom they make drunk to tackle the job. . . .
> Then, the great cities pour down their abominitions into the innocent Sea, waste matter that the Earth wants & craves.[64]

This concern for the environment shows strong signs of the influence of Fourier. In a 1902 review of *Selections from the Writings of Fourier,* O'Grady called the book "one of the greatest of the century," and all of his post-1900 writing reflects a sensibility in tune with Fourier's. Fourier's basic premise was that the order in the natural world would also exist in the social, moral world were it not for the warped intervention of "civilization." Charles Gide, who wrote the introduction to the *Selections* O'Grady reviewed in 1902, explains the essential premise of Fourier's thought:

> Fourier starts out with the *a priori* idea that there must be a plan of God, that is to say, a certain social order conformable to God's will, and such as may secure the perfect happiness of all mankind. The whole thing is to discover this plan: the entire social problem reduces itself to a sort of divining-rod task. . . . Assuming as a postulate the pre-established correspondence between the planetary and the social world, he asserts that the mechanism which causes both to move must be the same, namely: attraction. To Newton, to whom he constantly compares himself, the glory of having revealed the principle and expounded its laws as regards the material world; to him, Fourier, the honour of having revealed it and expounded its laws as regards the moral world.[65]

Fourier argued that ignorance of "passional attraction" in civilized societies had so constrained people as to force them constantly into unnatural work and life situations. O'Grady strongly concurred with Fourier in this regard, and much of what appears to have been O'Grady's last work, *Arcadia*, echoes Fourier. O'Grady castigates work in dimly lit factories and raves about life outdoors. His analysis of the effects of socialization upon children has the ring of Fourier:

> The natural man is seen best in the child, for as he grows he gradually assumes a second nature impressed upon him by the social world that surrounds him.[66]

The antedote to this socialization is simple; O'Grady advises parents:

> Don't force the young mind in any direction. Nature is infinitely wiser than we are, and may be trusted to take the best care of all the children whom she sends into the world.[67]

In short, the natural "attractions" of the children should be given free play.

O'Grady believed that a society so in tune with nature had existed in the primitive "Aryan Village Commune," and his treatise argues for a return to that state. His vision of the modern, corrupt state of affairs has an ominous ring to it:

> That universal and absolutely right and natural feeling of our Aryan ancestors has been obscured in more modern Europe by the prevalence of Semitic fanaticisms, the devotion to divers gods and demons made in the likeness of corrupt mankind; but it has been here always nevertheless; and always will be. The love of Nature, the all-Mother, has ever lain deep in the European heart. . .[68]

Thus, at the last O'Grady joined other twentieth century thinkers in seeing a Semitic origin for the corruption of Europe. As such, his personal intellectual history is an important record of the development of the Aryan myth in modern Europe. The above passage is the only specifically anti-Semitic remark I have found although it is implicit in much of his writing. Indeed, it is not surprising that a man who had inherited the nineteenth century notion of "race" should visualize his utopia as a "racially pure" state.

While O'Grady met with little success in promoting the idea of "race" in politics, he did succeed in making a generation of Irish writers believe that a national literature which was rooted in the distant past of the country was much to be desired in Ireland. While O'Grady's principal literary contributions to the Irish Revival were made in the early part of his career, he continued to encourage writers to write on Irish subjects and made the columns of his *All Ireland Review* available to them. Though many acknowledged their debt to O'Grady, Yeats and AE were perhaps influenced the most.

Less than two months after his 1926 letter to Yeats regarding sanitation, O'Grady again wrote to Yeats asking him if he had received it. O'Grady wanted "to know that my seed had dropped into such a fertile soil."[69]   The line may have been unconscious, but it has meaning for the relationship of the two men that far exceeds the issue immediately at hand. O'Grady at age 80 was still trying to light a fire under Yeats as he had so often done in the past.

At his worst O'Grady must have been a pest to Yeats. In

1900 he wrote him this sharp rebuke:

> Frankly, & quite between ourselves, I don't like at all the
> way you have been going on now for a good many years.
> You can't help it, I suppose, having got down into the
> crowds.[70]

O'Grady apologized for this intemperate remark in a letter
written the same day,[71] but he was also capable of issuing a
similar rebuke in public.   In 1900, O'Grady published the text
written by Yeats of "A Postscript to a Forthcoming Book of
Essays by Various Writers" in the *All Ireland Review*.   O'Grady
followed Yeats's "Postscript" with very harsh words:

> . . . I take this great liberty—for I confess that it is such—
> because too I have a certain personal grievance to allege
> against you and your friends.   This little essay or dis-
> course is a postscript to a book, the purpose of which is
> to exhibit the Irish mind in London, and I understand
> that among the other interesting barbarians whom you
> are exhibiting to the Philistines, I, too, am being trotted
> out and made to show my paces. Now is this right? You
> are at one with me about the iniquity of the tourist
> movement and the exploitation for commercial purposes
> of the beauty of our country. Yet holding such opinions
> you bring us all—we who in some poor way stand for
> Ireland—over to London and trot us round for the de-
> lectation of your clever London friends whose favourable
> opinion we don't want and can do very well without.[72]

It is hard to determine how much such rebukes shook
Yeats's high opinion of O'Grady. Apparently, they were minor
matters, for Yeats's imagination was deeply imbued with
O'Grady's spirit—a fact that he documented in his notes to the
poems in "The Wind among the Reeds." He mentions O'Grady
specifically several times.   One instance in particular reveals
the depth of Yeats's awareness of O'Grady's work. In the first
version of the notes Yeats refers to a story that he probably
found in O'Grady's *Finn and His Companions,* but at the time
of writing the notes he cannot recall that source: "I am writing
away from most of my books, and have not been able to find
the passage; but I certainly read it somewhere."[73]   In a later

version he hazards a guess: "But maybe I only read it in Mr. Standish O'Grady, who has a fine imagination, for I find no such story in Lady Gregory's book."[74]

Though Yeats may have been the most important "fertile soil" in which O'Grady sowed his "seed," no writer was more influenced by him than AE. Perhaps this influence was only appropriate: AE was a man much like O'Grady—both were visionaries and both were concerned with developing practical solutions to problems. AE's expression of his debt to O'Grady justifies O'Grady's title as the "Father of the Irish Revival" in AE's case at least:

> With reference to Ireland, I was at the time I read [O'Grady's "bardic history"] like many others who were bereaved of the history of their race. I was as a man who, through some accident, had lost memory of his past, who could recall no more than a few months of new life, and could not say to what songs his cradle had been rocked, what mother had nursed him, who were the playmates of childhood or by what woods and streams he had wandered. When I read O'Grady I was as such a man who suddenly feels ancient memories rushing at him, and knows he was born in a royal house, that he had mixed with the mighty of heaven and earth and had the very noblest for his companions. It was the memory of race which rose up within me as I read, and I felt exalted as one who learns he is among the children of kings.[75]

When O'Grady died in 1928 on the Isle of Wight, he was working on *Arcadia*—his program for a better Ireland. Death alone stopped him from trying to start things.

Notes

[1] I have read through the *Daily Express* for four years, 1895-1898, but I have been unable to identify positively any of the leading articles as O'Grady's. However, many of the opinions expressed do resemble his.

[2] Standish James O'Grady, "Chap. II: 'Greek Women,' " TS, pp. 7-8, The Standish De Courcey O'Grady Collection.

[3] Cf. pp. 120-121 for a discussion of this tract.

[4] Archibald P. P. Roseberry, quoted in Francis H. Herrick, "Lord Randolph Churchill and the Popular Organization of the Conservative Party," *Pacific Historical Review,* 15 (1946), 182.

[5] Cf. F. S. L. Lyons, *Ireland Since the Famine* (New York: Charles Scribner's Sons, 1971), pp. 178-179 and p. 291, for a discussion of Churchill's actions during this period.

[6] Ruskin's *Fors Clavigera* was a collection of letters on economic and social matters. They were published continuously between 1871 and 1884 and were subtitled *Letters to the Workmen and Labourers of Great Britain.* The reviewer in *Dublin University Review* 2 (1886), 368-369, stated that O'Grady in writing *Toryism and Tory Democracy* had written an Irish *Fors Clavigera.*

[7] *Toryism and the Tory Democracy,* p. 191.

[8] *Toryism and the Tory Democracy,* pp. 198-199.

[9] *Toryism and the Tory Democracy,* p. 199.

[10] *Toryism and the Tory Democracy,* p. 239.

[11] O'Grady's view of Parnell's funeral in *The Story of Ireland* became the basis for the mythology surrounding that event that Yeats employed in his poems, "Parnell's Funeral." For a full discussion of this subject, cf., Malcoln Brown, *The Politics of Irish Literature* (Seattle: University of Washington Press, 1972), pp. 373-374.

[12] Cf., e. g., Standish James O'Grady, *The Story of Ireland* (London: Methuen, 1894), p. 46:

> This was bribing [practiced by St. Patrick], no doubt, and whether right or wrong is a question I would leave to the casuists, but for the fact that I seem to see here the little rift within the lute, which in the end destroyed the music of Irish Christianity, a lack of straightforward, bald, and honest dealing, which afterwards became a notorious vice, so that many of our great saints were also great liars, and fell under the just scorn and contempt of those who had no religion at all but simply preserved the old instinctive Pagan abhorrence of falsehood and double dealing.

Twenty pages later, O'Grady ascribes the worship of saints to Irish Christianity—a traditional charge of Protestants against Roman Catholics (based on the notion that praying to saints violates the first commandment):

> . . . the founders [of the monasteries], Ciaran, Kevin, Columba,
> Bridget, and many others, descended visibly into the battles of
> men, and gave or withheld victory.   They were the Tuatha De
> Danan of a new and astonishing time when Irish Christianity
> became only a degraded form of Paganism with saints for its
> gods (p. 66).

(This description of Irish Christianity is interesting for another reason: it
is an euhemerist explanation of the religion and therefore denies any special
truth or spiritual transcendance to it.)

[13] *The Story of Ireland*, p. 64.

[14] This idea expresses O'Grady's belief that there are cycles in history.
Thus he saw the cycle of peasant ascendancy on its necessary way in the
Ireland of his own time.

[15] The following passages from one of the essays in O'Grady's series
entitled "The Great Enchantment" in the *All Ireland Review* (1 [24 March
1900] p. 5, col. 1) are perhaps his most direct and succinct explanations
of this point:

> Aristocracies come and go like the waves of the sea; and some
> fall nobly and others ignobly.   As I write this Protestant Anglo-
> Irish aristocracy which once owned all Ireland from the centre
> to the sea, is rotting from the land in the most dismal farce-
> tragedy of all time, without one brave deed, without one brave
> word.
>
>   Our last Irish aristocracy was Catholic, intensely and fanati-
> cally Royalist and Cavalier, and compounded of elements which
> were Norman-Irish and Milesian-Irish.   They worshipped the
> Crown when the Crown had become a phantom or a ghost, and
> the god whom they worshipped was not able to save them, or
> himself.   They were defeated and exterminated.   They lost every-
> thing; but they never lost honour; and because they did not
> lose that, their overthrown was bewailed in songs and music
> which will not cease to sound for centuries yet.
>
>   'Shaun O'Dwyer o'Glanna,
>   We're worsted in the game.'
>
>   Worsted they were, for they made a fatal mistake; and they
> had to go; but they brought their honour with them, and they
> founded noble or princely families all over the Continent.
>   Who laments the destruction of our present Anglo-Irish

aristocracy? Perhaps in broad Ireland not one. They fail from the land while innumberable eyes are dry, and their fall will not be bewailed in one piteous dirge or one mournful melody.

[16]Standish James O'Grady, "Preface," in Sir Thomas Stafford, *Pacata Hibernia,* ed. Standish James O'Grady (London: Downey & Co., 1896), I, xxx.

[17]"Preface," *Pacata Hibernia,* I, lii.

[18]In his preface O'Grady described *The Flight of the Eagle* as follows:

> This tale, in spite of its title, is not a romance, but an actual historic episode, told with hardly a freer use of the historical imagination than is employed by the more popular and picturesque of our professed historians. There is, however, this difference between my methods and theirs, viz. that while they write directly, I aim at a similar result through a certain dramatization. The same method has been adopted, I think very effectively, by Carlyle, at times, in his history of Frederick the Great.

Standish James O'Grady, *The Flight of the Eagle* (London: Lawrence and Bullen, 1897), p. v.

The Flight of the Eagle does resemble Carlyle's *Frederick the Great* in the manner that O'Grady suggests. Carlyle tries to make his readers see Frederick much as a novelist tries to create a picture of his or her characters. Consider the following introductory description of Frederick:

> The man is not of godlike physiognomy, any more than of imposing stature or costume: close-shut mouth with thin lips, prominent jaws and nose, receding brow, by no means of Olympian height, head, however, is of long form, and has superlative gray eyes in it. Not what is called a beautiful man; nor yet, by all appearance, what is called happy. On the contrary, the face bears evidence of many sorrows, as they are termed, of much hard labour done in this world; and seems to anticipate nothing but more still coming. Quiet stoicism, capable enough of what joy there were, but not expecting any worth mention; great unconscious and some conscious pride, well tempered with a cheery mockery of humor,—are written on that old face; which carries its chin well forward, in spite of the slight stoop about the neck; snuffy nose rather flung into the air, under its old cocked-hat, like an old snuffy lion on the watch; and such a pair of eyes as no

man or lion or lynx of that Century bore elsewhere, according
to all the testimony we have.

Thomas Carlyle, *History of Frederick the Great*, Vol. I, Vol. XII of *The
Works of Thomas Carlyle* (New York: Scribner's, 1897), p. 2.

[19]W. B. Yeats disagreed with O'Grady's depiction of Perrott. In
writing about the earlier version of the story, *Red Hugh's Captivity*, Yeats
says:

> [Love of force] is a fruit of a good quality, but none the less
> irritating at times, as when, for instance, Mr. Standish O'Grady
> in his incomparable monograph, *Red Hugh*, writes many pages
> to glorify the extremely murderous Sir John Perrot [sic].

Letters to the New Island (1934; rpt. Cambridge, Mass.: Havard University
Press, 1970), pp. 109-110.

[20]This is the political strategy of *All Ireland*. Cf. pp. 169-171.

[21]*The Flight of the Eagle*, p. 11.

[22]*The Flight of the Eagle*, pp. 156-157.

[23]*The Flight of the Eagle*, p. 255. Cf. Austin Clarke's statement in
A Penny in the Clouds (London: Routledge and Kegan Paul, 1968), p. 110,
on this passage: the last chapter of James Stephens' *The Crock of Gold*
"owes much to the vision of Red Hugh O'Donnell on Slieve Gullion in . . .
The Flight of the Earls [sic]."

[24]*The Flight of the Eagle*, p. 257.

[25]*The Flight of the Eagle*, p. 272.

[26]Cf. Standish James O'Grady, Letter to T. Fisher Unwin, 13 Feb.
[1895], Henry W. and Albert A. Berg Collection, The New York Public
Library, Astor, Lenox and Tilden Foundations. In discussing *The Chain of
Gold* with his publisher, O'Grady writes: "Even so great an artist as Wilkie
Collins adopted this mode of narration which possesses great advantages
from the point of view of verisimilitude, reality and close contact with the
facts. I adopted it in "Lost on Du-Corrig" & was not censured by a single
critic."

[27]Standish James O'Grady, *The Chain of Gold* (Dublin: Talbot, [n.
d.]), p. 4.

[28]Cf. pp. 11-12.

[29]The father of the two lost boys is a Church of Ireland clergyman like
O'Grady's father, and the boys' adventures resemble the descriptions of
O'Grady's childhood given by his son in *Standish James O'Grady: the Man
and the Writer*, pp. 24-28.

[30]*The Chain of Gold*, p. 263.

[31] *The Chain of Gold,* p. 264.

[32] *The Chain of Gold,* p. 264.

[33] Cf. pp. 83-85.

[34] Cf. pp. 118-119.

[35] *The Chain of Gold,* p. 247.

[36] O'Grady makes an important addition to Crusoe's ethic: Ned is more concerned than Jack with making the cave beautiful, and in fact he builds an arbour for both of them. In giving Ned this positive characteristic, O'Grady adds a purely aesthetic element to the strict Puritan work ethic that Defoe's Crusoe embodies, and to O'Grady's mind this probably represented a specifically Irish contribution to that ethic. O'Grady does not state that "Ned's Aesthetics" (the title of a chapter) are peculiarly Irish, but such an assignation fits with his omnipresent emphasis on the bardic legacy.

[37] *The Chain of Gold,* p. 103.

[38] Perhaps from the Aran Islands although O'Grady does not name the islands.

[39] *The Chain of Gold,* p. 293.

[40] Cf. Lyons, p. 207.

[41] He wanted to include Scotland in his All Ireland theory on the basis that the Scots in the bardic literature were indistinguishable from the Irish. He called the Scots "Irishmen through and through—of a purer race than ours, and who speak the Irish tongue." *All Ireland* (Dublin: Sealy, Bryers, and Walker; London: T. Fisher Unwin, 1898), p. 128.

[42] *All Ireland,* p. 142.

[43] *All Ireland,* p. 159.

[44] George Russell [AE], "Literature and Life: Standish O'Grady," *The Irish Statesman,* 10 (26 May 1928), 231. (An aside: AE's words reveal how well he knew O'Grady's works.)

[45] *All Ireland,* p. 72.

[46] *All Ireland,* p. 57.

[47] Standish James O'Grady, "Self-Reliance," *All Ireland Review,* 6 July 1901, p. 190, col. 1.

[48] Standish James O'Grady, *All Ireland Review,* 20 Sept. 1902, p. 457, col. 2.

[49] *All Ireland Review,* 20 Sept. 1902, p. 457, col. 2.

[50] Standish James O'Grady, Letter to John Quinn, 28 Nov. 1906, John Quinn Memorial Collection, Manuscripts and Archives Division, The New York Public Library, Astor, Lenox and Tilden Foundations.

[51] Ernest Boyd reports that O'Grady first advocated communism in *The Irish Peasant.* *The Peasant* was apparently preceded by a newspaper with that title. From what I can tell, *The Irish Peasant* was suppressed by

the Catholic Bishop of Dublin in 1907, and O'Grady may well have written for it in that year. Cf. Standish James O'Grady, *Selected Essays and Passages*, ed. Ernest A. Boyd (New York: Frederick A. Stokes, 1918), pp. 16-17.

[52] Cf., e. g., Ruskin's explanation of "Old Communism":

> First, it [Old Communism] means that everybody must work
> in common, and do common or simple work for his dinner. That
> much, perhaps, you thought you knew?—but you did not think
> we Communists of the old school knew it also?

Fors Clavigera, Vol. I, Vol. XXVII of *The Works of John Ruskin*, ed. E. T. Cook and Alexander Wedderburn (London: George Allen; New York: Longmans, Green, 1907), p. 117.

[53] [W. B.] Y[eats], quoted in Standish James O'Grady, "The Great Enchantment," *All Ireland Review*, 22 Sept. 1900, p. 4, col. 1.

[54] Standish James O'Grady, "The Great Enchantment," *The Peasant*, 20 June 1908, p. 2, col. 1.

[55] Cf. pp. 126-128.

[56] Standish James O'Grady, "The Making of Nations," *The Peasant*, 5 Sept. 1908, p. 7, col. 1.

[57] Standish James O'Grady, "Life and Liberty: Letters to a Dublin Clerk," *The Peasant*, 12 Dec. 1908, p. 5, col. 5.

[58] "Life and Liberty: Letters to a Dublin Clerk," *The Peasant*, 12 Dec. 1908, p. 5, col. 5.

[59] Standish James O'Grady, "Life and Liberty: an Explanation," *The Irish Nation*, 2 Jan. 1909, p. 5, col. 1-2. O'Grady speaks as if he is a Christian. He seems to have been one when it suited his purposes. In a 1918 letter to John Quinn he described his religion:

> I think my own religion is no more than this: "We come from
> God and we return to God. Therefore bear up stoutly and hold
> hard and steer straight forward, and deil take all whimpering and
> repining."
>   Not much of a religion, indeed, but I find it suits myself and
> seems to hold good for myself in all weather.

9 Nov. 1918, John Quinn Memorial Collection, Manuscripts and Archives Division, The New York Public Library, Astor, Lenox and Tilden Foundations.

[60] Standish James O'Grady, "Life and Liberty: Letters to a Dublin Clerk," *The Irish Nation*, 16 Jan. 1909, p. 5, col. 4.

[61] Ernest A. Boyd, "Introduction," in Standish James O'Grady, *Selected Essays and Passages*, p. 17.

[62] Cf., e. g., O'Grady's essay, "An Irish Sunrise," *The Irish Review*, 3 (1913), 462-469.

[63] Standish James O'Grady, "Life and Liberty: Letters to a Dublin Clerk," *The Irish Nation*, 16 Jan. 1909, p. 5, col. 4.

[64] Standish James O'Grady, Letter to W. B. Yeats, 24 April 1926, Vol. 7, Reel I, pp. 192-193, The W. B. Yeats Archives, State University of New York at Stony Brook.

[65] Charles Fourier, *Design for Utopia: Selected Writings of Charles Fourier* (1901; rpt. New York: Schocken Books, 1971), p. 17.

[66] Standish James O'Grady, "Chap. 6: 'Children and Animals,' " TS, pp. 5-6, The Standish De Courcey O'Grady Collection.

[67] "Chap. 6: 'Children and Animals,' " p. 11.

[68] Standish James O'Grady, "Part II: Nature & Man; Chap. 1: Natura Naturans," TS, p. 3, The Standish De Courcey O'Grady Collection.

[69] Standish James O'Grady, Letter to W. B. Yeats, 24 April 1926, Vo. 7, Reel I, p. 196, The W. B. Yeats Archives, State University of New York at Stony Brook.

[70] Standish James O'Grady, Letter to W. B. Yeats, 12 Dec. 1900, in *Letters to W. B. Yeats*, eds, Richard J. Finneran, *et al.*, (New York: Columbia University Press, 1977), I, 76-77.

[71] Standish James O'Grady, Letter to W. B. Yeats, 12 Dec. 1900, in *Letters to W. B. Yeats*, I, 77.

[72] Standish James O'Grady, Untitled reply to W. B. Yeats, *All Ireland Review*, 1 Dec. 1900, p. 6, col. 1-2. In *Yeats and the Beginning of the Irish Renaissance* (Ithaca, NY: Cornell University Press, 1970), Phillip Marcus argues that Yeats, not O'Grady, ought to be considered the "Father of the Irish Renaissance." O'Grady's reply to Yeats here illuminates the differences in what both men set out to achieve.

[73] W. B. Yeats, *The Variorum Edition of the Poems of W. B. Yeats*, eds. Peter Allt and Russell K. Alspach (New York: Macmillan, 1957), p. 813.

[74] *Variorum Yeats*, p. 814.

[75] George Russell [AE], "Standish O'Grady: a Tribute," in Standish James O'Grady, *The Coming of Cuculain* (Dublin: Talbot; London: T. Fisher Unwin, [n. d.]), pp. x-xi.

Bibliography

I. *Books and Articles by Standish James O'Grady*
(in chronological order)

[Clive, Arthur] . "Shelley's 'Prometheus Unbound.' " *The Gentleman's Magazine*, NS 12 (1874), 421-437.

—. "Boswell and His Enemies." *The Gentleman's Magazine*, NS 13 (1874), 68-77.

—. "*Kottabos.*" *Dublin University Magazine*, 84 (1874), 565-579.

—. "Stone Worship: Ireland." *Dublin University Magazine*, 85 (1875), 60-74.

—. "The Trammels of Poetic Expression." *The Gentleman's Magazine*, NS 14 (1875), 184-197.

—. "Lord Chesterfield." *Dublin University Magazine*, 85 (1875), 52-66.

—. "Druidism." *Dublin University Magazine*, 86 (1875), 513-532.

—. "Walt Whitman, the Poet of Joy." *The Gentleman's Magazine*, NS 15 (1875), 704-716.

—. "St. Patrick." *Dublin University Magazine*, 87 (1876), 257-271.

—. "Irish Archaeology." *Dublin University Magazine*, 88 (1876), 641-651.

—. "The Milesian Invasion of Ireland." *Dublin University Magazine,* 89 (1877), 673-682.

"The Falstaff of Ossian." *Belgravia,* 36 (1878), 203-210.

History of Ireland: the Heroic Period. Vol. I. 1878: rpt. New York: Lemma, 1970.

Early Bardic Literature, Ireland. 1879; rpt. New York: Lemma, 1970.

"The Irish Small Farmer." *Fortnightly Review,* NS 27 (1880), 568-579.

History of Ireland: Cuculain and His Contemporaries. Vol. II. 1880; rpt. New York: Lemma, 1970.

History of Ireland: Critical and Philosophical. Vol. I. London: Sampson Low; Dublin: E. Ponsonby, 1881.

The Crisis in Ireland. Dublin: E. Ponsonby: London: Simpkin and Marshall, 1882.

Cuculain: an Epic. London: Sampson Low, Searle, Marston and Rivington; Dublin: E. Ponsonby, 1882.

"Irish Conservatism and Its Outlooks." *Dublin University Review,* (1885), 4-15.

Rev. of *Anecdotes of the Connaught Circuit, from Its Foundation in 1604 to Close upon the Present Time,* by Oliver J. Burke. *Dublin University Review,* 1 (1885), 316-317.

"Carlyle as a Political Teacher." *Fortnightly Review,* NS 38 (1885), 516-530.

Toryism and the Tory Democracy. London: Chapman and Hall, 1886.

Red Hugh's Captivity. London: Ward and Downey, 1889.

"The Last Kings of Ireland." *English Historical Review,* 4 (1889), 286-303.

Finn and His Companions. London: T. Fisher Unwin, 1892.

The Bog of Stars. 1893; rpt. Freeport, NY: Books for Libraries Press, 1973.

"Scintillae Hibernicae; Parnell—Some Personal Reminiscences." *The Daily Express* [Dublin], 18 Dec. 1893.

The Story of Ireland. London: Methuen, 1894.

The Coming of Cuculain. London: Methuen, 1894.

Lost on Du-Corrig. London, Paris and Milbourne: Cassell, 1894.

The Chain of Gold. London: T. Fisher Unwin, 1895.

"I Give my Heart to Thee," and "Lough Bray." In *Dublin Verses by Members of Trinity College.* Ed. H. A. Hinkson. London: Elkin Mathews; Dublin: Hodges, Figgis & Co., 1895, pp. 31-32 & p. 69.

"The New Irish Movement." *The New Review,* 15 (1895), 666-676.

In the Wake of King James. London: J. M. Dent; Philadelphia: J. B. Lippincott, 1896.

Ulrick the Ready. London: Downey, 1896.

"The New United Ireland." *The New Review,* 16 (1897), 129-142.

"Ireland; the New Irish Movement." *Fortnightly Review,* NS 81 (1897), 170-179.

The Flight of the Eagle. London: Lawrence and Bullen, 1897.

"Imagination in History." *The New Review,* 17 (1897), 657-665.

All Ireland.   Dublin: Sealy, Bryers and Walker; London: T. Fisher Unwin, 1898.

"The End of Black Donal."   *English Illustrated Magazine,* 18 (1897-1898), 603-607.

"The Awakening of the Ultonians."   *The Irish Homestead,* 4 [Christmas Supplement] (1898), 2-4.

"The Fight at the Ford."   *Kilkenny Moderator,* (Christmas-tide) 1898, p. 9, cols. 2-3; p. 10, cols. 1-3.

"A Wet Day."   *The Irish Homestead,* 5 [Christmas Supplement] (1899), 9.

[Netterville, Luke] . *The Queen of the World.* London: Lawrence and Bullen, 1900.

Mr. Goodenough.   All Ireland Review, 24 Feb. 1900, p. 3; 3 Mar. 1900, p. 3; 10 Mar. 1900, p. 3; 17 Mar. 1900, p. 3; 24 Mar. 1900, p. 3; 31 Mar. 1900, p. 3; 7 Apr. 1900, p. 6; 14 Apr. 1900, p. 6; 21 Apr. 1900, p. 6; 28 Apr. 1900, p. 6; 5 May 1900, p. 5; 19 May 1900, p. 5; 26 May 1900, pp. 2-3; 2 June 1900, p. 5; 9 June 1900, p. 5; 16 June 1900, p. 5; 23 June 1900, p. 3; 30 June 1900, p. 4; 7 July 1900, p. 4; 14 July 1900, p. 4; 21 July 1900, p. 4; 28 July 1900, p. 4; 11 Aug. 1900, p. 3; 18 Aug. 1900, p. 3; 25 Aug. 1900, p. 6; 1 Sept. 1900, p. 6.

"The Great Enchantment."   In *Ideals in Ireland.*   Ed. Lady Isabella Augusta Gregory.   1901; rpt. New York: Lemma, 1973.

In the Gates of the North.   Kilkenny: Standish O'Grady, 1901.

Hugh Roe O'Donnell.   Belfast: Nelson and Knox, 1902.

"Hugh O'Neill."   *Ulster Journal of Archaeology,* 14 (1903), 1-6.

"The Battle of the Curlew Mountains."   *The Gael,* 22 (1903), 201-214.

"On Reading the Fragments of Early Greek Lyric Poetry." In *Echoes from Kottabos*. Eds. R. Y. Tyrell and Sir Edward Sullivan. London: E. Grant Richards, 1906, p. 15.

The Masque of Finn. Dublin: Sealy, Bryers and Walker, 1907.

"The Wisdom of the Ant." *The Peasant and Irish Ireland*, 25 Apr. 1908, p. [5], cols. 2-4.

"The Great Enchantment." *The Peasant and Irish Ireland*, 2 May 1908, p. [4], col. 5; p. [5], col. 1; 9 May 1908, p. [5], cols. 2-4; 16 May 1908, p. [5], cols. 3-4; 23 May 1908, p. [5], cols. 4-5; 30 May 1908, p. [5], cols. 4-5; 6 June 1908, p. [5], cols. 3-4; 20 June 1908, p. [2], cols. 1-3.

"About Paradises: A Conversation." *The Peasant and Irish Ireland*, 16 May 1908, p. [2], cols. 1-2; 28 May 1908, p. [3], cols. 2-3; 30 May 1908, p. [3], cols. 2-3; 6 June 1908, p. 3, cols. 2-4; 20 June 1908, p. [5], cols. 1-3; 7 June 1908, p. [6], col. 4.

"About Getting On." *The Peasant and Irish Ireland*, 27 June 1908, p. [5], cols. 3-4; 4 July 1908, p. [5], cols. 4-5; 18 July 1908, p. [5], cols. 2-3; 25 July 1908, p. [5], cols. 3.

Note to "Wealth in Lavish Floods: Wonders of the New Gardening," by W. Beach Thomas. *The Peasant and Irish Ireland*, 25 July 1908, p. [2], cols. 4-5.

"About the Making of Nations." *The Peasant and Irish Ireland*, 1 Aug. 1908, p. [5], cols. 1-3; 8 Aug. 1908, p. [5], cols. 1-2; 15 Aug. 1908, p. [5], cols. 1-3; 22 Aug. 1908, p. [6], cols. 1-3; 29 Aug. 1908, p. [5], cols. 1-3; 5 Sept. 1908, p. [7], col. 1.

"Liberty and Life: Letters to a Dublin Clerk." *The Peasant and Irish Ireland*, 19 Sept. 1908, p. [2], cols. 1-3; 26 Sept. 1908, p. [5], cols. 1-3; 10 Oct. 1908, p. [5], cols. 1-3; 17 Oct. 1908, p. [5], cols. 1-2; 24 Oct. 1908, p. [5], cols. 1-3; 31 Oct. 1908, p. [5], cols. 1-3; 7 Nov. 1908, p. [5], col. 2; 14 Nov. 1908, p. [4], col. 5; p. [5], cols. 1-4, 21 Nov. 1908, p. [4], col. 5; p. [5], cols. 1-4; 28 Nov. 1908,

p. [5], cols. 1-5; 5 Dec. 1908, p. [5], cols. 2-4; 12 Dec. 1908, p. [5], cols. 4-5; p. [8], col. 5; 19 Dec. 1908, p. [1], cols. 4-5; p. [5], cols. 4-5.

"The Holy Family: Christmas 1908." *The Peasant and Irish Ireland*, 26 Dec. 1908, p. [5], cols. 2-4.

"Life and Liberty: An Explanation." *The Irish Nation and the Peasant*, 2 Jan. 1909, p. [5], cols. 1-2.

"Life and Liberty: Letters to a Dublin Clerk." *The Irish Nation and the Peasant*, 16 Jan. 1909, p. 5, cols. 2-4; 23 Jan. 1909, p. 5, cols. 1-2; 30 Jan. 1909, p. 5, cols. 1-4.

"The First Irish Commune of the New Order." *The Irish Nation and the Peasant*, 29 Jan. 1910, p. 5, col. 4; 5 Feb. 1910, p. 5, cols. 3-4; 26 Feb. 1910, p. 5, cols. 3-4; 5 Mar. 1910, p. 5, col. 4; p. 8, col. 4; 19 Mar. 1910, p. 5, cols. 2-3; 26 Mar. 1910, p. 5, cols. 2-3; 13 Apr. 1910, p. 5, col. 4; p. 8, cols. 2-4; 21 May 1910, p. 5, col. 4; p. 8, col. 4.

"An Event of World History." *The Irish Review*, 1 (1911), 161-164.

"The Silent Race." *The Irish Review*, 1 (1911), 313-321.

"Paganism—Greek and Irish." *The Irish Review*, 2 (1912), 57-67.

"Sun and Wind: about Heroes and the Heroic." *The New Age*, NS 13 (1913), 261-263.

"An Irish Sunrise." *The Irish Review*, 3 (1913), 462-469.

The Departure of Dermot. Dublin: Talbot, 1917.

Selected Essays and Passages. Ed. Ernest A. Boyd. New York: Frederick A. Stokes, 1918.

"British Record in Ireland Examined." *Christian Science Monitor,* 14 Sept. 1918, p. 6, cols. 1-3; 16 Sept. 1918, p. 8, cols. 1-2; 17 Sept. 1918, p. 7, cols. 1-2.

The Triumph and Passing of Cuculain. Dublin: Talbot Press; London: T. Fisher Unwin, [1920].

"Foreward." In *Essays*, by John Todhunter. London: Elkin Mathews, 1920, pp. 5-10.

Eulogy for T. W. Rolleston. *The Irish Times*, [6?] Dec. 1920.

"Poems of Standish O'Grady." In *Standish O'Grady: the Man and the Writer*, by Hugh Art O'Grady. Dublin and Cork: Talbot, 1929, pp. 49-62.

Eadar Muir Is Tir [Lost on Du-Corrig]. Tr. Niall O Domhnaill. Dublin: Oific Dioita failleacain Riaitais, 1935.

II. *Works Edited by Standish James O'Grady*
(in chronological order)

[Clive, Arthur]. *Scintilla Shelleiana: Shelley's Attitude towards Religion.* Dublin: William McGee; London: Simpkin, Marshall, 1875.

Pacata Hibernia; or, a History of the Wars in Ireland during the Reign of Queen Elizabeth, Especially within the Province of Munster under the Government of Sir George Carew, and Compiled by his Direction and Appointment by Sir Thomas Stafford. London: Downey, 1896, 2 vols.

Kilkenny Moderator, 1898-1900. [Note: O'Grady probably wrote most of this newspaper].

All Ireland Review. Kilkenny and Dublin, 6 Jan. 1900—Jan. 1907. [Note: O'Grady himself wrote about one-half to two-thirds of each issue of this weekly publication].

III. *Published Letters of Standish James O'Grady*
(in chronological order)

"Irish Land Question." Letter. *The Times* (London), 24 Nov. 1880, p. 6.

Letter to Walt Whitman. 5 Oct. 1881. In Horace Traubel, *Walt Whitman in Camden.* New York: Rowman and Littlefield, 1961. Vol. I, pp. 399-400.

"How the Irish State Papers are Edited." Letter. *Athenaeum,* 97 (1891), 568-569.

"Irish Literature and Mr. Dowden." Letter. *Daily Express* [Dublin], 28 Jan. 1895, p. 5, col. 8, p. 6, col. 1.

"Literature in Ireland." Letter. *Daily Express* [Dublin], 2 Feb. 1895, p. 5, col. 8.

Letter to W. B. Yeats. 16 July 1899. In *Letters to W. B. Yeats.* Ed. Richard J. Finneran, *et al.* New York: Columbia University Press, 1977. Vol. I, pp. 57-58.

Letter to W. B. Yeats. 12 Dec. 1900. In *Letters to W. B. Yeats.* Ed. Richard J. Finneran, *et al.* New York: Columbia University Press, 1977. Vol. I, pp. 76-77.

Letter to W. B. Yeats. 12 Dec. 1900. In *Letters to W. B. Yeats.* Ed. Richard J. Finneran, *et al.* New York: Columbia University Press, 1977. Vol. I, p. 77.

"The 'Cooking' of Irish History: A Letter to T. Kettle." *St. Stephen's,* 2 (Dec. 1903), 5-6.

Letter. *The Peasant and Irish Ireland,* 16 May 1908, p. 5, col. 3.

"Central." Letter. *The Irish Nation and the Peasant,* 6 Feb. 1909, p. 5, col. 4.

"Agriculture and the War." Letter. *The Irish Times,* [29?] June 1915, p. 5, col. [5?]; p. 6, col. 4.

"The Exclusion of Ulster." Letter. *The Irish Times,* 2 July 1916.

Letter to W. B. Yeats. Jan. 1924. In *Letters to W. B. Yeats.* Ed. Richard J. Finneran, *et al.* New York: Columbia University Press, 1977. Vol. II, pp. 445-446.

IV. *Unpublished Letters of Standish James O'Grady*

A. Henry W. and Albert A. Berg Collection
The New York Public Library
Astor, Lenox, and Tilden Foundations

Letter to Lady Isabella Augusta Gregory. 10 Jan. 1898.

Letter to Lady Isabella Augusta Gregory. 16 Aug. 1898.

Letter to Lady Isabella Augusta Gregory. 16 Apr. 1899.

Letter to Lady Isabella Augusta Gregory. 20 June 1899.

Letter to Lady Isabella Augusta Gregory. 24 June 1899.

Letter to Lady Isabella Augusta Gregory. 14 July [1899].

Letter to Lady Isabella Augusta Gregory. 1 Mar. [1900].

Letter to Lady Isabella Augusta Gregory. 7 Mar. [1900].

Letter to Lady Isabella Augusta Gregory. 8 July [1900].

Letter to Lady Isabella Augusta Gregory. 15 July 1900.

Postcard to Lady Isabella Augusta Gregory. 14 Nov. 1900.

Postcard to Lady Isabella Augusta Gregory. 2 Dec. 1900.

Letter to Lady Isabella Augusta Gregory. 14 Jan. [1902].

Letter to Lady Isabella Augusta Gregory. 1 June [1902].

Letter to Lady Isabella Augusta Gregory. 25 July [1904].

Letter to Lady Isabella Augusta Gregory, 26 Dec. [1904?].

Letter to Algernon Charles Swinburne. 19 Jan. [n. y.].

Letter to T. Fisher Unwin. 19 Jan. [1892].

Letter to T. Fisher Unwin. 13 Feb. [1895].

B. John Quinn Memorial Collection
Manuscripts and Archives Division
The New York Public Library
Astor, Lenox, and Tilden Foundations

Postcard to John Quinn. 17 Nov. 1904.

Letter to John Quinn. 25 [?] 1904.

Letter to John Quinn. 21 Mar. 1905.

Letter to John Quinn. 13 Apr. 1905.

Letter to John Quinn. 11 May 1915.

Letter to John Quinn. 16 June 1915.

Letter to John Quinn. 18 Sept. 1915.

Letter to John Quinn. 13 Apr. 1905.

Letter to John Quinn. 11 May 1915.

Letter to John Quinn. 16 June 1915.

Letter to John Quinn. 28 Nov. 1906.

Letter to John Quinn. 10 Sept. 1907.

Letter to John Quinn. 7 Jan. 1908.

Letter to John Quinn. 15 Mar. 1914.

Letter to John Quinn. 26 Feb. [1916].

Letter to John Quinn. 10 Oct. 1917.

Letter to John Quinn. [?] Mar. [1918].

Letter to John Quinn. 27 Oct. 1918.

Letter to John Quinn. 9 Nov. [1918].

Letter to John Quinn. 10 Oct. 1917.

C.` Charles E. Feinberg Collection

Letter to Walt Whitman. 8 Mar. 1892.

D. James Augustine Healy Collection
Colby College Library

Letter to Miss [Ella] Young. 26 Dec. [?].

E. Special Collections
The Stanford University Libraries

Photocopy of Letter to Mr. Colles. 24 Mar. [1893].

Photocopy of Letter to Mr. Colles. 11 Apr. [1893].

Photocopy of Letter to Mr. Colles. [received 11 May 1893].

Photocopy of Letter to Mr. Colles. [received 13 May 1893].

Photocopy of Letter to Mr. Colles. 5 Jun. [1893].

Letter to Mr. Colles. 15 Jun. [1893].

Photocopy of Letter to Mr. Colles. 11 July [1893].

Photocopy of Letter to Mr. Colles. 8 Dec. [1893].

Photocopy of Letter to Mr. Colles. 20 Dec. [1893].

Photocopy of Letter to Mr. Colles. 22 Dec. [1893].

Photocopy of Letter to Mr. Colles. 10 Jan. [1894].

Letter to Mr. Colles. 11 Apr. [?].

Letter to "Dear Manager." 31 Dec. [n. y.].

Letter to Mr. Moores. 11 Jan. [1894].

Letter to George Russell [AE]. 5 Sept. [n. y.].

Photocopy of Letter to "Dear Sir." 13 Jan. 1893.

Letter to "Dear Sir." 6 Feb. [1893].

Letter to "Dear Sir." 9 Mar. [1893].

Photocopy of Letter to "Dear Sir." 15 Aug. [1893].

Photocopy of Letter to "Dear Sir." 20 Sept. [1893].

Letter to "Dear Sir." 2 Apr. [1895].

F. Hutzler Collection
The Milton S. Eisenhower Library
The Johns Hopkins University

Letter to John Stuart Mill. 9 Jan. [1869].

G. The William Butler Yeats Archives
State University of New York at Stony Brook

Photocopy of Letter to Lady Isabella Augusta Gregory. 14 Dec.
     [n. y.]. Vol. 7, Reel I, pp. 179-180.

Photocopy of Letter to W. B. Yeats. 9 Mar. [1926]. Vol. 7,
     Reel I, pp. 192-193.

Photocopy of Letter to W. B. Yeats. 24 April 1926. Vol. 7,
Reel I, p. 196.

H. National Library of Ireland

1. MS. 10,043

Letter to Edmund Downey. 20 May 1895.

Letter to Edmund Downey. 22 Jan. [1895].

Letter to Edmund Downey. 24 Mar. [1895].

Letter to Edmund Downey. 27 June [1895].

Letter to Edmund Downey. 26 Dec. [n. y.].

Letter to Edmund Downey. 17 Dec. [n. y.].

Letter to Edmund Downey. 15 Dec. [n. y.].

Letter to Edmund Downey. 15 Dec. [n. y.].

Letter to Edmund Downey. 14 Dec. [n. y.].

Letter to Edmund Downey. 4 Feb. [n. y.].

Letter to Edmund Downey. 27 Jan. [n. y.].

Letter to Edmund Downey. 13 Jan. [n. y.].

Letter to Edmund Downey. 26 Jan. [n. y.].

Letter to Edmund Downey. 26 Apr. [n. y.].

Letter to Edmund Downey. 5 Feb. [n. y.].

Letter to Edmund Downey. 15 Feb. [n. y.].

Letter to Edmund Downey. 22 Feb. [n. y.].

Letter to Edmund Downey. 25 Mar. 1896.

Letter to Edmund Downey. 1 Apr. [n. y.].

Letter to Edmund Downey. 10 Dec. [n. y.].

Letter to Edmund Downey. 26 Feb. [n. y.].

Letter to Edmund Downey. 10 May [n. y.].

Letter to Edmund Downey. 21 Mar. [n. y.].

Letter to Edmund Downey. 19 Mar. [n. y.].

Letter to Edmund Downey. 3 June [n. y.].

Letter to Edmund Downey. 6 July [n. y.].

Letter to Edmund Downey. [n. d.].

Letter to Edmund Downey. 5 June [n. y.].

Letter to Edmund Downey. 9 Sept. [n. y.].

Letter to Edmund Downey. 24 Mar. [n. y.].

Letter to Edmund Downey. 7 Jan. [n. y.].

Letter to Edmund Downey. [?] Oct. [n. y.].

Letter to Edmund Downey. 8 May [n. y.].

Letter to Edmund Downey. 4 Mar. [n. y.].

Letter to Edmund Downey. 27 May [n. y.].

2. MS. 15,713

Letter to Alfred Percival Graves. 2 Aug. [n. y.].

Letter to Miss [?] Doyle. 15 Aug. [n. y.].

Letter to Mr. Colles. 23 Nov. [1894].

Letter to "Dear Sir." 3 Sept. [n. y.].

3. MS. 8600

Letter to Mr. Gwynne. 3 Feb. [n. y.].

4. MS. 8001

Letter to John O'Leary. 20 Dec. [n. y.].

Postcard to John O'Leary. 18 Sept. [n. y.].

Letter to John O'Leary. [?] Sept. [n. y.].

I. Special Collections
Kenneth Spencer Research Library
University of Kansas

Letter to Mr. Colles. MS. P401 Ba: 1. [received 2 Jan. 1893].

Letter to Mr. Colles. MS. P401 Ba: 2. 24 Aug. [1893].

Letter to Mr. Colles. MS. P401 Ba: 3. 9 May [1894].

Letter to William Morris. MS. P401 Bb: 1. 1 June [c. 189?].

Letter to Edward Martyn. MS. P401 Bc: 1. 2 July [1900 or 1901].

Letter to Edward Martyn. MS. P401 Bc: 2. 6 July [1900 or 1901].

Letter to "Dear Sir" [Martyn?]. MS. P401 Bd: 1. 28 Sept. [c. 189?].

Postcard to Patrick Kelly. MS. 120 C: 1. 22 Feb. 1928.

V. *Unpublished Manuscripts of Standish James O'Grady*

A. Special Collections
Kenneth Spencer Research Library
University of Kansas

Autobiographical Sketch. [c. 1892]. 5 pp. MS. P401A.

B. The Standish De Courcey O'Grady Collection
(in possession of Edward A. Hagan)

Copy of "An Event of World History" torn out of *The Irish Review*, with pencil corrections and four additional pages in holograph. "Chap. 3" is written above the title of the article.

The Departure of Dermot. TS. 13 pp.

Render to Caesar: Social Essays. O'Grady's columns in *The Peasant* and *The Irish Nation*, clipped from the newspapers and pasted to 8 1/2 x 13 sheets of paper [apparently from the ledger book of the *All Ireland Review*]. Numerous corrections of the newspaper articles and several whole sheets have been written in O'Grady's own hand. Material was apparently assembled in preparation for publication in book form. 123 pp.

"Chap. 3: Air & Light & the Heroic." TS. 12 pp.

"Chap. V: 'Arcadia.' " TS, with corrections in O'Grady's hand. 14 pp.

"A Short Novel up to Date." TS. 12 pp.

"Chap. 4: A Welcome Visitor." TS, with corrections in O'Grady's hand.

"Chap. 6: 'Children and Animals.' " TS, with corrections in O'Grady's hand. 13 pp.

"Chap. 5: 'Child, Teacher, and Book.' " TS. 1 p. Title page only.

"Part II: Nature & Man; Chap. 1: Natura Naturans." TS, with corrections in O'Grady's hand. 26 pp.

"Sun and Wind; Chapter I: An Irish Sunrise." TS, with corrections in O'Grady's hand. 14 pp.

"Primitive Aryan City; Age of Innocence." TS, with corrections in O'Grady's hand. 16 pp. [Also another copy of this TS with a larger number of corrections and entitled "Chap. 12; A Picture."].

"Chap. 11; 'Greek Women.' " TS, with corrections in O'Grady's hand. 10 pp.

"Chap. 10: Homer's Men." TS, with corrections in O'Grady's hand. 19 pp.

"Chap. IV: The Greek Polis." TS, with corrections in O'Grady's hand. 17 pp.

"Chap. III: Nations and Nations." TS, with corrections in O'Grady's hand. 20 pp.

"Chap. 2: 'The Great Psalm.' " TS, with corrections in O'Grady's hand. 11 pp.

"Chap. 4: 'A Little Epic and a Small Hero.' " TS, with corrections in O'Grady's hand. 12 pp.

Render to Caesar: The Social Problem from an Irish Point of View. Title page, followed by a dedication to Ellen, Countess of Desart, and a six page "Introduction to English Readers."

"To the Leaders of Our Working People." Newspaper columns pasted to pages of a notebook with corrections in O'Grady's hand in the margins. Place of publication of newspaper columns unknown, but published sometime after 1911. 44 pp.

"To the Leaders of Our Working People." TS, with corrections in O'Grady's hand. 8 pp.

C. Jeanne R. Foster-William M. Murphy Collection of Irish and Anglo-Irish Miscellanea

"Chap. 7: 'Arcadia.' " TS, with corrections in an unknown hand [O'Grady's?]. 15 pp.

VI. *Published Bibliographies*

Marcus, Phillip L. "Bibliography." In *Standish O'Grady*. Lewisburg, PA: Bucknell University Press, 1970.

McKenna, John R. "The Standish O'Grady Collection at Colby College." *Colby Library Quarterly*, 4 (1958), 291-303. [Note: Most of the letters listed as the property of Colby are not in fact located there].

O'Hegarty, Patrick Sarsfield. *A Bibliography of Books Written by Standish O'Grady*. Dublin: Printed for the author by A. Thom & Co., 1930. Also published anonymously as: "Bibliographies of Irish Authors: No. 2. Standish O'Grady." *Dublin Magazine*, NS 5 (1930), 49-56.

"Standish O'Grady." *The Complete Catalogue of the Library of John Quinn*. New York: Anderson Galleries, 1924. Vol. II, pp. 721-726.

VII. *General Bibliography*

Alspach, Russell K. *Irish Poetry from the English Invasion to 1798*. Philadelphia: University of Pennsylvania Press, 1959.

—. "Some Sources of Yeats's *The Wanderings of Oisin*." *PMLA*, 58 (1943), 849-866.

Arnold, Matthew. *On the Study of Celtic Literature and Other Essays.* London and Toronto: J. M. Dent; New York: E. P. Dutton, 1910.

Atkinson, Ernest G. "How the Irish State Papers are Edited." Letter. *Athenaeum,* 97 (1891), 606.

Bigger, Francis Joseph. " 'Hugh Roe O'Donnell': an Irish Historical Masque." *Ulster Journal of Archaeology,* 2nd Series, 8 (1902), 172.

Blodgett, Harold. *Walt Whitman in England.* New York: Russell and Russell, 1973.

Boyd, Ernest A. *Appreciations and Depreciations.* New York: John Lane, 1918.

—. *Ireland's Literary Renaissance.* New York: Alfred A. Knopf, 1922.

Brown, Malcolm. *The Politics of Irish Literature.* Seattle: University of Washington Press, 1972.

[Cara]. "Mr. Standish O'Grady and an Irish Renaissance." Letter. *The Peasant and Irish Ireland,* 3 Oct. 1908, p. 2, cols. 3-4.

Carlyle, Thomas. "Boswell's Life of Johnson." In *Critical and Miscellaneous Essays.* Vol. XXVIII of *The Works of Thomas Carlyle.* New York: Scribner's, 1899.

—. "Burns." In *Critical and Miscellaneous Essays.* Vol. I, Vol. XII of *Carlyle's Complete Works.* Boston: Dana Estes and Charles E. Lauriat, 1884, pp. 256-314.

—. "Chartism." In *Critical and Miscellaneous Essays.* Vol. IV, Vol. XVI of *Carlyle's Complete Works.* Boston: Dana Estes and Charles E. Lauriat, 1884, pp. 36-117.

—. *Frederick the Great.* Vols. V-XI of *Carlyle's Complete Works.* Boston: Dana Estes and Charles E. Lauriat, 1884.

—. *The French Revolution.* Vols. III-IV of *Carlyle's Complete Works.* Boston: Dana Estes and Charles E. Lauriat, 1884.

—. *On Heroes, Hero-Worship and the Heroic in History.* Ed. Carl Niemeyer. Lincoln: University of Nebraska Press, 1966.

—. "On History." In *Critical and Miscellaneous Essays,* Vol. II. Vol. XIV of *Carlyle's Complete Works.* Boston: Dana Estes and Charles E. Lauriat, 1884, pp. 60-71.

—. "On History Again." In *Critical and Miscellaneous Essays,* Vol. III. Vol. XV of *Carlyle's Complete Works.* Boston: Dana Estes and Charles E. Lauriat, 1884, pp, 74-82.

—. *Past and Present.* Vol. XII of *Carlyle's Complete Works.* Boston: Dana Estes and Charles E. Lauriat, 1884, pp. 1-286.

—. *Sartor Resartus and Selected Prose.* New York: Holt, Rinehart and Winston, 1970.

—. "Shooting Niagara: and After?" In *Critical and Miscellaneous Essays,* Vol. IV. Vol. XVI of *Carlyle's Complete Works.* Boston: Dana Estes and Charles E. Lauriat, 1884, pp. 421-465.

Chadwick, H. M. and Nora. *The Growth of Literature.* Vol. I. Cambridge University Press, 1932.

Chadwick, H. M. *The Heroic Age.* Cambridge University Press, 1912.

—. *The Nationalities of Europe and the Growth of National Ideologies.* Cambridge University Press, 1945.

Clarke, Austin. *A Penny in the Clouds.* London: Routledge and Kegan Paul, 1968.

—. "Standish James O'Grady." *Dublin Magazine,* NS 22, No. 1 (1947), 36-40.

Clissmann, Anne. *Flann O'Brien: a Critical Introduction to His Writings.* Dublin: Gill and Macmillan; New York: Barnes and Noble, 1975.

Collingwood, R. G. *The Idea of History.* New York: Oxford University Press, 1956.

Corbet, W. J. "Elizabethan Ireland." *The Evening Herald,* 21 Mar. 1895.

Cox, T. W. "Life and Liberty." Letter. *The Peasant and Irish Ireland,* 26 Sept. 1908, p. 8, col. 5.

Curtis, Jr., L. P. *Anglo-Saxons and Celts.* Bridgeport University Press, 1968.

—. *Apes and Angels.* Washington, D.C.: Smithsonian Institution Press, 1971.

Dale, Peter Allan. *The Victorian Critic and the Idea of History.* Cambridge, Mass. and London: Harvard University Press, 1977.

Davitt, Michael. "Irish Conservatism and Its Outlooks." *Dublin University Review,* (Sept. 1885), 93-108.

deJubainville, H. D'Arbois. *The Irish Mythological Cycle and Celtic Mythology.* Tr. Richard Irvine Best. 1903; rpt. New York: Lemma, 1973.

deVere, Aubrey. *The Foray of Queen Maeve and Other Legends of Ireland's Heroic Age.* London: Kegan Paul, Trench, 1882.

Diskin, Patrick. "A Source for Yeats's 'The Black Tower.' " *Notes & Queries,* NS 206 (1961), 107-108.

—. "Yeats's 'The Black Tower.' " *Notes & Queries,* 210 (1965), 278-279.

Dowden, Edward. "Sir Samuel Ferguson's Poetry." Letter. *The Irish Times,* 16 Jan. 1896, p. 6, col. 5.

Dume, Thomas Leslie. "William Butler Yeats: a Survey of His Reading." Diss. Temple 1950.

Eglinton, John (W. K. Magee). *Pebbles from a Brook.* Kilkenny: Standish O'Grady, 1901.

"Elizabethan Ireland: Lecture by Mr. Standish O'Grady." *Daily Express,* 5 Feb. 1897, p. 7. col. 5.

Ferguson, Sir Samuel. *Congal.* Dublin: E. Ponsonby; London: Bell and Daldy, 1872.

"Fionn and His Companions in Dublin." Editorial. *The Irish Nation and the Peasant,* 27 Mar. 1909, p. 5, cols. 1-2.

Fourier, Charles. *Design for Utopia: Selected Writings of Charles Fourier.* 1901; rpt. New York: Schocken Books, 1971.

Froude, J. A. *The English in Ireland in the Eighteenth Century.* New York: Charles Scribner's Sons, 1888. 3 vols.

[Gael]. "A Note on Standish O'Grady." *The Irish Review,* 1 (1911), 215-216.

Gregory, Lady Isabella Augusta. Ed. and tr. *Cuculain of Muirthemne.* New York: Oxford University Press, 1970.

—. *Gods and Fighting Men.* New York: Oxford University Press, 1970.

—. *Seventy Years: Being the Autobiography of Lady Gregory.* Ed. Colin Smythe. Gerrards Cross, England: Colin Smythe, 1974.

Gwynn, Denis. "Standish O'Grady." *Old Kilkenny Review,* No. 22 (1970), pp. 11-14.

Herrick, Francis H. "Lord Randolph Churchill and the Popular Organization of the Conservative Party." *Pacific Historical Review,* 15 (1946), 178-191.

"History and Biography." Rev. of *Ireland: Her Story* [*sic*], by Standish O'Grady. *Westminster Review,* 141 (1894), 219-221.

Hume, David. *The Natural History of Religion.* Ed. H. E. Root. London: Adam and Charles Black, 1956.

Joyce, P. W. *Old Celtic Romances.* London: Kegan Paul, 1879.

Keating, Geoffrey. *The History of Ireland.* Tr. John O'Mahony. New York: P. M. Haverty, 1857.

Kelleher, John V. "Yeats's Use of Irish Materials." *Triquarterly,* (Fall 1965), 122-123.

Kinsella, Thomas, tr. *The Tain.* London and New York: Oxford University Press, 1970.

Kozicki, Henry. "Philosophy of History in Tennyson's Poetry to the 1842 *Poems.*" *ELH*, 42 (1975), 88-106.

Kropotkin, Petyr A. *Fields, Factories and Workshops.* 1913; rpt; New York and London: Benjamin Blom, 1968.

Lecky, W. E. H. *A History of Ireland in the Eighteenth Century.* London: Longman's, Green, 1892.

Literary Ideals in Ireland. 1899; rpt. New York: Lemma, 1973.

Loebell, [Prof.]. "On the Character of Niebuhr as an Historian." In *The Life and Letters of Barthold Georg Niebuhr.* New York: Harper, 1852.

Maine, Sir Henry Sumner. *Lectures on the Early History of Institutions.* 1914; rpt. Port Washington, NY: Kennikat Press, 1966.

Macaulay, Thomas Babington. *The History of England.* 6 vols. Ed. Charles Harding Firth. 1913; rpt. New York: AMS Press, 1968.

[Mac Dare, Curoi]. Rev. of *In the Gates of the North*, by Standish James O'Grady. *The Peasant and Irish Ireland*, 28 Nov. 1908, p. 3, cols. 2-3.

Manuel, Frank E. *The Eighteenth Century Confronts the Gods*. New York: Atheneum, 1957.

Marcus, Phillip L. *Standish O'Grady*. Lewisburg, PA: Bucknell University Press, 1970.

—. *Yeats and the Beginning of the Irish Renaissance*. Ithaca: Cornell University Press, 1970.

Martyn, Edward. *The Heather Field and Maeve*. London: Duckworth, 1899.

—. *The Tale of a Town and an Enchanted Sea*. Kilkenny: Standish O'Grady, 1902.

Matthews, W. G. "The Irish State Papers." Letter. *Athenaeum*, 97 (1891), 668.

Mercier, Vivian. "Standish James O'Grady." *Colby Library Quarterly*, 4 (1958), 285-290.

—. "Standish James O'Grady." *The Irish Times*, 28 July 1956; 4 Aug. 1956.

Mill, John Stuart. "To Standish O'Grady." 16 Jan. 1869. Letter 1378. In *The Later Letters of John Stuart Mill, 1849-1873*. Ed. Francis E. Mineha and Dwight W. Lindley. Toronto University Press, 1972, XVII, 1545-1546.

"Mr. Standish O'Grady on 'Elizabethan Ireland.' " *Daily Express*, 20 Mar. 1895, p. 6, col. 6.

Moore, George. *Hail and Farewell: Ave, Salve, Vale*. Gerrards Cross, England: Colin Smythe, 1976.

Müller, E. Rev. of *History of Ireland: the Heroic Period*, by Standish James O'Grady. *Revue Celtique*, 3 (1876-78), 476-478.

Niebuhr, Barthold G. *The History of Rome.* Tr. Julius Charles Hare and Connop Thirlwall. London: Taylor, Walton, and Maberly, 1851. 3 vols.

O'Curry, Eugene. *Lectures on the Manuscript Materials of Ancient Irish History.* 1861; rpt. New York: Burt Franklin, 1964.

—. *On the Manners and Customs of the Ancient Irish.* London and Edinburgh: Williams and Norgate; Dublin: W. B. Kelly; New York: Scribner, Welford, 1873. 3 vols.

O'Daly, John. Tr. *Tan-bo-Cooalney.* Royal Irish Academy. MS. 24. M. 39.

O'Donovan, John, ed. and tr. *Annals of the Four Masters.* 8 vols. 1854; rpt. New York: AMS Press, 1966.

O'Driscoll, Robert. *An Ascendancy of the Heart: Ferguson and the Beginnings of Modern Irish Literature in English.* Dublin: Dolmen, 1977.

—. "Ferguson and the Idea of an Irish National Literature." *Eire-Ireland.* (Spring 1971), 82-95.

O'Grady, Hugh Art. *Standish James O'Grady: the Man and the Writer.* Dublin: Talbot, 1929.

—. *Strafford and Ireland, the History of His Vice-royalty with an Account of His Trial.* 2 vols. Dublin: Hodges, Figgis, 1923.

O'Halloran, Sylvester. *A General History of Ireland.* London: Printed for the author by A. Hamilton, 1778.

Omond, T. S. "Is Verse a Trammel?" *The Gentleman's Magazine,* NS 14 (1875), 344-354.

Orage, A. R. *Readers and Writers.* London: Allen and Unwin, 1922.

Pearse, Padraic. "Padraic Mac Piarais on the Old Heroes and the New Students." *The Irish Nation and the Peasant,* 27 Mar. 1909, p. 3, cols. 1-2.

—. *The Story of a Success.* Dublin and London: Maunsel, 1917.

Petrie, George. *The Ecclesiastical Architecture of Ireland, Anterior to the Anglo-Norman Invasion.* Dublin: Hodges and Smith, 1845.

—. "On the History and Antiquities of Tara Hill." *Transactions of the Royal Irish Academy,* 18 (1839), 25-232.

Poliakov, Leon. *The Aryan Myth.* Tr. Edmund Howard. New York: Basic Books, 1974.

"Prominent Penmen: Standish O'Grady." *The Irish Book Lover,* 11 (1920), 76-77. Originally published in *The Nation.*

Reid, B. L. *The Man from New York: John Quinn and His Friends.* New York: Oxford University Press, 1968.

Renan, Ernest. *The Poetry of the Celtic Races.* Tr. William G. Hutchinson. London: W. Scott, 1896.

[Report on an O'Grady Lecture]. *Daily Express,* 20 Mar. 1895, p. 4, col. 5.

Rev. of *History of Ireland: the Heroic Period,* by Standish James O'Grady. *The Celtic Magazine,* 4 (1878), 396-399.

Rev. of *History of Ireland: the Heroic Period,* by Standish James O'Grady. *Hibernia,* 1 (1882), 14.

Rev. of *History of Ireland: the Heroic Period,* by Standish James O'Grady. *Light,* 20 April 1878.

Rev. of *History of Ireland: the Heroic Period,* by Standish James O'Grady. *The Spectator,* 51 (1878), 799-800.

Rev. of *In the Wake of King James,* by Standish James O'Grady. *Bookman* [London] , 10 [1896] , 120.

Rev. of *In the Wake of King James,* by Standish James O'Grady. *Bookman* [New York] , 4 [1896] , 76.

Rev. of *Lost on Du-Corrig,* by Standish James O'Grady. *Bookman* [London] , Vol. 59.

Rev. of *The Flight of the Eagle,* by Standish James O'Grady. *Athenaeum,* 109 (1897), 533-534.

Rev. of *The Story of Ireland,* by Standish James O'Grady. *Athenaeum,* 103 (1894), 835.

Rev. of *The Story of Ireland,* by Standish James O'Grady. *Spectator,* 72 (1894), 473-474.

Rev. of *Toryism and the Tory Democracy,* by Standish James O'Grady. *Dublin University Review,* 2 (1886), 368-369.

Rev. of *Ulrick the Ready,* by Standish James O'Grady. *Athenaeum,* 107 (1896), 376.

Rhys, John. *Celtic Britain.* London: Society for Promoting Christian Knowledge, 1882.

—. *Lectures on the Origin and Growth of Religion as Illustrated by Celtic Heathendom.* London: Williams and Norgate, 1888.

Rolleston, C. H. *Portrait of an Irishman.* London: Methuen, 1939.

Ruskin, John. *Sesame and Lilies, The Two Paths, and The King of the Golden River.* London and Toronto: J. M. Dent; New York: E. P. Dutton, 1907.

Russell, George [AE] . "The Dramatic Treatment of Heroic Literature." *Samhain,* (Oct. 1902), 11-13.

—. *Imaginations and Reveries.* Dublin: Maunsel, 1915.

—. *The Inner and the Outer Ireland.* London: T. Fisher Unwin, 1921.

—. *Letters from AE.* Ed. Allan Denson. London: 1961.

—. *The Living Torch.* Ed. Monk Gibbon. New York: Macmillan, 1938.

—. "Literature and Life: Standish O'Grady." *The Irish Statesman,* 10 (1928), 231.

—. "Standish O'Grady." In *Irish Literature.* Ed. Justin McCarthy. Chicago: deBower-Elliot, 1904, VII, 2737-2740.

Ryan, W. P. *The Irish Literary Revival.* London: Ward and Downey, 1894.

[Sliabh Mor]. "Clerk's Appeal to Mr. O'Grady." Letter. *The Peasant and Irish Ireland,* 26 Sept. 1908, p. 7, cols. 3-4.

"Standish O'Grady." *The Irish Book Lover,* 11 (1920), 77-78.

Stephens, James. *The Crock of Gold.* New York: Macmillan, 1913.

Stokes, Whitley. "Cuchulainn's Death." *Revue Celtique,* 3 (1876-78), 175-185.

Summerfield, Henry. *That Myriad-minded Man.* Gerrards Cross, England: Colin Smythe, 1975.

Thompson, William Irwin. *The Imagination of an Insurrection.* New York: Oxford University Press, 1967.

Todhunter, John. *The Banshee and Other Poems.* London: Kegan Paul, 1888.

Upton, William C. *Cuchulainn: The Story of His Combats at the Ford.* Dublin: M. H. Gill and Son, 1887.

Whitaker, Thomas R. *Swan and Shadow.* Chapel Hill: University of North Carolina Press, 1964.

White, Sean J. "Standish O'Grady." *Kilkenny Magazine,* 2 (Autumn 1960), pp. 10-26.

Whitman, Walt. "Democratic Vistas." In *Leaves of Grass and Selected Prose.* New York: Modern Library, 1950, pp. 460-516.

—. *Walt Whitman: the Correspondence.* Vols. II, III, and V. Ed. Edwin Haviland Miller. New York University Press, 1961.

Whitney, Lois. "Primitivist Theories of Epic Origins." *Modern Philology,* 21 (1924), 337-378.

Yeats, William Butler. *The Autobiography of William Butler Yeats.* New York: Collier Books, 1965.

—. "Battles Long Ago." Rev. of *The Coming of Cuculain,* by Standish James O'Grady. In *Uncollected Prose by W. B. Yeats: First Reviews and Articles, 1886-1896.* Vol. I. Ed. John P. Frayne. New York: Columbia University Press, 1970, pp. 350-351.

—. *The Collected Plays of W. B. Yeats.* New York: Macmillan, 1953.

—. *Essays and Introductions.* New York: Macmillan, 1961.

—. Letter to Standish James O'Grady. 31 Aug. [n. y.]. MS 25 Wa: 8:1. Department of Special Collections. Kenneth Spencer Research Library. University of Kansas.

—. *The Letters of W. B. Yeats.* Ed. Allan Wade. New York: Macmillan, 1955.

—. *Letters to the New Island.* 1934; rpt. Cambridge, Mass.: Harvard University Press, 1970.

—. *Memoirs.* Ed. Denis Donoghue. New York: Macmillan, 1972.

—. "Mr. Standish O'Grady's 'Flight of the Eagle.' " Rev. of *The Flight of the Eagle,* by Standish James O'Grady. In *Uncollected Prose by W. B. Yeats: Reviews, Articles and Other Miscellaneous Prose, 1897-1939.* Vol. II. Ed. John P. Frayne and Colton Johnson. New York: Columbia University Press, 1975, pp. 47-51.

—. Rev. of *The Chain of Gold,* by Standish James O'Grady. In *Uncollected Prose by W. B. Yeats: Reviews, Articles and Other Miscellaneous Prose, 1897-1939.* Vol. II. Ed. John P. Frayne and Colton Johnson. New York: Columbia University Press, 1976, p. 515.

—. *The Variorum Edition of the Poems of W. B. Yeats.* Ed. Peter Allt and Russell K. Alspach. New York: Macmillan, 1957.

—. *A Vision.* New York: Collier Books, 1966.

Young, Ella. *Flowering Dusk.* New York and Toronto: Longman's, Green, 1945.

Appendix A

This poem by O'Grady appeared in *Kottabos,* probably sometime between 1869 and 1874. It was reprinted in *Echoes from Kottabos,* ed. R. Y. Tyrell and Sir Edward Sullivan (London: E. Grant Richards, 1906), p. 15.

On Reading the Fragments of Early Greek Lyric Poetry

We have all Tupper—not one thunder—tone
    Hath ceased to bellow through the British sky,
And ladies tell us that the great trombone
    Will sound again, and laughing fools defy;
But where are ye, whose broken harmony
    Makes discord shriek where music seem'd to flow,
Clear stars of song, to whom our best can be
    Nought but loose clouds, that shift and toil below;
Hand breadths of wondrous streams, joyous and free,
    That leap and foam and flash, and have no peers,
Sounded by darkness; wafts of strange melody
    Heard in the loud wild night of wasteful years?
Ah, bleeding mouths! ah, smitten tuneful lips!
    He is the same who mightily lifts the sun
Majestical, and blacks it with eclipse,
    And wastes the pleasant slopes of Helicon—
The law that bound the Israelites of old
Slays you, the firstlings of Apollo's fold.

Appendix B

This letter from O'Grady to John Stuart Mill is located in the Hutzler Collection in the Milton S. Eisenhower Library of the Johns Hopkins University.

> Majourney glebe
> Couchford, Co. Cork
> Jan. 9 [1869]

My dear Sir,

In your chapter on Disbelief in the "Inductive Logic" you say that no amount of testimony for a miracle can convince one of the existence of God who does not admit the fact already.

I have no doubt, Sir, but that if I understand the whole of the question I should see that you are right. But as you have not adduced as far as I can see any arguments in support of this assertion and as I do not think it self-evident I have taken the liberty of asking you why this must be the case.

Suppose I had the testimony of my own senses and the testimony of the senses of hundreds of my neighbours for the appearance in this country of a great public teacher proclaiming that he is in direct communication with a supernatural power the maker of the world and in proof of his words breaking at will the established laws of nature. Even this may not convince many of the existence of this power. They may attribute the phenomena to some cause known to exist, but why could not my belief in that supernatural being be established and legitimately established thus. I have to choose between several possible causes why ought I as a scientific man to reject this one?

If you would drop me a few lines as soon as you have leisure I should be much obliged for I am preparing a paper bearing upon this subject for the Fortnightly Review.

> I remain
>   My dear Sir,
> Your affecte [sic] Student
> Standish O'Grady

Appendix C

The following is the text of the initiation rite of Cuculain as it appears in John O'Daly's translation, MS. 24. M. 39., The Royal Irish Academy, pp. 90-92.

Levarcan the daughter of Hugh perceived them. "There is a chariot approaching, Conor" said she, and it advances furiously. The bloody heads of our foes are in that chariot and beauteous white birds are fastened to it and wild deer able to run are bound to it and a servant is with him in the chariot also, And if he [Cuchullin] be not attended to now by him will the Chiefs of Uladh fall." "I know that chariot" says Conor, "it is that boy of my sisters that went so lately to the land that don't belong to us, and I hope he has bloodied his hand and unless his anger be attended to the youths of Eamhna will fall by him."

Then the Rulers held a Council, namely, the women of the Harem of Eamhna, and they came to the resolution to send forth to meet the youth thirty women, and they active and blushing naked, exposing their persons and their shame before him. And the youth hid his face and his countenance from them and turned his face towards the body of the chariot as soon as he perceived the nakedness and the shame of the women.

Then descended he from the chariot and he was placed in a bath of cold water and the first vessel he was placed in the hoops and the staves burst like nuts under him and the water run out of the second vessel and the third vessel no one could stand the water at all, then in the long run the anger left the youth and he put his beauteous raiment upon him and his comeliness and his form came back to him and he was changed into a crimson pillar from his head to the ground; and beauteous was the youth. He had

seven toes on each of his feet and seven fingers on each
of his hands, seven pupils in each of his eyes, and a bunch
of Eye Bright in each separate pupil; and he had four
Dimples in each of his cheeks, viz. a blue Dimple, a
crimson Dimple, a green Dimple and a yellow Dimple—
fifty auburn locks had he from one ear to the other like
the yellow wast [?] of the bees, or like a brooch of fine
gold opposite a bright Sun-cloud. A green cloak was
upon him and a silver pin in the cloak over his breast
which had gold embroidered linen on it.

Index